The Disinterred Muse

ALSO BY DAVID NOVARR

The Making of Walton's *Lives*

The Disinterred Muse

Donne's Texts and Contexts

DAVID NOVARR

Cornell University Press

Ithaca and London

First published 1980 by Cornell University Press.
Published in the United Kingdom by Cornell University Press Ltd., 2-4 Brook Street, London W1Y 1AA.

International Standard Book Number 0-8014-1309-5
Library of Congress Catalog Card Number 80-66967
Printed in the United States of America
Librarians: Library of Congress cataloging information appears on the last page of the book.

Here lies a King, that rul'd as hee thought fit
The universall Monarchy of wit;
Here lie two Flamens, and both those, the best,
Apollo's first, at last, the true Gods Priest.

THOMAS CAREW
"An Elegie upon the Death of the
Deane of Pauls, Dr John Donne"

Contents

Contents

Preface

This book is about some of John Donne's poetry, secular and religious. First, I examine two of the most familiar love poems, so quintessentially Donnean that to study them is to open up matters of thought, wit, and technique which are central to an understanding of the poet. Then I consider two poems in other genres, in order to account for the discordant tone of one and to establish for both their dates of composition and their relation to other poems of Donne's. Last, I deal with all the poems Donne wrote after 1614, some of them not very well known, to show what he accomplished when he was simultaneously God's priest and Apollo's. Throughout, I rely on crucial contexts that refine our understanding of particular poems and of Donne as poet.

The belief that scholarship can work in important ways to help us understand literary texts is not so self-evident as it used to seem. The kidnapping of an earlier poet by a later one has, lately, been given the inevitability and respectability of a general principle; the legislators of the world have now been granted license by the critics for the kind of misinterpretation that they have ever taken to be their right. Gentle readers have never needed permission to find in a literary text what they wished to find, but even they have received critical sanction to identify personal response with truth. Practical critics have given us as many ambiguities as answers, but, for all the narrowness of their focus, at least they focused on the poem. With the intent of broadening their view, many of their successors have been so busy formulating blueprints for *the* superhighway to heaven that they have forgotten why they want to get there. A scholar begins to have mixed feelings when he realizes that what Merritt Hughes called "the ungrateful task of recovering historical reality" has been left to him.

It is easy to see that Donne has been imprisoned by Izaak Walton, enthralled by Dr. Johnson, ravished by T. S. Eliot, taken by innumerable critics and readers. It is generally assumed that he has been freed by Louis L. Martz, Rosalie Colie, and Barbara K. Lewalski, and made chaste by Herbert J. C. Grierson, Helen Gardner, and Evelyn M. Simpson. But historical reality depends, among other things, on perspective, emphasis, selection. Scholars, like critics, enlarge our understanding of poetry by hanging up looking glasses at odd corners, and it becomes necessary to compensate for the distortion of their angle of vision. The whole business is sometimes disheartening, but it's the only real business in town. Here, as elsewhere, our solace comes from Milton — not every piece of the building can be of one form: "the perfection consists in this, that out of many moderate varieties and brotherly dissimilitudes that are not vastly disproportional, arises the goodly and the graceful symmetry that commends the whole pile and structure." A little generous prudence, a little forbearance of one another, some grain of charity, joining into one general and brotherly search after truth.

Some years ago, J. B. Leishman suggested that it was natural that most of us who meddle with poetry should talk a great deal of nonsense. "Perhaps the best we can hope for," he said, "is that we should gradually come to perceive that it *was* nonsense, and that we should contrive to talk less nonsense as we grow older." With modesty and foresight, he admitted that there might be a considerable residuum of nonsense in *The Monarch of Wit*, and said he would not be offended with any who thought so, for tomorrow he might think so too. I wish I could take his mature and disarming attitude, but the very makeup of this volume shows I can't.

The second and fifth essays, which comprise about three-quarters of the volume, are new. The second essay confronts the problem of multiple historical realities and maintains that one may be more relevant to a particular poem than others. The last essay seeks to reshape the stones in the building of Donne's career as poet after he had taken orders, to refine the chronology, the meaning, the achievement of the poems he felt impelled to write after he had renounced verse. As my work on Donne goes back thirty years, I should like to think these essays wiser than the three earlier ones. That would be easier to believe if I could honestly admit that I now see major flaws in those. I don't (and I don't know whether to be saddened or pleased), and I reoffer them for various reasons.

The essay which points out that Donne's intent in the Lincoln's Inn epithalamion is broadly satiric has, to be sure, drawn readers' attention to the satire in the poem, but there is still some disposition to see the poem as an unsuccessful imitation of Spenser rather than as a successful frolic of Donne's or to fault it because it does not decorously fuse satire and celebration to provide moral enlightenment. Moreover, my tentative proposal that Donne wrote the poem for performance at the Midsummer revels at the Inn in 1595 has been called untenable on the basis that there is no evidence that revels were ever held there at any time other than the Christmas season; careful reading of the essay will show, I think, that though there is some evidence that revelry at Christmas had been reduced, perhaps even discontinued, in Donne's day, there is no evidence that the revels so long celebrated at Midsummer and at other times did not continue while he was at the Inn. The essay as printed here differs from the original only in that I have substituted for one of the footnotes a longer one for which *The Review of English Studies* could not find space; that I have updated. My argument that *La Corona* was not written in 1607 has been generally accepted. At a time when some scholars postdate "Satyre III" by two decades and "A Nocturnall upon S. Lucies Day" by one, it may seem a quibble to reemphasize that the date I proposed for *La Corona* was not 1609 but "late in 1608 or early in 1609"; the small difference is not negligible, for I mean to suggest that *La Corona* was written after "Upon the Annunciation and Passion falling upon one day. 1608" and before the first of the Holy Sonnets. My concern to reprint the essay on "The Exstasie" has another motive. I had wished to arrive at a right reading of the poem, which had already received extraordinarily careful scrutiny, by means of an even more careful reassessment that stressed Donne's wit in the context of the casuistry of love. Unfortunately, the first printing of my essay departed from my manuscript in many places and introduced serious errors. The version printed here follows my manuscript, with a few modifications.

I have a larger purpose, too, in reprinting these essays. I see them, like the new essays here, as pieces different in form but similar in their function of helping to construct the "reality" of Donne and his poetry. I have not built either a wholly new pile and structure or a whole one. My detailed examination of the work of others, my dependence on them and my differences with them — these are evidence enough that I think the whole will arise from a long collaboration. I have contributed only where I thought I could perhaps say something significant about some of Donne's verse. I cannot even say, "The method only is mine own." I wanted only to demonstrate once again the utility of a kind of architecture, old enough and laborious enough that the legitimacy of its claims needs to be reasserted in practice.

My footnotes merely begin to acknowledge how much I owe to others. My debt to the work of Herbert J. C. Grierson, Helen Gardner, R. C. Bald, Wesley Milgate, and Evelyn M. Simpson is immense; theirs is the foundation I have built on. My students and my colleagues, particularly Ephim Fogel and Charles Levy, have listened endlessly and sympathetically and have advised and instructed magnanimously. The staff of the Cornell Libraries has given me help and refuge. The grant of a fellowship by the Huntington Library in early 1978 made possible some inquiries I could not otherwise have pursued; and James Thorpe, the staff at the Library, and the devotees of The Footnote made real for me the Idea of the brotherly search after truth. I could not have done what I have done without the generous prudence, extraordinary forbearance, and infinite charity of my wife.

I am grateful to Edmund Miller, who kindly read for me "On Taking Orders: Donne, Herbert, Tilman," a shorter version of two sections of Chapter 5, at the Modern Language Association's Special Session on George Herbert, held in New York on December 29, 1976.

I am indebted also to the Pennsylvania State University Press for permission to reprint "'The Exstasie': Donne's Address on the States of Union," which appeared in *Just So Much Honor: Essays Commemorating the Four-Hundredth Anniversary of the Birth of John Donne*, ed. Peter Amadeas Fiore (University Park, 1972), pp. 219–43; to the Clarendon Press for permission to reprint "Donne's 'Epithalamion made at Lincoln's Inn': Context and Date," which was printed in *The Review of English Studies*, 7 (July 1956), 250–63; and to the University of Iowa for permission to reprint "The Dating of Donne's *La Corona*," which appeared in *Philological Quarterly*, 36 (April 1957), 259–65. I have made some changes in accidentals.

DAVID NOVARR

Ithaca, New York

Abbreviations
of Periodicals

EIC	Essays in Criticism
ELH	Journal of English Literary History
ES	English Studies
HLQ	Huntington Library Quarterly
JEGP	Journal of English and Germanic Philology
MLN	Modern Language Notes
MLR	Modern Language Review
N&Q	Notes and Queries
PMLA	Publications of the Modern Language Association of America
PQ	Philological Quarterly
RES	The Review of English Studies
SEL	Studies in English Literature, 1500–1900
TLS	[London] Times Literary Supplement

The Disinterred Muse

1

"The Exstasie": Donne's Address
on the States of Union

> From thinking us all soule, neglecting thus
> Our mutuall duties, Lord deliver us.
>
> —"A Litanie," ll. 143–44

"We are at last becoming aware, in general, that our primary office for this poet is . . . to establish a full technical context, and to trace material sources." The words of A. J. Smith, written in 1958,[1] may serve to remind us that Donne scholarship has come a long way since the pioneering work done by Sir Herbert Grierson in his commentary on the poems (1912), by Mary Paton Ramsay in *Les doctrines médiévales chez Donne* (1917), and by Charles M. Coffin in *John Donne and the New Philosophy* (1937). The last decade or two have seen the publication of contextual and source studies even for individual poems, such work as that of Louis L. Martz, Frank Manley, and O. B. Hardison on *The Anniversaries*, Jay A. Levine on "The Dissolution," John Freccero on "A Valediction: forbidding Mourning," Robert Silhol on "A Litanie," and A. B. Chambers on "Goodfriday, 1613. Riding Westward."[2] The reconstruction of traditions and conventions, the explications of the course of ideas in

---

[1] A. J. Smith, "The Metaphysic of Love," *RES*, ns 9 (1958), 363.

[2] Louis L. Martz, *The Poetry of Meditation* (New Haven, 1954); Frank Manley, *John Donne: The Anniversaries* (Baltimore, 1963); O. B. Hardison, *The Enduring Monument* (Chapel Hill, 1962); Jay A. Levine, "'The Dissolution': Donne's Twofold Elegy," *ELH*, 28 (1961), 301–15; John Freccero, "Donne's 'Valediction: forbidding Mourning,'" *ELH*, 30 (1963), 335–76; Robert Silhol, "Réflexions sur les sources et la structure de *A Litanie* de John Donne," *Etudes Anglaises*, 15 (1962), 329–46; A. B. Chambers, "Goodfriday,

history (especially in nonliterary disciplines) have enriched the knowledge and deepened the understanding of Donne scholars. The studies have provided us with the climate of opinion in which Donne worked, and, with varying success, have illuminated poems or passages in poems. Our debt to them is immense. But R. S. Crane has brilliantly pointed out some of the pitfalls of the study of the history of ideas,[3] and others are so readily apparent that we overlook them. It is perhaps worth reminding ourselves, for instance, that *Zeitgeist* explanations are likely to be most useful when we are dealing with second-rate writers rather than first-rate ones. Again, though the thoroughness of the immersion of some authors in some ideas is not to be questioned, others have merely tested the temperature of the water from time to time. Donne has told us that he "survayed and digested the whole body of Divinity, controverted betweene ours and the Romane Church,"[4] and that "an Hydroptique immoderate desire of humane learning and languages"[5] diverted him from the law; Walton says that among the "visible fruits of his labours" in his study, Donne left "the resultance of 1400. Authors, most of them abridged and analysed with his own hand."[6] The breadth of his interests and the extent of his learning are hardly in question, but his "voluptuousnes" toward languages did not make him a skilled Hebraist, and it is unlikely that he had the technical command of alchemy, astronomy, and philosophy which some modern historians of ideas have of particular disciplines (and which they have attributed to him). Moreover, even though we may have reservations about the dictum that "in poetry, all facts and beliefs cease to be true or false and become interesting possibilities," there is no one-to-one relation

1613. Riding Westward: The Poem and the Tradition," *ELH*, 28 (1961), 31-53. See, too, my "Donne's 'Epithalamion made at Lincoln's Inn': Context and Date," reprinted here as Chapter 3.

[3]R. S. Crane, "The Houyhnhnms, the Yahoos, and the History of Ideas," in *Reason and the Imagination*, ed. J. A. Mazzeo (New York, 1962), pp. 231-53.

[4]*Pseudo-Martyr* (London, 1610), sig. B3[r].

[5]*Letters to Severall Persons of Honour* (London, 1651), p. 51.

[6]Izaak Walton, *The Lives of D[r] John Donne* . . . (London, 1675), p. 60.

between a poet's learning and that learning as he draws upon it and tempers it in a particular poem. *De Doctrina Christiana* is not *Paradise Lost*, and when Milton forces Adam to choose between the basic tenet of man's superiority and the equally basic tenet that Eve's will is free and must not be forced, interesting things start to happen.

About a decade ago, Helen Gardner and A. J. Smith published major articles which combined the study of material source or technical context with a detailed reading of "The Exstasie."[7] More recently, A. R. Cirillo has published an article in which he says, "There is no need to prolong further the still unresolved controversy about the tone of that poem and its attitude toward human love. All I want to suggest is that the *topos* of the hermaphrodite is basic to its context, whether Donne was using it seriously or cynically."[8] Cirillo's interest in an idea for its own sake needs no justification; his candor in separating the idea from the uses made of it in the poem is commendable. Most students of literature are not willing, however, thus to compartmentalize their concerns. In what follows, I should like to look closely at the approaches and interpretations of Gardner and Smith. Then, building on a number of their suggestions, for they have immeasurably increased our sensitivity to "The Exstasie," I should like to try to resolve the controversy about the tone of the poem and its attitude toward human love. I shall assume three things: that Donne did not research "The Exstasie" as he did *Biathanatos* and *Pseudo-Martyr*; that in "The Exstasie" he was not only interested in the casuistry of love but even more interested in a poetic construct; that he was not only the first poet in the world in some things, but also that the

[7] Helen Gardner, "The Argument about 'The Ecstasy,'" in *Elizabethan and Jacobean Studies Presented to Frank Percy Wilson*, ed. Herbert Davis and Helen Gardner (Oxford, 1959), pp. 279–306; Smith, "The Metaphysic of Love," pp. 362–75. I single these out because they are most relevant to my purpose here. Among other major studies, those of Merritt Y. Hughes are invaluable: "The Lineage of 'The Extasie,'" *MLR*, 27 (1932), 1–7, and "Some of Donne's 'Ecstasies,'" *PMLA*, 75 (1960), 509–18.

[8] A. R. Cirillo, "The Fair Hermaphrodite: Love-Union in the Poetry of Donne and Spenser," *SEL*, 9 (1969), 90.

level of his customary achievement is so high that "The Exstasie" is a fine poem.

Gardner regards "The Exstasie" as "wholly serious in intention" ("The Argument," p. 284). "As the title tells us," she says, Donne's "subject is ecstasy. He is attempting to imagine and make intellectually conceivable the Neo-Platonic conception of ecstasy as the union of the soul with the object of its desire, attained by the abandonment of the body." But, she continues, "it is the essence of ecstasy that while it lasts the normal powers of soul and body are suspended, including the power of speech, and the soul learns and communicates itself by other means than the natural." It is, then, the very nature of the experience which Donne is trying to render (ecstasy can only be spoken about in the past tense) which makes him choose a narrative form unusual for him; moreover, with "characteristic daring and a characteristic ingenuity," he attempts by introducing a hypothetical ideal listener "to render the illumination of the soul in ecstasy as a present experience" (p. 285).

Gardner is persuaded that Donne derived his conception of "amorous ecstasy" from Leone Ebreo's *Dialoghi d'Amore*, and she says that "The Exstasie" "originated in Donne's interest in Ebreo's long description of the semi-death of ecstasy and in the idea that the force of ecstasy might be so strong that it would break the bond between soul and body and lead to the death of rapture."

> This death in ecstasy his lovers withdraw from, to return to life in the body. What they are concerned to argue, in the concluding section of the poem, is that the bond of the "new soul" will still subsist when their souls once more inhabit their separate bodies, and that they have a function to fulfil in the world of men which justifies their retreat from the blessed death of ecstasy. [P. 295]

According to Gardner, the ecstasy of the lovers reaches its climax by line 48 of the poem, with the revelation that their love is immortal. "Unless they are to enjoy the 'blessed death' of ec-

stasy," she says, "they must now return to their bodies" (p. 300).
The conclusion of the poem (ll. 49–76) justifies this return by
reference to Ebreo's doctrine of the circle of love:

> The inferior desires to unite itself in love with what is superior;
> but equally the superior desires to unite itself in love with what is
> inferior. The inferior desires the perfection which it lacks; the
> superior desires to bestow its own perfection on what lacks it. . . .
> The blood strives to become spiritual, to produce the spirits, or
> powers of the soul, which are necessary to unite the intellectual
> and corporal in man. Conversely souls must condescend to the
> affections and faculties of the bodies in order that man's sense
> organs may become rational. . . . [A soul's] duty is to take "in-
> tellectual life and knowledge and the light of God down from the
> upper world of eternity to the lower world of decay" and thus
> realize the unity of the Universe. A soul that does not perform
> this divinely appointed function is like a prince in a prison. . . .
> If the soul does not thus animate the body in all its parts, it
> is imprisoned in a carcass instead of reigning in its kingdom.
> [Pp. 301–3]

The only "proposal," then, which Gardner finds in the last section of the poem is "the perfectly modest one that the lovers'
souls, having enjoyed the rare privilege of union outside the
body, should now resume possession of their separate bodies
and reanimate these virtual corpses" (p. 283). She reads the last
lines of the poem as a further justification for life in this world —
the duty to reveal love to men (p. 303): "The final and, one
must suppose from its position, the conclusive reason for such a
return of the separated souls is not that it will in any way benefit
the lovers; but that only in the body can they manifest love to
'weake men'" (p. 283).

If Donne's subject is "ecstasy," the structure of his poem is
strange, though its proportions are symmetrical. The heart of
the poem must be thought to lie in the central section, which,
as Gardner says, "contains the illumination which the lovers received in their ecstasy" (p. 298). Since these twenty lines are
flanked by a twenty-eight-line "prelude" (p. 295) and by a

twenty-eight-line "conclusion" (p. 300) justifying a return to bodies, the illumination, central though it is, seems foreshortened. But, Gardner thinks that Donne's poem originated in his interest in Ebreo's description of the semi-death of ecstasy, and we should look for evidence of that aspect of ecstasy in the poem. The climax of the ecstasy of the lovers, as Gardner sees, is reached with the revelation that their love is immortal (p. 300). As she says, the central section of the poem describes "the union of their intellectual souls, or spiritual minds": "This union is indissoluble because it is a union of perfect with perfect, or like with like. It is only those things which are unequally mixed which are subject to decay or mutability" (p. 299). Now, this kind of emphasis on immortality and indissolubility perhaps carries, suppressed beneath the surface, the seed of the idea of the semi-death of ecstasy, but Donne's focus and perspective seem at odds with the concept of death. In "The Exstasie," the idea of death is at best implied in two places: in the "sepulchrall statues" of line 18 and in the "great Prince in prison" of line 68. Nowhere does Donne make explicit the idea of rapturous death. Had he done so, he must certainly have done so at the beginning of his last section. But the culminating words of the second section are "no change can invade"; in their emphasis on permanence, perfection, immortality, these words seem to preclude rather than to include the idea of death. Gardner, then, reads the last section of the poem as an alternative to a proposition which is not stated, a proposition to which Donne does not direct us but from which he diverts us.

When Gardner asks how successfully Donne has achieved his purpose in "The Exstasie," she finds the poem remarkable among Donne's lyrics for its lack of metrical interest and variety. She finds fine lines and fine passages in it, but thinks that "it lacks, as a whole, Donne's characteristic *élan*, and at times it descends to what can only be described as a dogged plod" (p. 303). She finds, moreover, that "there is a tone of argument throughout the lovers' speech which is out of keeping with the poem's subject." "The essence of any illumination received in ecstasy," she says, "is that it is immediate and not arrived at by the normal processes of ratiocination," and Donne's lovers seem far from the holy stillness, the peace of union, the blissful quiet characteristic of ecstasy. She rightly feels that the tone of the poem is that of "an ordinary dialogue in which points are being made and objections met" (p. 304), and she would explain this by saying that in "The Exstasie," Donne is "too tied to his source. It smells a little of the lamp" (p. 306): "When Donne was inspired by the *Dialoghi d'Amore* to write a poem showing the achievement of union in love, he caught from his source that tone of persuasion which has misled readers. The poem *sounds* as if someone is persuading someone. The defect of 'The Ecstasy' is that it is not sufficiently ecstatic. It is rather too much of an 'argument about an ecstasy'" (p. 304). But Gardner goes further: "I do not believe that Donne was very deeply moved by the conception of ecstasy. He too often in his sermons disparages the idea of ecstatic revelation for me to feel that it had ever a strong hold on his imagination." She points out, however, that Donne was profoundly moved by the conception of love as union, and she would in some measure attribute the deficiencies of "The Exstasie" to the fact that it was one of Donne's earliest poems on love as union, written as a result of his recent discovery of Ebreo (p. 304).

In the last paragraph of her essay, Gardner reiterates, notwithstanding what she has so candidly said of Donne's general lack of sympathy for the conception of ecstasy, her opinion that he is here writing seriously about ecstasy. She is concerned to defend his artistic and intellectual integrity against the critics who so exalt his wit that they "deny that ideas had any value to him as a poet except as counters to be used in an argument." She holds, quite correctly, that "no poet has made greater poetry than Donne has on the theme of mutual love. . . . The poems which Donne wrote on the subject of love as the union of equals, such poems as 'The Good-morrow', 'The Anniversary', or 'A Valediction: Forbidding Mourning' are his most beautiful and original contribution to the poetry of human love; for poets have written very little of love as fullness of joy" (p. 304). Since she finds in "The Exstasie" "the key to Donne's greatest love-poetry" (p. 304), she finds it important to read the poem as "wholly serious in intention" in order to protect Donne's integrity and sincerity. She is willing to grant that "the language of the first twelve lines is 'pregnant' with sexual meanings," that the lovers are young and fit for all the offices of love; she has no objection to Legouis's suggestion that, although hands and eyes are so far the only physical means the lovers have employed, they will soon enjoy bodily union (p. 296). She is even right to insist that the *main* meaning in these lines is that so far the lovers' only union is "through the corporal sense of touch and the spiritual sense of sight" (p. 296).[9] When she shows that Ebreo sanctions what has been called "Donne's metaphysic of love" — that bodily love is not incompatible with spiritual love, and that spiritual love can exist after bodily love has been satisfied — Gardner grants that the words of Ebreo which she cites make the same point "as it has been assumed [by others] that Donne was making in his poem: that lovers who are united in soul must, in order that their union should be complete, unite also in body." But, she insists, in this particular poem this conclusion is not being argued for, "although it is implied" (p. 295). She does not wish to deny that the poem "implies the lawfulness and value of physical love," but she denies that "the poem is in the least concerned to argue to this particular point"; it is merely a corollary to its main line of thought (p. 284). Gardner, then, makes it quite clear that she is aware of the sexuality in the poem, but at the same time she works heroically to free it from the charge of libertinism. She seems to feel that unless Donne is serious about ecstasy in this crucial poem, the precursor of the

[9]There is, of course, no necessary contradiction between this statement and those that Gardner makes in Appendix D (p. 262) of her edition of *John Donne: The Elegies and the Songs and Sonnets* (Oxford, 1965): "I do not know why it is always assumed that so far they have only loved chastely"; "'One another's best' at least implies that there has been no question of one refusing the other." Still, in the edition, Gardner glosses "sexe," in the line "Wee see by this, it was not sexe," as "all the desires and impulses that arise from differentiation of sex," not as "indulgence in physical intercourse." I think she is right. The "all our meanes to make us one" of line 10, like the reference to "sexe," seems to describe the lovers' general relation to this time, not merely the isolated experience described in the poem.

24

great love poems, he has somehow compromised the integrity of his basic belief about love. To that we may answer that it is frequently the committed man who dares to explore and exploit alternatives and that it in no way undercuts a man's integrity if he chooses to be witty about a subject that matters to him.

A. J. Smith reads "The Exstasie" as a witty poem which has its context not only in Ebreo's metaphysic of love but also in the theories of other sixteenth-century Italian writers. To establish the full technical context, he demonstrates the range of these theories, from Ficino's pure idealism, which emphasized the essential independence of the soul from the body, to the modified empiricism of commentators who, building on the ideas of Aristotle and Aquinas, made the perfect love of souls inseparable from or dependent upon the love of bodies. Whether or not Donne actually read Ficino, Ebreo, Speroni, Varchi, Tullia d'Aragona, Betussi, Tasso, and others, Smith says, he was exposed to "a varied and malleable body of public material." Donne, he thinks, used this material eclectically, and his "individual contribution to the theory of love in this poem is, to all appearance, not great": "one's attention is on the whole less usefully directed to what he used than to how he used it. In other words, it is in that measure a typical piece of witty writing" ("The Metaphysic of Love," p. 370).

Smith is, I think, right. He concludes that "The Exstasie" is a "remarkably 'witty'" poem (p. 375); still, he does not seem to find the wit very remarkable when he discusses it. Part of the difficulty stems from the fact that, for all he has to say about Italian love theory and Donne's eclectic use of it, he is disposed to attribute to Donne a position which Donne does not hold in the poem.

The "stereotyped and emblematic" situation with which the poem begins, Smith finds "tricked out with every convenient quirk of current poetic wit" (p. 370). He speaks of the "little play" on the stock Petrarchan properties by which Donne describes the ecstatic posture of the lovers in order to show the depth and fixity of their trance. He sees the "erotic motivation" provided by "Pillow" and "Pregnant banke," he starts to enunciate Donne's general attitude toward love when he says that the coupling of contemplating eyes "would have satisfied an Aristotelian only as a preliminary," and he finds that in the first dozen lines Donne "unambiguously motivates his later position": "A deft exploitation of the even more Petrarchan play of the picture in the eye enables him to refer to the normal end of physical union, and the whole extent of the present deficiency is shown. Moreover, his 'as yet,' in line 9, promises a remedy." He mentions the "comic literalness" of the description of the emanation and coupling of souls, and calls attention to the cleverness by which Donne has the souls as armies not contend against each other but augment themselves by the closest alliance, the perfecting power of the ecstatic union (p. 371).

Though Smith is content to describe the hypothetical listener as "an amusing and also a pointed device," he explains admirably the function of the listener in the poem:

> Donne is able at once to claim that there is a kind of arcanum of love, a soul-language for initiates, and, parenthetically, to assert the perfect oneness of these loving souls. But he has another point too, no less neatly made. This bystander is an initiate, and some way advanced in the mystery — besides being "refin'd" by love, he has by his good love "growen all minde." Yet if he listens carefully here he will learn much; will indeed take "a new concoction" ("the acceleration of anything towards purity and perfection," Johnson says), and "part farre purer then he came." But the lovers who grew all mind in the process, spurning the body, were the strict Neoplatonists. Donne is certainly not condemning them. He only suggests pleasantly they have still a great deal to learn, and that he is about to show them what it is. [Pp. 371-72]

Smith has little to say of the five stanzas which describe the knowledge granted to the lovers in their ecstasy, "the climax of the first half of the poem." Like Gardner, he states that this knowledge lies in an awareness of the fusion of souls and a realization of eternal fidelity. Where wit is concerned, he merely says that Donne "dresses up" the "one and four" of the theorists by an analogy from Plotinian metaphysics (p. 372).

Of the last section of the poem, Smith says, "One is not unprepared for Donne's return to the incompletely united bodies. . . . His concern now, in this latter part of the poem, is to develop the assertion that the lovers' state cannot be perfect while their bodies remain in unsatisfied singleness." He considers the treatment in lines 51–56 of the notion that the body is the instrument of the soul "not remarkable," and he continues,

> What is curious is to find Donne all but compromising his argument, and certainly reducing its possible effectiveness, by his apparent adoption of the Augustinian — and Ficinian — dichotomy in this section: "They are ours, though they are not wee." This is much more like Ficino's "the soul is the man" than Speroni's figure of the centaur, and Aquinas's assertion that the man is neither body nor soul alone, but a complex of both. It is, I suppose, with the analogy of "intelligences" and "spheres," capable of bearing a Thomist construction. "They are not wee" — we are no more bodies alone than we are souls alone. But there would seem a maladroitness in that way of presenting it unlooked for in so accomplished a rhetorician. [Pp. 372–73]

Donne is not, however, compromising *his* assertion but one which Smith has pushed on him. He is not in the last section of "The Exstasie" stating that "the lovers' state cannot be perfect while their bodies remain in unsatisfied singleness." In no way does he undercut the perfection of the ecstatic union of souls; he wishes, rather, to demonstrate conclusively the interrelations of souls and bodies in order to make a persuasive case for the propriety of physical love. Smith says that the very end of the poem "seems" to be "an assertion that the lovers' resort to their bodies now will mean no debasing of their love, or sundering of their eternally faithful souls" (p. 375). It *is* such an assertion, and the reason Smith finds the conclusion of the poem "somewhat enigmatic" is that he has pushed Donne too far into the Aristotelian camp.

27

Of Donne's use of spirits intermediary between body and soul, Smith says, "his metaphysics are ordinary in doctrine as in production": "He has merely made a pleasant (or perhaps tendentious) figure of that physiological explanation of the hypostatic union" (p. 373). He works hard to show that Donne may have used the figure of "a great Prince in prison" with originality, but his suggestion that Donne may be saying that the joint soul of lovers has not attained its full prerogatives until their joined bodies release it through physical intercourse (p. 375) seems farfetched. The last lines of the poem Smith treats as a "winding-up, chiefly by means of the comic pretence of the arcana of love": "The idea that bodily union might be desired 'as sign of the primary conjunction' is deftly dressed, the body becoming love's book wherein he reveals his spiritual mysteries to uninitiates. We have, again, the point that the speech of the loving souls is intelligible only to another lover — with the weak joke added that it has been a 'dialogue of one,' a novel and mysterious sort of *dialogo d'amore*" (p. 375).

If Smith's statement about what Donne wishes to assert in "The Exstasie" is too extreme, his statement about its conclusion puts him in the ranks of most critics, excepting Gardner, who, as she says, "take it for granted that the main point of the poem is a justification of physical love as not incompatible with the highest form of ideal love" (p. 283). But neither Gardner's dissatisfaction with Donne's achievement in the poem nor Smith's account of the wit of the poem vindicates the fascination it has had for scholars, anthologists, and readers. The critics are right, I think, about the intent of the poem, but, I think, too, that some aspects of its wit have not been sufficiently emphasized. I shall now try to underscore aspects of the wit which have been in some degree neglected or misinterpreted.

"The Exstasie" opens with the description of a strange, an extraordinary, experience.[10] The situation is imprecise, full of ill-

[10]Whether or not the modern reader approaches the poem with the "convention" delineated by Morris W. Croll and George Williamson in mind (Williamson, "The Convention of *The Extasie*," in *Seventeenth Century Contexts*

sorting details, mysterious. The oddness of the condition of the lovers is emphasized, the extent to which they are abstracted from nature and reality. The first stanza seems to show us two lovers who are sitting with their backs against a bank. We revise this picture when we learn that they sit facing each other, staring into each other's eyes, their fingers intertwined. But, it turns out, "sit" may be wrong, for we find out that they have been lying all day "like sepulchrall statues." Did they first sit, and then shift position so that they are on their backs, gazing at the heavens? Or have they been leaning, even reclining, on the bank, facing each other, their hands intergrafted? We cannot be sure, but we are sure that we have been projected into an unusual situation, and its strangeness is intensified when we are told that the lovers' souls have left their bodies, to hang in mid-air between the bodies in order to "negotiate." Puzzled by lovers who are sitting or lying, by lovers "cimented / With a fast balme" and entranced by twisted eyebeams (who yet make us aware explicitly of propagation), by unspeaking bodies and articulate souls, we are not surprised to learn that only a very special listener will be able to comprehend the negotiation. The negotiation, in fact, is also puzzling, for the souls have no differences of opinion; they speak as one.

The situation is, then, a highly rarified one. Quite suddenly, certainly without the careful step-by-step procedure we are familiar with in discourses about love, we have been taken to the top of the ladder of love. We are face-to-face with ecstatic rapture; we have ascended "to the lofty mansion where heavenly, lovely, and true beauty dwells, which lies hidden in the inmost secret recesses of God, so that profane eyes cannot behold it."[11] Donne starts where Bembo ends. He *assumes* that glorified

[London, 1960], pp. 63–77), it is fair to say that the convention probably did not exist for Donne's first readers. If the opening reminded them vaguely of poems about a springtime dialogue of love, reminiscence would serve only to set "The Exstasie" apart from the usual shepherd and his lass in a pastoral setting.

[11]Baldesar Castiglione, *The Book of the Courtier*, trans. Charles S. Singleton (Garden City, 1959), p. 355.

state of love which the philosophers and courtiers seek to reach. By a wonderful turn of wit, he has placed us in a position where we shall not hear about the gradual attainment of spiritual love from the lips of a virtuoso or from the dialogue between a lover and his beloved, but where we shall learn about love from the most highly qualified of all commentators — the "abler soule" which has divined all mysteries.[12]

The voice of the "abler soule" is, of course, authoritative. Having achieved the acme of the experience of love, the "abler soule" is perfect, immutable, at one with itself, and it soliloquizes. The "dialogue of one" is not a "weak joke." It is the keystone of Donne's arching wit. The "abler soule" has no doubts as it speaks; it knows. Its certainty is reflected in the metrical regularity of "The Exstasie," in the patness of its stanzaic form.

In five stanzas, the "abler soule" describes its exalted state. If, as C. S. Lewis says, most of Donne's love poetry is "less true than that of the Petrarchans, in so far as it largely omits the very thing that all the pother is about,"[13] so his ecstasy is less "true" than that of the Neo-Platonists. If the love poetry is *Hamlet* without the prince, the ecstasy lacks the soaring rapture of Bembo, himself almost inebriated as he envisions "that inexhaustible fountain of contentment that ever delights and never satiates."[14] In "Satyre III," Donne had said that it is easy enough to apprehend mysteries: they "are like the Sunne, dazling, yet plaine to all eyes"; but they are difficult to comprehend: the mind must extend itself to reach "hard knowledge." As Gardner says, Donne's "abler soule" is not ecstatic as it

[12]To be sure, the ecstasy described by Bembo arises from his perception of the Idea of beauty. Donne's ecstasy arises from an ecstatic union of lovers. Ebreo's discussion of ecstasy arises from Philo's experience of an ecstatic union with the idea of Sophia's beauty. As Gardner says, he is still in the process of wooing her, and they have not reached the state of Donne's lovers, in which each is equally lover and beloved (pp. 290-91). The point I am trying to make, however, is that Donne is less interested in the method of attainment of ecstasy than in what is to be learned from having attained it.

[13]C. S. Lewis, "Donne and Love Poetry in the Seventeenth Century," in *Seventeenth Century Studies Presented to Sir Herbert Grierson* (Oxford, 1938), p. 81.

[14]*The Book of the Courtier*, p. 356.

es. It starts by expressing gratitude and appreciation to es for their role in making ecstasy possible. Since the bodies responsible for conveying the souls to each other, they are drosse" to souls, but "allay"; not the scum thrown off from en ore or metal, but a less valuable metal added to one valuable in order to provide it with qualities of worth uld not otherwise have. Unlike the conventional Neo- nic advocate who is anxious to divorce body and soul, to the body behind so that he may focus on soul, the "abler " in its infinite wisdom about love, makes it clear that it is rned not merely with soul, but with *man*, and the word rs three times in the last five stanzas.

> On man heavens influence workes not so,
> But that it first imprints the ayre.

asic doctrine here, that heavenly influence works not di- out through an intermediary, is used to explain the inter- y function of the body in the union of souls, and the two re developed in the next three stanzas. The "abler soule" s the truth of the doctrine that man reaches wholeness iring to spirituality: the blood produces intermediary " which unite the corporal to the intellectual. Its special n is, however, to announce that the inverse of this is true, and the "abler soule" enunciates with authority trine that if man is to be whole, souls, too, must worl intermediary "affections" and "faculties" (passions an ns) in order to "reach and apprehend" sense; that is, i affect and inform the activities of the body.[17] For th

e lines "So must pure lovers soules descend / T'affections, and / Which sense may reach and apprehend," Gardner emen o "That"; she reads "sense" as subject of "may reach and app d thinks a purposive clause is needed, not a relative one (*The Eleg ongs and Sonnets*, p. 187). I agree with René Graziani ("Jo he Extasie' and Ecstasy," *RES*, ns 19 [1968], 134–35) that it is o emend; "Which," referring to "affections" and "faculties," is s ense" an inverted object. My paraphrase differs very little f

speaks of ecstasy; refined by love, it has "grown all minde," and it tries to make its experience comprehensible. Therefore it speaks logically, dispassionately; its aim is explicatory.

Its first statement defines the nature of love by telling what it is not: "Wee see by this, it was not sexe." Since the situation of the lovers has already made this abundantly clear, the statement seems almost superfluous; indeed, like the earlier descriptions of intergrafted hands and propagating eyes, it seems to intrude sexuality at the same time that it denies it. And what does the hypothetical listener, so exquisitely refined by love that he is able to understand the language of souls, so purified that he has "grown all minde," learn from such a statement which would give him additional insight into love? Indeed, what lessons can so devoted a believer in spiritual love learn from anything the "abler soule" says in the five stanzas describing ecstasy? He may be edified, he must get immense pleasure in being reassured of his own beliefs, not by a fellow Neo-Platonist, but by the "abler soule" which has attained the heights of spiritual love; however, the doctrine of the mixture, interanimation, and perfection of lovers' souls is not new to him.

If the refined listener hardly needs to be reminded that it was not sex which led to ecstasy, if what he learns in the five stanzas which elucidate the state of ecstasy is merely confirmatory, why should it be necessary for the "abler soule" to indulge in the analogy of the violet in order to enlighten him? Gardner says, "Like a modern scientist, trying to explain some scientific mystery to laymen, Donne refers to something rather similar in nature to the union which love effects in souls" (p. 299).[15] Her own analogy, though faulty, is provocative. The "abler soule" is, to

[15]Gardner's use of "Donne refers" indicates that she is looking at the passage not in terms of its speaker and listener, but in terms of the poet and his audience. There is no question that the poet's analogy aids his readers to comprehend the mysterious union being described by referring to seventeenth-century horticultural speculations about transplantation and "commixtion of seeds," though Gardner's informed account of this speculation shows that Donne was clarifying a larger mystery by a somewhat smaller one (p. 300). But Donne has been very careful to define the speaker and the listener in his poem, and *their* points of view are crucial to the intent of the poem.

be sure, in the position of a modern scientist who reports his findings. The listener, however, is not a layman but another qualified scientist, an expert in the same field. Given his special qualifications, he surely does not need a simplified or popularized or analogized explanation. But, like many experts, he has so specialized that he needs to be reminded of the relation between pure science and life. The burden of what the "abler soule" as scientist has to tell his proficient listener about the experiment he is describing has precisely to do with its relation to nature. The description of ecstatic union which Gardner calls a "scientific mystery" is not a mystery to the listener; this he knows. The mystery is in the violet, the link between spiritual and natural phenomena. The violet, here linked to the soul, had in the first stanza been juxtaposed to the lovers' bodies. Like the earlier mention of "sexe," the reference to the violet also serves as a reminder of the physical world in the midst of a spiritual experience. The middle section of the poem, then, like the first section, has in it elements which serve not only to define the situation and experience, but which also, at the same time, point away from them, beyond them.

Smith has noticed that in concluding the first section of "The Exstasie" Donne has unambiguously motivated his later position and that the "as yet" in line 9 promises a remedy. "One is not unprepared," he says, "for Donne's return to the incompletely united bodies. But his transition is dramatic, and the rhetoric of memorable cadence" (p. 372). He is quite right. Still, the "abler soule," that most competent exponent of spiritual love, having quickly and dispassionately summarized the state of ecstasy, surprises us and the listener when, instead of providing answers, it asks a question. The question is rhetorical, to be sure, but the lines "But O alas, so long, so farre / Our bodies why doe wee forbeare?" are the only ones in the long speech which are infused with feeling. Certainly, the question must stir the listener. If he has to this point merely received corroboration of his opinions, if he has thus far learned nothing new, he can hardly "part farre purer then he came." Now he is about to hear the ablest, the most authoritative of all speakers

---

instruct him not on the love of souls but [...] and important that it preempts the larg[...] (seven stanzas, as compared to the five [...] That question concerns the role of the [...] doctrine announced must, of course, g[...] speaker, be definitive.

What the listener hears, what it is [...] far purer than he came, is a justificatio[...] this is made clear in the first argument [...] propounds:

> They [our bodies] 'are ours, though th[...]
>   The'intelligences, they the sphear[...]

The lines contain a textual difficul[...] "spheare"; the editions, "spheares." [...] fer "spheare"; and Grierson explains, [...] the Sphere in which the two Intelligen[...] Smith finds this gloss "attractive[...] "spheares" on the ground that the us[...] pation of Donne's argument" (p. 37[...] patory quality of "spheare" which a[...] forward to rolling all strength and a[...] just as other obtrusive details in t[...] over, the argument which the "ab[...] pends on the singular "spheare," f[...] tery which the "soule" has already [...] that the lovers have been refined [...] soule," souls, too, may interact s[...] fruition in bodily union. Since th[...] static doctrine of the "abler soule[...] will certainly find persuasive the [...] the role of the body, new and st[...] The "abler soule" proceeds n[...]

[16]Herbert J. C. Grierson, ed., *The P[...]

3[...]

"abler soule's" major assumption about heaven's influence working by indirection, Donne could have relied on several classical sources,[18] but he probably had in mind also the dangers expressed in Exod. 33:20 about the direct apprehension of God: "And he said, Thou canst not see my face: for there shall no man see me, and live."[19] The "abler soule" in a state of ecstasy has looked directly on the face of God, but God reveals himself to *men* through acts, signs, words, and laws. Only an "abler soule" can perceive directly the mysteries of love which grow in souls; men, who are weak,[20] can perceive these mysteries not directly, but only as they are made manifest in the

[18]Grierson (*The Poems of John Donne*, II, 44) quotes a passage from Du Bartas which refers to Pliny, Plutarch, Plato, and Aristotle. Gardner (*The Elegies and the Songs and Sonnets*, p. 186) cites a passage from Paracelsus.

[19]Merritt Y. Hughes ("Some of Donne's 'Ecstasies,'" p. 514) quotes Donne's opinion that in this world we can see only through a glass darkly: "neither *Adam* in his ecstasie in Paradise, nor *Moses* in his conversation in the Mount, nor the other Apostles in the Transfiguration of Christ, nor S. *Paul* in his rapture to the third heavens, saw the Essence of God, because he that is admitted to that sight of God, can never look off, nor lose that sight againe. Only in heaven shall God proceed to this patefaction, this manifestation, this revelation of himself" (*The Sermons of John Donne*, ed. George R. Potter and Evelyn M. Simpson [Berkeley, 1953-62], VIII, 232). Donne utilizes the idea in his epithalamion for Somerset; he tells the bride, "Pouder thy Radiant haire, / Which if without such ashes thou would'st weare, / Thou, which, to all which come to looke upon, / Art meant for Phoebus, would'st be Phaëton." See, too, "Goodfriday, 1613. Riding Westward": "Who sees Gods face, that is selfe life, must dye."

[20]Gardner's reading of the lines "To'our bodies turne wee then, that so / Weake men on love reveal'd may looke" makes for difficulties. The introduction so late in the poem of a second audience, "weake men" or "layetie," not only makes diffuse the focus and point of view which Donne has carefully established, but it also assumes that the refined listener will be moved by an argument which calls for consideration of and generosity toward "prophane men." Moreover, the reading introduces a purpose which has no intrinsic value for the lovers, which will in no way benefit them, but which calls upon their magnanimity and sense of duty.
Gardner's reading depends too much on her recognition that "in his 'Platonic' poems Donne's lovers often speak as if they had a kind of mission to the world, to impart a glimmering of 'love's mysteries' to the 'laity' in love. . . . Donne's lovers always assume their superiority to the rest of mankind; and these have just given proof that they are extraordinary." She finds it impossible that the lovers should include themselves among "weake men" (*The Elegies and the Songs and Sonnets*, p. 261, n. 1).

body. The soul is subject to direct revelation; man learns the same truths by relying on the Scripture of the body.

The "abler soule," having described the nature of the union of souls in ecstasy, takes great pains to make it clear that there is little to choose between the love of souls and the love of bodies. The listener to the "abler soule" of the lovers "will not be aware of much difference between their union when 'out of the body' and *their union* when they have resumed possession of their" bodies. The quoted words are Gardner's (p. 303); the italics are mine. The emphasis in Gardner's words here is a little different from her insistence that the proposal in the last part of the poem is "the perfectly modest one that the lovers' souls, having enjoyed the rare privilege of union outside the body, should now resume possession of their separate bodies and reanimate these virtual corpses" (p. 283). To be sure, the last lines of the poem do not so much point directly to physical intercourse as do other, earlier lines; they are, rather, directed to clarifying the relation between souls and bodies. Still, there is little doubt about Donne's direction throughout the poem and about its end doctrine: a justification of bodily love as not incompatible with spiritual love.

But, Gardner says, the fact that an ideal lover is invited to "marke" the lovers when they are "to bodies gone" "surely makes the notion that the poem culminates in an 'immodest proposal' absolutely impossible." "It is one thing," she explains, "for a narrative poet to describe two lovers in passionate embrace oblivious of a bystander, as Spenser does at the original ending of Book III of the *Faerie Queene*; it is quite another for lovers themselves to call for an audience at their coupling." And, she

---

Donne has in "The Exstasie" underscored the extraordinary nature of the ecstatic experience. The "abler soule" is uniquely qualified to speak about love. What is surprising about its speech is that it is not content to exalt souls in ecstasy, but that it still cares about bodies. It recognizes, refined as it is, its link to the body and it holds that man ("weake men") is composed of body as well as soul. It recognizes, too, that ecstasy is customarily beyond a mortal's share, reached only by casting the body's vest aside, and it therefore justifies man's cultivation of a garden less pure and sweet than the landscape of heaven.

continues, "M. Legouis himself thought it particularly shocking that 'the hypothetical listener of the prelude re-appears and turns spectator at a time when the lovers as well as we could wish him away'" (p. 284). It is, of course, possible to defend Donne by asserting that the ideal listener and voyeur is hypothetical, not real. He is, in fact, not present to hear the words of the "abler soule" or to view the union of bodies; his presence is imagined. This defense is not, however, necessary. If the proposal at the end of the poem is considered "immodest," the wit in the poem leads us to insist that the immodesty is in the eye of the beholder. Who are we, who is the ideal listener, to doubt the authority and the propriety of what is proposed by the "abler soule"? Can we deny the truths which it has propounded about the relation between soul and body? The conclusion of the poem follows logically and wittily from what has preceded. We must be strange believers, indeed, if we find it immodest to read Scripture. The chief stroke of wit in "The Exstasie" is Donne's tactic of having the "abler soule" make the case justifying the role of the body in love and educating not "the layetie" but the refined Neo-Platonist who must be persuaded of the prerogatives of the body. This listener has no use for the softnesses of love; he will be persuaded only by the nice speculations of philosophy. In the amorous verses of "The Exstasie," Donne affects the metaphysics so that nature may reign.

What of Donne's "sincerity" in "The Exstasie"? All we can say is that he is here concerned to make a case for physical love; here he asserts, above all else, the prerogatives of the body. Is his justification seriously meant? If it is not, it is hard to see why Donne would have bothered to write the poem; he means seriously what he says about the role of the body in love. Does he, in fact, believe what he propounds about spiritual love, about ecstasy? There is no reason to deny his belief in the situation and doctrine he sets forth. We must admit, however, that the first sections of the poem are used to point toward and reinforce the last section, that it is most useful for Donne, indeed crucial for him, in this poem to assume the validity and value of the ecstatic experience so that he can through his speaker make the most authoritative and convincing statement possible about the role of the body to a listener who has "grown all minde." "But," one asks, "is the whole argument intentionally sophisticated?" The question seems to imply that, if Donne was not a firm believer in ecstasy as he described it, there is something immoral, lacking in integrity, in his feigning such a belief. We must judge intent by performance and we must not confuse literature with life. The whole of Donne's argument is coherent and effective; the argument itself is not sophisticated, whatever his own beliefs and motives may have been. "Is somebody being 'led up the garden path'"? The question begs a question, or two. Is it wayward to sing the Song of Songs? May it not be therapeutic to impart the wisdom of Solomon to a congregation grown all mind?

"The Exstasie" is not a moving celebration of mutual love like "The Good-morrow" or "A Valediction: forbidding Mourning." It is not so great a poem about love as "The Canonization," for, because of the kind of poem Donne wanted to write, it lacks feeling except in the communication of the mystery at its beginning and in the two lines which introduce the last section. Its doctrinal content contains no startling truths or insights for the modern reader, who, in fact, must acquaint himself with the subtleties of ideas long since outmoded[21] in order to understand what Donne is saying about spiritual and physical love. But the arid air of refined doctrine provides a fertile atmosphere for crisp argument and dry wit. No one will deny that Donne was profoundly moved by the concept of love as union; however, the concept took not one shape but several in his poetry. If "The Exstasie" holds the key to Donne's greatest love poetry, it opens only the door of his subject matter, not of his feeling. For all

[21]They were probably outmoded, too, for many of Donne's contemporaries. Hughes says ("Some of Donne's 'Ecstasies,'" p. 515), "Donne wrote for an audience which had rejected its faith in ecstasy as Aquinas understood it." He holds that "by the end of the sixteenth century, if ecstasy in any of its meanings was to be taken seriously," it had to be used imaginatively or ingeniously by a poet.

that, I agree with Gardner that "it is a wonderful poem and a poem that only Donne could have written" (p. 304), the inventive, cerebral, imperious Donne who ruled as he saw fit the universal monarchy of wit.

2

Contextual Study and Donne's "A Valediction: forbidding Mourning"

> The body will not last out to have read
> On every part, and therefore men direct
> Their speech to parts, that are of most effect.
>
> —"An Anatomy of the World," ll. 436–38

Readers of literature readily assume the utility of studies of context and source, especially for works written long ago, and particularly for a poet like Donne, who confessed to a preoccupation with learning[1] and whom Dr. Johnson placed in a school of learned poets whose sole endeavor was to show their learning.[2] If scholars admired Grierson's text, it was his Commentary that was thumbed for light on allusions, parallels, *topoi*, conventions. In the Introduction to his *Metaphysical Lyrics & Poems of the Seventeenth Century*, Grierson described Donne's poetry as intellectual, learned, ratiocinative, but he considered Donne "metaphysical" only by virtue of his familiarity with the definitions and distinctions of scholasticism and his deep and reflective psychological curiosity into the experiences of love and religion. Donne, he insisted, was not a metaphysical poet in the full sense of the term, not, like Lucretius or Dante or Goethe, a poet inspired by a philosophical conception of the universe.[3] The most extremely reductionist expression of this statement was

[1]*Letters to Severall Persons of Honour* (London, 1651), p. 51.
[2]*Lives of the English Poets by Samuel Johnson*, ed. George Birkbeck Hill (Oxford, 1905), I, 19.
[3]Herbert J. C. Grierson, ed., *Metaphysical Lyrics & Poems of the Seventeenth Century* (Oxford, 1921), pp. xiii–xvi.

the assertion of C. S. Lewis that ideas in Donne's poetry have "no value or even existence except as they articulate and render more fully self-conscious the passion" of a particular moment.[4] In an article (discussed in Chapter 1) in which she sought to show that Donne's Platonism as it related to love derived from Leone Ebreo's *Dialoghi d'Amore*, Helen Gardner chided Lewis and other scholars who tried to exalt Donne's wit "at the expense of his artistic and intellectual integrity, and to deny that ideas had any value to him as a poet except as counters to be used in an argument." "Donne's greatness needs restating," she said; "One element in that greatness is that certain ideas mattered to him intensely and that he made them wholly his own."[5] Recently, A. J. Smith stated that if Donne's love poems do not offer us a Lucretius, a Dante, or a Michelangelo, they still add up to a metaphysic of love: "Donne's wit is purposeful and expresses a settled way of encountering experience which *is* his philosophy of love. The love poems cohere overall. They don't say the same thing by a long way but they don't exclude each other either; they refer back convincingly to the realities of erotic life in which a committed passion will subsume sexuality rather than reject or transcend it." In dealing with "The Canonization," Smith speaks of "the embodied passion of two people whose sexual expressions only confirm their deeper sense of oneness," and he maintains that what holds the love poetry together is "a coherent vision of human nature and a consistent temper of mind." When he says that Donne would have been chagrined to find people talking of Neo-Platonic ideas in his verse, Smith reflects his own chagrin, not Donne's; he admits

[4]C. S. Lewis, *English Literature in the Sixteenth Century* (Oxford, 1954), p. 549. T. S. Eliot had expressed almost the same opinion two decades earlier: "His learning is just information suffused with emotion, or combined with emotion not essentially relevant to it"; "His attitude toward philosophic notions in his poetry may be put by saying that he was more interested in *ideas* themselves as objects than in the *truth* of ideas" ("Donne in Our Time," in *A Garland for John Donne 1631–1931*, ed. Theodore Spencer [1931; rpt. Gloucester, Mass., 1958], pp. 8, 11).

[5]Helen Gardner, "The Argument about 'The Ecstasy,'" in *Elizabethan and Jacobean Studies Presented to Frank Percy Wilson*, ed. Herbert Davis and Helen Gardner (Oxford, 1959), pp. 282, 305.

that "The Exstasie" has Platonic or Neo-Platonic properties. What really bothers him is not the presence of Neo-Platonic ideas in Donne's poetry but what he feels to be a mistaken estimate of their importance to Donne.[6] Still, it was he who had stressed, elsewhere, the necessity of meticulous study of Donne's technical contexts and material sources.[7] The "dismal sound" of Smith's formulation, Patrick Cruttwell said, made his heart sink, though his own bias was on the side of historical truth, and he confessed that he could not imagine "how any young reader, who reads poetry simply to be moved and instructed in the 'context' of his own life, would not be immediately and finally deterred from the reading of *that* poet at least."[8]

These opinions may serve to remind us that study of the context of a literary work, particularly the study of ideas (rather than, say, biographical or political or social context), is complicated by the degree of consistency in an author's world-view, by the change or development of his views about a subject or concept, by the relations between his thought and his feeling and by his expression of these. In my essay on "The Exstasie," I paid homage to contextual studies of Donne which reconstructed traditions and conventions, clarified the climate of opinion, explicated the historical course of ideas, and thereby illuminated poems or passages in them, but I pointed also to the danger of too ready acceptance of explanations based on *Zeitgeist*, of assuming that incidental mention of a subject indicated depth of knowledge, of underestimating the pressures exerted on ideas in a work of art. I tried to show that brilliant exposition of relevant ideas in "The Exstasie" had not, in fact, resolved the controversy about Donne's attitude toward love and about the tone of the poem, that recognition of the propriety and centrality of certain ideas was no guarantee of proper comprehension of

[6] A. J. Smith, "The Dismissal of Love, or, Was Donne a Neoplatonic Lover?" in *John Donne: Essays in Celebration*, ed. A. J. Smith (London, 1972), pp. 90, 124, 128, 131.

[7] Idem, "The Metaphysic of Love," *RES*, ns 9 (1958), 363.

[8] Patrick Cruttwell, "The Love Poetry of John Donne: Pedantique Weedes or Fresh Invention?" in *Metaphysical Poetry* (Stratford-upon-Avon Studies 11), ed. Malcolm Bradbury and David Palmer (New York, 1970), pp. 36–37.

what was being said about the ideas, that there was a gap between context and interpretation.[9]

Unlike "The Exstasie," "A Valediction: forbidding Mourning" has rarely provoked controversy about its attitude toward love and about its tone. When Izaak Walton said of Donne's "Copy of Verses," "I beg leave to tell, that I have heard of some Criticks, learned, both in Languages and Poetry, say, that none of the Greek or Latine Poets did ever equal them," he assumed that the "Valediction," like "Sweetest love, I do not goe," expressed Donne's affection for his wife.[10] Grierson thought the two poems "almost identical in tone": "They are certainly the tenderest of Donne's love poems, perhaps the only ones to which the epithet 'tender' can be applied."[11] Since there has been virtual unanimity about Donne's attitude toward love and his tone, scholars have been content merely to gloss the "Moving of th'earth," "trepidation of the spheares," the alchemical terms in the following two stanzas, and to focus their attention on the source of the compass image.[12] W. A. Murray moved beyond source when he pointed out in conjunction with the line before the image, "Like gold to ayery thinnesse beate," that the chemical symbol for gold in Donne's day was ☉ and that the "transitional association" was self-evident.[13] Robert F. Fleissner cited Murray's words that Donne's conceits often turn out to be connected by complex associations which, discovered, give his

[9]See Chapter 1.

[10]Izaak Walton, *The Lives of Dr John Donne* . . . (London, 1675), pp. 29–33. Walton provides no evidence that the poem was written for Ann Donne or that it was written on the occasion of Donne's accompanying Sir Robert Drury to the continent in 1611–12. His own understanding of the poem persuaded him that he was right about addressee and date.

[11]Herbert J. C. Grierson, ed., *The Poems of John Donne* (Oxford, 1912), II, 40.

[12]See, for example, Mario Praz, *Secentismo e Marinismo in Inghilterra* (Florence, 1925), p. 109; F. P. Wilson, *Elizabethan and Jacobean* (Oxford, 1945), pp. 30, 133; Josef Lederer, "John Donne and the Emblematic Practice," *RES*, 22 (1946), 196–200; D. C. Allen, "Donne's Compass Figure," *MLN*, 71 (1956), 256–57; Doris C. Powers, "Donne's Compass," *RES*, ns 9 (1958), 173–75.

[13]W. A. Murray, "Donne's Gold-Leaf and His Compasses," *MLN*, 73 (1958), 329–30.

poetry greater coherence, and he asked, "What constitutes the most *significant* associations?" He maintained that a correct answer "should entail a consideration of those factors which relate most pertinently to the basic considerations of Donne's age," but he would distinguish associational patterns which are "historically essential" from those which are "merely essentially historical": "The literary historian is obliged to select an attitude toward the integrity of the poem in which the image occurs, one which conforms to what best typifies the milieu of which it is a part and to which its own uniqueness contributes." Fleissner held that "the circle transcribed by the compasses has more poetic significance than the compasses themselves (the design composed being more relevant to Donne's intentions than merely the instrument for constructing it)," and he would find the primary source of Donne's figure in Dante's picture of Love occupying the very center of a circle and in his use of the circle as a symbol of the perfection of love.[14]

More recently, John Freccero has concerned himself in "Donne's 'Valediction: forbidding Mourning'"[15] with the compass image, but he copes with it in a long and learned article which sets forth a formidable intellectual context in, among other things, astronomy, metaphysics, and alchemy. Like most readers of the "Valediction," Freccero feels that Donne's purpose in the poem is to assert the humanity of love. Freccero's title implies that his interest is to explicate the poem, not merely to provide a context. His scholarship is extraordinarily impressive, and every diligent reader will profit from his discussion of ideas which undoubtedly enrich the poem. But his article has been somewhat neglected;[16] I think it fair to say that its effect

[14]Robert F. Fleissner, "Donne and Dante: The Compass Figure Reinterpreted," *MLN*, 76 (1961), 315-20.

[15]John Freccero, "Donne's 'Valediction: forbidding Mourning,'" *ELH*, 30 (1963), 335-76.

[16]Freccero's article may have affected the interpretation by John T. Shawcross in *The Complete Poetry of John Donne* (Garden City, N.Y., 1967), pp. 87-88, 400; it certainly affected the strained speculations of Eugene R. Cunnar's "Donne's 'Valediction: forbidding Mourning' and the Golden Compasses of Alchemical Creation" in Luanne Frank, ed., *Literature and the*

on critics, who felt that they knew what Donne was getting at, has been depressing because it leaves the impression that only a reader of prodigious intellect can properly appreciate the poem. Perhaps it is not a bad thing to leave a reader shaky about his own capacities and newly impressed by the learning and intelligence of a poet, and, after all, the purpose of contextual study is to provide information which a reader is not likely to have. Freccero, however, pursues ideas so intently that, except when he quotes a line of verse, one is never aware that he is dealing with a poem. He treats the "Valediction" as though it is not a song but a subtle treatise, a hermetic text, "The Law, the Prophets, and the History" which others have let fall, and whose incomprehensibleness will not deter him from trying to imprison Donne's sense. Although most of the context he sets forth is relevant, I should like to show that he gives some of it greater importance than it deserves and that some of it perhaps contains some special pleading. I should like to show, too, that though he illuminates the general intellectual context in which Donne works, he does not take sufficiently into account the poetic context within which Donne uses ideas. And, finally, I hope to present an essential context for the poem, which Freccero dismisses out of hand.[17]

Almost at the outset of his article, Freccero finds it important to establish the fact that the idea of resurrection is introduced in the first stanza of the poem and is central to the meaning of

---

Occult (Arlington, Tex., 1977), pp. 72–110. It has been reprinted by John R. Roberts in *Essential Articles for the Study of John Donne's Poetry* (Hamden, Conn., 1975), pp. 279–304, 518–27.

[17]My friend and former colleague would be wholly right to suggest that I call this essay "Yet Once More." We first argued about the poem when he read his paper, prior to its publication, at a meeting of the English Club at Cornell, and again when it was the subject of an interdepartmental colloquium. My comments here, then, constitute triple jeopardy, and no one ought be plagued with that. Freccero's work was instrumental in shaping my own ideas about the utility of scholarship, especially in relation to the teaching of poetry. I trust that my essay will not be read as a denial of my admiration of his learning, my gratitude for its stimulation, my appreciation of his good-natured tolerance of our differences.

the poem. Virtuous men, he says, pass mildly away and confidently whisper to their souls to go because they are convinced that their death is not a definite separation but only a pause in the life of body and soul (p. 358). He quotes from Donne's sermons to show that Donne writes about death and resurrection in figurative terms of the separation and reunion of husband and wife: "As farre as man is immortall, he is a married man still, still in possession of a soule, and a body too"; "Death is the Divorce of body and soule: Resurrection is the Re-union" (p. 337). In the poem, where, Freccero says, the first two stanzas are a simile comparing the death of virtuous men to the parting of two lovers (p. 372), Donne reverses the analogy found in the sermons and writes "to his beloved" of their separation and eventual reunion in figurative terms of death and resurrection (p. 338). "The union of husband and wife, their love," Freccero says, is like the union of body and soul; "it is Love incarnate, possessed of a single soul," and though Love dies a physical death when the lovers part, its soul lives on "in the comfort of the Resurrection, when husband and wife, the components of Love's body, will cleave together once more." The "Valediction," then, not only precludes grief in the same way that the death of virtuous men forbids mourning, but the first simile hints that "just as the righteous soul will at the Last Judgement return to its glorified body, so the voyager will return to his beloved" (p. 338).

Attractive as these suggestions are, they get us into problems. First, Donne's use of an analogy in the sermons does not *prove* that he had used the same analogy and, moreover, reversed its terms, in a poem written some years earlier. Second, the analogy allegorizes the relation of body and soul in terms of the relation of husband and wife, *not* of man and woman. Freccero is careful to refer to the woman in the "Valediction" as the "beloved," though he twice calls her a wife (pp. 341, 355). Donne may feel in some of the *Songs and Sonets* that lovers are "more than maryed," but that doctrine is not easily yoked to a Christian context and, as Freccero himself points out, "the doctrine of the Resurrection can be of little comfort to lovers whom death parts, since there is no marriage in heaven" (p. 338). Third, the idea of resurrection is not central to the first stanza; it is, at most, implied as the reason that virtuous men pass mildly away and whisper to their souls to leave their bodies. The idea is contained in the first two lines of the stanza. What is its relation to the other two lines? Freccero maintains that lines 3 and 4 present a simile antithetical to the first one, which compares the death of virtuous men to the parting of two lovers: the sad friends, who cannot determine when the separation of body and soul is definitive because they cannot discern the breathing, are "like the 'layetie' who cannot understand the mystery of love" (pp. 372-73). They are sad because they "lack an intimate assurance of the Resurrection and therefore cannot be sure that they will ever see the dying man again. This may well be the moment of definitive separation and it therefore seems a matter of some importance to watch the purely material breath (which is all they can perceive) as it leaves the body once and for all" (p. 358). Freccero forces us to ask what kind of friends virtuous men have. Are virtuous men likely to have friends who lack an intimate assurance of the Resurrection? Do their friends have no belief in the doctrine? Do they question that the dying men are virtuous enough for resurrection? Are they unsure about their own resurrection? Their "debates," Freccero says, "are irrelevant to the dying man who, like the historian of ideas, knows that the 'breath' which is expired in time is intimately connected with the soul which is 'inspired' in eternity" even though he cannot communicate his confidence to the "layetie" (p. 358). But if the friends' words are not relevant to the dying men, it is obvious that Donne does not consider their sadness and their observations to be irrelevant to his stanza. The friends are not carrying on a debate (the slow and soft escape of sound is equally reflected in the *s*'s of lines 1 and 2 and of lines 3 and 4). They are quietly, laconically, almost reverently remarking on the attenuation of the breath of friends. More likely than not, they, too, believe in the Resurrection, but Donne does not raise the question. He stresses their very human sadness as they watch friends depart this life.

At one point, in a footnote, Freccero sees fit to say that "the traditional identification of a peaceful death with virtue and a violent death with vice explains the association here of 'virtuous men' and passing 'mildly away'" (p. 360). He is quite right, and it is interesting that in this *topos* there is no mention of resurrection. What was Donne's opinion of the *topos*? The question itself is irresponsible, for it does not ask *when* he had an opinion, whether he may have changed his opinion, whether he may on occasion have exploited a *topos* he did not believe in. Donne comments most memorably on the *topos* in *Deaths Duell*, his last sermon. He says, "we have no . . . rule or art to give a *presagition* of *spirituall death* & damnation upon any such *indication* as wee see in any *dying man*." We must draw no ill conclusions from a man's loathness to die; and "upon *violent deaths* inflicted, as upon malefactors, *Christ* himselfe hath forbidden us by his owne death to make any *ill conclusion*." Although Donne sees that we pray "for a *peaceable life* against *violent death*, & for *time* of *repentance* against *sudden death*, and for *sober* and *modest assurance* against *distemperd* and *diffident death*," he says that we must never make "*ill conclusions* upon persons overtaken with such deaths." He maintains that "Our *criticall* day is *not* the *very day* of our *death*, but the whole course of our life."[18] Donne's opinion here is precisely the opposite of that expressed in the first two lines of the "Valediction." Regardless of what his opinion was when he wrote the "Valediction," he saw fit on that occasion to assume the justness of the *topos*. Perhaps he believed it; perhaps he didn't. If he didn't, he was not averse, in a poem, to taking advantage of a stereotype when it served his purpose to do so. It is clear, however, that even in his most memorable discussion of the stereotype Donne's emphasis is on the relation, or lack of it, between the way of life and the way of death; his sole allusion to resurrection is in his refutation that the way of death presages "*spirituall death* & damnation." Nevertheless, Freccero maintains that the strategy of the "Valediction" is that "the 'body' of Love dies

[18]*Deaths Duell* (London, 1632), pp. 25–27.

when the lovers part and is 'resurrected' when they are reunited" (p. 346), and the rest of his argument is predicated on this assumption.

It is the compass image, Freccero says, which manages to span the two moments between the death of the body of Love when the lovers part and its resurrection when they are reunited (p. 346). Because the compass image symbolizes "the principle which governs the movement of the poem" (p. 353), Freccero must explicate the principle in detail, and he finds that its context is primarily astronomical (p. 348). But all movement or motion must take place in some medium, and Freccero is then concerned to show that "the vital reality underlying the compass image is *pneuma*, or *spiritus*," the mysterious substance or breath of the universe which the ancients thought to be "the medium of the soul's action on the body, as well as the medium of the planetary soul's action on the heavenly body" (p. 357). The establishment of this context is important to him because he holds that in the "Valediction" "a symbolic *pneuma* joins the body and soul of Love, and therefore is the symbolic medium through which the poem moves" (p. 357). Moreover, since he feels that the utilization of such a fundamental principle "lacks the symbolic concreteness which we have come to expect from Donne" and that Donne must somehow root the "spirit" of Love to the real world, he must explore still another context (p. 362). He maintains that in Donne's time the science of alchemy predicated a theoretical continuity between matter and spirit and that Donne borrowed some of its principles in order to give a symbolic consistency to his poem. He must, then, probe the mysteries of alchemy in order to show how "an allegory based on the Hermetic science resolves the complexity of the poem into a unified and poetically meaningful statement" (p. 362). Before we can properly understand the poem, we must be familiar, among other things, with Aristotle on the cognitive and appetitive powers of the soul (p. 351), the principles of the cosmic year (p. 355), the reversibility of spiritual and chemical orders built into the language of alchemy and its use of sexual allegory (pp. 364–65), the planetary course of Mercury through the Zodiac (p. 370), and the doctrine of the ecstatic kiss of rational lovers (pp. 374–76).

The massive erudition in Freccero's article tends to overwhelm, almost to run counter to, his thesis that Donne's purpose in the "Valediction" is to assert the humanity of love. The compass image, he says,

> protests, precisely in the name of incarnation, against the neo-Petrarchan and neoplatonic dehumanization of love. It makes substantially the same point made by Love to the young Dante three hundred years before: angelic love is a perfect circle, while beasts move directly and insatiably to the center; *tu autem non sic*.
>
> Human love is neither because it is both; it pulsates between the eternal perfection of circularity and the linear extension of space and time. The compass which Donne uses to symbolize it, therefore, traces not merely a circle but a dynamic process, the "swerving serpentine" of Donne's poetry and of his thought. . . . With its whirling motion, Love's compass describes the expansion of the lovers' spirit from eternity to time and back again.
>
> This motion is the archetypal pattern of Love's universe, the principle of coherence joining matter and spirit throughout all levels of reality. [Pp. 336–37]

Because the compass image has always fascinated readers and because perhaps the most fascinating part of Freccero's article is his explanation of what has long been thought to be an inconsistency in the image, I should now like to focus on it.

> If they be two, they are two so
>   As stiffe twin compasses are two,
> Thy soule the fixt foot, makes no show
>   To move, but doth, if th'other doe.
>
> And though it in the center sit,
>   Yet when the other far doth rome,
> It leanes, and harkens after it,
>   And growes erect, as it comes home.

Such wilt thou be to mee, who must
 Like th'other foot, obliquely runne;
Thy firmnes makes my circle just,
 And makes me end, where I begunne.

The second of these stanzas has generally been thought to describe movement along a radius, from a center to a circumference and back again; the third, or at least its last two lines, has been thought to describe circular motion. The "inconsistency" in the last two lines has most recently been commented upon by James Winny: "The analogy is not exact, for when the outer leg of the compasses completes its circle it is at the same distance from the centre as during its movement; and obviously Donne means the closing of the circle to represent reunion at the end of the journey."[19] Freccero points to the "epigrammatic quality" of the last line and says, "If we were to take 'end' to mean some point on the circumference, then the feet would remain equidistant throughout such an image, whereas the meaning is that the lover begins from the center, beside his beloved, is separated from her and finally will return" (pp. 340–41). His explanation of the logic of the compass image is wonderfully ingenious:

> The beginning of the poem states the relationship of the lover to his beloved in terms of the union of body and soul. The ending of the poem traces the emblem of that union, the geometric image of a soul that cannot be perfect while it remains disembodied and therefore cannot be represented in the same way that Dante represented angelic love. In other words, the "circle" which ends the poem is no circle in the ordinary sense, but is rather a circle joined to a rectilinear "otherness" distinguishing man from the angels. . . . With its whirling motion, the compass synthesizes the linear extension of time and space with the circularity of eternity. [P. 339]

Referring to the commentary of Chalcidius on the *Timaeus*, Freccero explains that in antiquity the *spiral* was considered to

[19]James Winny, *A Preface to Donne* (London, 1970), p. 140.

be the harmonization of rectilinear motion with circularity (p. 341). He maintains that Donne uses the compass image in the same way as Chalcidius, "to describe a wandering path which is nevertheless rooted in circular regularity," and that Donne's use of the word "rome" shows that he had in mind the exemplar of such orbits, the path described by the planets or "wandering" stars (p. 342). He finds confirmation of Donne's dependence on the spiral in "obliquely runne." That phrase, he says, not only describes planetary motion quite accurately but it also indicates that Donne is referring not to a path or a line but to a "kind" of motion, "the motion which in the Latin neoplatonic tradition was referred to as the *motus obliquus*" (p. 345). He concludes, then, that "a compass can lean or grow erect *at the same time* that it describes a circle only if that 'circle' is in fact a spiral. The next to the last line of the poem does indeed indicate diurnal, circular motion, the fixity of love, while the last refers to a dyastolic and systolic pulsation, the 'zodiacal' exigencies of life, for these two patterns are combined in the figure that 'obliquely' runs" (p. 346).

Freccero's resolution of the "inconsistency" is learned and complicated, but Donne is a learned and complicated poet. Freccero's gloss of "obliquely" as "spirally" would be more persuasive if he could illustrate the usage in some English text; normally, the term has linear reference: it refers to a slanting direction, to a diagonal, to a line inclined at some angle other than a right angle. But his gloss is not impossible and it is tempting in his astronomical context. He shows, too, the astronomical relevance of such words as "rome," "home," "lean," and "erect," and he would lay to rest the erotic interpretation sometimes given the last two by demonstrating that the Hebrew letters kaph and samekh may stand for the words *inclinatio* and *erectio* and may be considered hieroglyphs for separation and reunion (p. 350). He calls erotic interpretation of the words psychologically naive, and in the light of his own abstruse and Pierian reading, the intrusion of eroticism would indeed be jarring. But the fact is that he is not interested in the psychology of the poem.

Freccero classifies the "Valediction" as a *congé d'amour* (p. 353), and he is aware that Donne has written other poems of this kind. But when he speaks of "vital reality" it is to discuss *pneuma* and when he speaks of the "real world" it is to discuss alchemy. For all his emphasis on the humanization of love, he is oblivious to the humanity of the situation which the poem predicates and to the humanity of the lovers involved. About a quarter of the *Songs and Sonets* deal with the departure of love or the parting of lovers, and Donne's attitude and approach differ from poem to poem. In "Sweetest love, I do not goe," for instance, "Donne *speaks* to his woman"; as Wilbur Sanders reminds us, we have a "real speech to a real person." Sanders sees that the speaker takes the "woman's fears" of his beloved into his own consciousness and gives them back to her "clothed in his man's tenderness." "That tonal sensitivity," he wisely insists, "the voice responding subtly and feelingly to the woman's presence, has a great deal to do with Donne's authority as a love-poet."[20] Similarly, in contrasting the "Valediction" with "The Valediction: Of Weeping," Winny is sensitive to its "inhibition of emotional display": "Donne does not merely urge the lady to be reticent, but shows restraint himself by adopting a simple poetic form and a manner which invites none of his characteristic flamboyance."[21] Freccero, on the other hand, focuses exclusively on nice speculations of philosophy, and though he says that the speculations are used in the service of the humanity of love, he sees none of the softnesses of love in the poem. The speaker in the poem is, for him, an ingenious prodigy of learning. If we ask what kind of woman Freccero assumes to be addressed,[22] we must try to imagine the Renaissance equivalent of a disciple of Arthur O. Lovejoy with a lot of time on her hands.

[20]Wilbur Sanders, *John Donne's Poetry* (Cambridge, 1971), pp. 11–12.
[21]*A Preface to Donne*, p. 138.
[22]The poem is, of course, a monologue. The woman in the poem is never addressed directly, as she is in "Sweetest love, I do not goe" and in "A Valediction: of Weeping." But I know of no sensible critic who looks upon the poem as a soliloquy, as an effort by the poet to persuade himself that he ought not mourn. The voice in the poem has always been thought to be responsive to the presence of a woman, not to be indulging in meditation or self-persuasion.

The vital reality in the "Valediction" inheres in a common human situation: a lover must part from his beloved. This woman, like many in such a situation, cannot control her emotions; she is carrying on. How can one forbid mourning, how command that tears stop, how argue with emotions? Even Dr. Johnson saw that one "must divert distressing thoughts, and not combat with them"; "To attempt to *think them down* is madness"; the mind must fly from itself—to chemistry, to rope-dancing, to anything.[23] If Donne's speaker is a sensible man, we may assume that his words are not imperative, not intended to argue his lady down. They are hortatory: he wishes to quiet her, to comfort her. He knows that no argument will by the force of its logic stem tears; one might better argue with the ocean tide. Moreover, any such argument must argue against nature. If, however, in these circumstances, argument cannot itself be persuasive, the very attempt at argument may be. He may perhaps divert or distract his lady from her emotion by trying to get her to follow an argument. Even if his argument has a hole in it, as indeed it must have if he argues against nature, it may persuade her to let up a little. She will perhaps find some comfort in the very effort he is making to comfort her. And, of course, even as heartless logic and relentlessly pedantic reason may increase her tears, so a calm and controlled voice, speaking mildly and naturally, not dogmatically, may influence her mood.

It is just such a voice which Donne uses in the "Valediction." For this occasion, he does not see fit to carve out an eccentric stanzaic form of his own; he uses the conventional cross-rhyming tetrameter quatrain. On this occasion, he keeps accent, modulating the perfect regularity of his beat only so that one hears a natural, conversational inflection. The first stanza of his argument is no rigid first step in a syllogistic formulation; he approaches his subject indirectly, with an analogy which can only show that for him, too, parting is like dying. The deathbed

[23]*Boswell's Life of Johnson*, ed. George Birkbeck Hill and L. F. Powell (Oxford, 1934), II, 440.

scene he evokes is almost as inhumanly still as it is, humanly, sad, and he would endow his love with the virtue, faith, holiness, and human caring implicit in such a scene. His exhortation for quiet is based on degree and hierarchy: the lovers are priests who would not profane their belief by revealing it by acts and signs to the laity; their love is not earthbound but partakes of the magnitude of the universe. It is not, like the love of most people, entirely dependent upon sensual desire. It is characterized by a mysterious refinement, by so perfect and constant an interpenetration of minds that its purity is unalterable and its security is confident. That is not to say that sensual desire is not part of it. The love of dull, sublunary lovers depends entirely on their physical proximity. When Donne says that he and his lady "Care lesse, eyes, lips, and hands to misse," he is not dismissing what is physical from his love. His very naming of bodily parts calls them into prominence, and he does not say that he and his lady care nothing for them but that they care less for them; they are less essential to their love than they are to that of others. Their love, holy, aristocratic, refined, partaking of the mind, is far from mundane; it is a love which has, indeed, united their very souls so that they are one, and souls so united can never be parted. Donne had introduced a metal image when he had said, "So let us melt"; he had utilized the elements of alchemy to characterize the refinement of their love; he clinches his argument that he and his lady can never be severed by likening their separation to gold beat to airy thinness. The gold image serves also, of course, to signify that their love is rich and precious.

Another poet would have been content to end on this note. Donne has, after all, presented an interesting and coherent argument based on a rarified concept of love, one that makes an appeal to exclusivity, magnitude, spirituality, preciousness. But to a woman made of flesh and blood, his last image, for all its refinement and delicacy, is somewhat thin. How comforting will she find the doctrines that their love is preeminent in its adherence to soul, that their one soul is capable of almost infinite expansion? Even gold leaf will not expand infinitely, and of what value is it when it is thinned to transparency or invisibility? Donne's conclusion is about as comforting as the adolescent Dryden's to the fiancée of the recently deceased Lord Hastings:

> With greater then Platonic love, O wed
> His soul, tho' not his body, to thy bed:
> Let that make thee a mother; bring thou forth
> Th' *ideas* of his virtue, knowledge, worth.

Moreover, though Donne would seem to have conceded the element of humanity in their love in "sad friends" and in "Care lesse,"[24] whatever human feeling his words communicate is mainly in the strenuous effort of mind he has made and in the tenderness of his own voice. Since the poem continues after the gold image, we can be sure that his lady has not ceased to mourn and that he himself feels some urgency to do more.

Cognizant, it would seem, of an inadequacy both in his general argument and in this last image, Donne violates one of the rules of argument by making a concession at the close of his speech. Having stated that two souls were one, he now says, "If they be two." Still, he continues to talk about souls, and, as though his equation of souls and gold has reminded him that the symbol of gold is ☉ and that reminds him of the center and circumference of a circle drawn by a compass, he now talks about the compass. For all these connections, the compass image comes as a surprise. Neither souls nor compasses strike us as subjects conducive to a concession about the humanity of love. If the appeal to souls seems rarified, that to geometry seems totally lacking in humanity. Moreover, if the argument about the nature of their love has to this point been made quietly, indirectly, associatively, the demonstration of the force of the compass analogy is made with attention to detail and to logic. It is developed at length, step by step, as though Donne is intent to prove his point, to make the firmest case he can. He first shows that even if he concedes that their souls are two, they are

---

[24]See, too, Freccero (p. 365) for the erotic connotations of "melt."

united as the legs of a compass are united and that, therefore, they are in harmony with one another since the foot at the center ("fixt" = stable, constant, unmoved, not affected by circumstance), stationary though it seems, moves if the other leg moves. He then shows that the unity and harmony of souls persists even when one leg moves some distance along a radius, since the other inevitably reacts to its motion away from and back to the center. In the third demonstration, he would show that the lovers themselves, not their souls alone, remain unified and harmonized. If one leg runs obliquely, that is, moves out along a radius to a certain point, the firmness of the other forces it to move round in a perfect circle and makes it end where it began. But, as Winny points out, the circle begins at some distance from its center and it is completed not at the center but on the circumference. The legs — and the lovers — are not reunited. The closing lines do have an epigrammatic quality; Donne *seems* to imply in them that both the perfection of the circle and the reunion of the lovers are inevitable and just, so long as his lady is stable, constant, unaffected by circumstance. But we are aware that the legs of the compass have not come together, that there is a gap between the lovers, that Donne's final image is as inadequate in its way as was the image of gold beat to airy thinness.[25]

We must assume, moreover, that Donne is sufficiently accomplished a poet not to huddle up an analogy; if his analogy is inexact, he means us to see that it is inexact and that its inexactness undercuts his overt argument.[26] It is likely, too, that his lady will see that it is inexact. His conclusion cannot comfort

[25]I prefer Winny's description to Freccero's. If to run "obliquely" indicates a spiral motion, the return motion must also be spiral, and though this motion is circular, it is not a "just" circle which is described. Even Freccero's description, then, leaves a hole in the argument.

[26]The last stanza describes two actions, one in line 2 ("obliquely runne") and one in line 3 ("circle just"). The efficacy of Donne's overt argument depends on the equivalence of the closing of the circle (the symbol of perfection) and the inevitable reunion of the lovers (perfect love). The semicolon after line 2, which is a common modern emendation of the full stop in the early printed editions, and Donne's emphasis on the justness of the circle in line 3 so

her, for what has geometry to do with human emotion? No geometrical proof, not even a perfect one, could comfort her. Her
lover has, however, been sensitive to her tears. She is aware of
the effort he has made to plead for her firmness. He has tried to
moderate, if not to stop, her mourning by demonstrating his
concern for her mood, by speaking quietly and calmly to her,
by showing her how highly he values their love, by making as
good a case against mourning as can be made. He has tried to
prove what he knows he cannot prove. He knows that at parting
sighs and tears are natural and human, but he has exercised all
his control and his ingenuity, particularly in his elaboration of
the compass image, both to divert her from her sadness and to
show her how much he cares. The very failure of his proof is itself a manifestation of the humanity of his love.

This his lady will perceive, and it is likely that she will also
perceive that both his ingenuity and the humanity of his love
are greater than I have thus far demonstrated. Her comprehension of the compass image is hardly dependent on a deep understanding of astronomy. What is so striking about the image
is Donne's clear, precise, methodical demonstration of how the
action of one leg affects the action of the other. If his lady
catches an overtone beyond the purely geometrical, it is not
likely that she hears the music of the spheres, though terms like
"home" and "erect" may be familiar to her as part of the vocab-
ulary of astronomy. It is more likely that to a woman reacting
emotionally to a physical separation from her lover such a collo-
cation of words as "stiffe," "foot," "center," "erect," "firmnes,"
and "circle" would carry erotic overtones, even though (or, even
because) they perversely fly in the face of the impersonality of
geometry and even though, in context, they ludicrously turn

focus attention on the action of completing the circle that for a moment we
believe that Donne has indeed ended where he began — until we realize that he
has ended at a point on the circle and has not been reunited with his lady.

It is not impossible to argue that Donne may have wished us to read the last
two lines to mean that the woman's firmness not only closes the circle which
the man makes but also causes him to retrace the oblique path which he origi-
nally took. If Donne intended this, he wrote less precisely and even more ellip-
tically here than he usually did, and the last action is one which detracts from
the perfection of the circle.

customary sexual connotations upside down.[27] The geometrical proof goes one way; at the very least, the *words* of the proof, their natural or physical denotations, jostle against the proof and, perhaps, even undermine it. Moreover, the sign of the compass image, which calls up its fundamental components of a point and a circle, the ⊙ which was also the recognized symbol of gold, is likely to call up customary associations so strong that they subvert the novelty and eccentricity of Donne's stipulative definition of the components.

When Burns exclaims that the sweetest hours he ever spent were spent "amang the lasses O," his *O* is not exclamatory, and it is in a long tradition. When the Nurse tells Romeo to cease his lamentation and be a man, she says, "For Juliet's sake, for her sake, rise and stand! / Why should you fall into so deep an O?" (III.iii. 89–90). When Benvolio says that conjuring Romeo by Rosaline's fair parts will anger him, Mercutio replies, "'Twould anger him / To raise a spirit in his mistress' circle / Of some strange nature, letting it there stand / Till she had laid it and conjured it down" (II.i. 23–26). In "Loves Alchymie" Donne asks where the "centrique happinesse" of "loves Myne" lies, and in "Loves Progress" he says "we love the Centrique part." In *Eastward Ho!* Gertrude asks Quicksilver, "Dost remember since thou and I clapped what-d'ye-call-'ts in the garret?" (III.ii), and we understand, if only in retrospect, that Quicksilver was not merely describing a country estate when Security had asked (in II.[ii]), "You know his wife's land?"

> *Quick.* Even to a foot, sir; I have been often there; a pretty fine seat, good land, all entire within itself.
> *Sec.* Well wooded?
> *Quick.* Two hundred pounds' worth of wood ready to fell. And a fine sweet house, that stands just in the midst on 't, like a prick in the midst of a circle.

We have no reason to believe that Donne's lady was any more skilled in music than in alchemy or astronomy. She may not

---

[27]See Eric Partridge, *Shakespeare's Bawdy* (London, 1947), and E. A. M. Colman, *The Dramatic Use of Bawdy in Shakespeare* (London, 1974).

have known, nor is it at all important that we know, that the sign of "*the moode perfect of the more* [prolation]" is "a whole cirkle with a prick or point in the center or middle thus: ⊙ ."[28] We can, however, assume her general familiarity with prick-song and also her awareness that the extended image which concludes Donne's argument is a reversal or rebuttal of the kind of "pricksong" of which modest ladies feign to be ignorant.[29] Donne has, as it were, set his words about his refined and spiritual love to the tune of a bawdy song. He has argued as effectively as he could for a kind of love which would preclude mourning, and even on its own merits, his argument has not been entirely successful, since its conclusion is inexact and inadequate. In addition, he has argued in terms which conjure up meanings other than those he stipulates; they are a constant reminder of a context different from his own, a context so familiar that it works against the thrust of his argument. His own words are a denial of what is natural, customary, and human, but his very choice of such words shows how much a part of him they are, how aware he is of his own humanity.

What effect does the compass image have on the lady? She will see that Donne has made a concession, will appreciate that

---

[28]Thomas Morley, *A Plaine and Easie Introduction to Practicall Musicke* (London, 1597), p. 18; rpt. Shakespeare Association Facsimiles No. 14 (1937).

[29]See George Chapman's *Bussy d'Ambois* (1607), I [ii]:

Monsieur I have here a friend / That I would gladly enter in your graces.

Bussy Save you, ladies.

Duchess If you enter him in our graces, my lord, methinks by his blunt behaviour he should come out of himself.

Tamyra Has he never been courtier, my lord?

Monsieur Never, my lady.

Beaupré And why did the toy take him in th' head now?

Bussy 'T is leap-year, lady, and therefore very good to enter a courtier.

K. Henry Mark, Duchess of Guise, there is one is not bashful.

Duchess No, my lord, he is much guilty of the bold extremity.

Tamyra The man 's a courtier at first sight.

Bussy I can sing pricksong, lady, at first sight; and why not be a courtier as suddenly?

Beaupré Here 's a courtier rotten before he be ripe.

Bussy Think me not impudent, lady; I am yet no courtier; I desire to be one, and would gladly take entrance, madam, under your princely colours.

he is being responsive to her in making one. Still, the concession, it turns out, is not truly one; Donne continues to try to
prove the same point he has made before. But, since he has got
hold of such a striking image, since he is arguing logically
rather than associatively, he has caught her attention and she
starts to follow his step-by-step demonstration. The compass
image is probably absurd and ingenious enough to distract her.
She weeps still, we may imagine, but more quietly, for she is lis-
tening intently. Donne's words confuse her; she blushes, perhaps, for though his words say one thing, they remind her of
another tune. When he ends, she is aware of a flaw in his argument, and she is aware that he must be very much aware of another point as he writes his counterpoint. She understands that
he is not without feeling, that he is so sensitive to her feelings
that he has used all his resources to make a case he can't make
successfully, that his solicitude and love for her are reflected in
his attempt to calm her. In some measure, he has succeeded.
She appreciates his high-minded expression of what their love
means to him; she sees how much he cares for her in the pains
he has taken for her; she sees that for all his effort to prove
otherwise, he, too, feels that sadness and weeping at parting are
natural and human. She may even smile a little through her
tears as she realizes that, for all his artful manipulation, her
lover, too, knows that compasses are not made of flesh and blood.

My own discussion of the "Valediction" has, of course, been
contextual in two ways. I have emphasized the context, the dramatic human situation, which the poem itself implies, and I
have sought to show the relevance of the erotic context which
has been vaguely sensed by modern readers and on which, I
maintain, Donne's contemporaries would have seen his compass image to turn. Are these contexts right? Are they better,
more useful, than the contexts in astronomy, metaphysics, and
alchemy emphasized by Freccero?

As scholars and critics, we base most of our work on the assumptions that contextual study is a useful accessory to the understanding of a work, that awareness of the proper context of a

noncontemporary work or a contemporary one which predicates a society different from our own is a necessary and proper counterweight to the contemporary context which a reader is otherwise likely to assume. In Spenser's day, for example, the context or contexts of his "Epithalamion" would have been self-evident, though not all his readers would have been fully aware of the generic context he utilizes and individualizes so sweetly and so magnificently. Most of them would have appreciated immediately the pastoral freshness, the delicate sensuality, and the high seriousness with which he endows the occasion of his marriage. Some of them may even have glimpsed the mysterious arithmetic of his poem, the context which modern scholars have recently emphasized. In our time, what most young readers may need to be reminded of above all else if they are ever to see sympathetically what strikes them as frigidly and endlessly monumental is that their relaxed, individualized, secular view of marriage differs substantially from the formal, ceremonious, sacramental, and ordered view of past generations.[30] Any number of contexts may be relevant to a poem; in some degree, almost everything we can bring to bear on a work is likely to help open it up or enrich it. We frequently need to distinguish, however, between the context which is necessary to an accurate and central understanding of a work and one which may shed light on an aspect of it which is subordinate or less crucial. Most scholars engaged in contextual study have in mind a "normative" reader; it is hopeless to contend with the eccentric reader who will not listen to a work, who colors everything with his own predispositions, obsessions, interests, or concerns, who will make no effort to project himself into a world different from his own, who is not willing to suspend belief. As scholars, we hate, of course, to think that our explorations of context may be at-

[30]Other generations have had their problems with the poem. Palgrave omitted the "Epithalamion" from the *Golden Treasury* "with great reluctance as not in harmony with modern manners," along with other love poetry which he considered "too high-kilted" and too "decidedly amorous." See Kathleen Tillotson, "Donne's Poetry in the Nineteenth Century (1800–72)," in *Elizabethan and Jacobean Studies Presented to Frank Percy Wilson*, p. 322.

tributed to our own predispositions, obsessions, interests, or concerns. Freccero, I know, has no fixation on the stars or on alchemy; I like to think I'm not a dirty old man.[31]

We can fairly say that the climate of opinion in Donne's time, the ideas that were part of the Renaissance atmosphere, even the ideas that are present in Donne's works other than the "Valediction" provide us, when we focus on the "Valediction," with ideas that are to be tested, not with presumptions to be argued from; they give us outside limits or contextual boundaries which are feasible. Their very presence in the "Valediction" needs to be demonstrated, and we cannot assume that Donne's use of them and his attitude toward them is consistent throughout his works, that he does not change them or manipulate them from poem to poem.[32] I would not deny Donne's erudition or even his general familiarity with a number of the ideas which Freccero stresses (though I doubt that he had Freccero's technical and detailed knowledge), but I have tried here to set forth other ideas which were equally prevalent and which may be more relevant to the poem. Donne's exploitation of the dramatic aspects of a situation has long been considered a hallmark of his verse (and of his sermons); his bawdy is a recognizable strain in a large part of his poetry, and it was so clear to his contemporaries that five of the love elegies were in 1632 excepted from publication by the licenser. Neither Freccero nor I have offered an obvious exegesis which most common readers in our time have spontaneously arrived at; our exegeses have this merit, at least, in common: both of us agree with and seek to confirm the common readers' feeling about the humanity of the concept of love expressed in the poem. We have called attention to different contexts. Freccero has sought to provide intellectual justification for the rightness of human love in the

[31]Only once have I been accused of being a dirty younger man. See Pierre Legouis, "Donne, l'Amour et les Critiques," *Etudes Anglaises*, 10 (1957), 115–22.

[32]See, for example, the discussion of Donne's views on what happens to a soul at the moment of death, in Helen Gardner, ed., *John Donne: The Divine Poems* (Oxford, 1952), pp. xliii–xlvii and Appendix A.

astronomy, metaphysics, and alchemy which informed Donne's thought. I have sought to provide affective justification for the rightness of human love in exploring the psychology of the situation which the poem implies and in showing that Donne's geometry in the poem has its counterpart in bawdy.

Three questions remain. (1) Does either of our contexts provide, facilitate, or support the kind of interpretation which is, upon its first production, acknowledged to be just? (2) Which context explains more completely, more accurately, more simply the particulars of the poem?[33] (3) (This makes me end where I began. I would, however, rephrase Cruttwell's question about the depressing effect of technical context on readers and place it within the context of Wordsworth's statement: "It is the honourable characteristic of Poetry that its materials are to be found in every subject which can interest the human mind. The evidence of this fact is to be sought, not in the writings of Critics, but in those of Poets themselves."[34]) Does Freccero's context or mine — or do both of them — have such a dismal effect on the discriminating reader that he is immediately and finally deterred from reading the "Valediction" or other poems of Donne's?

[33]I am indebted here, and elsewhere, to R. S. Crane's "The Houyhnhnms, the Yahoos, and the History of Ideas," in *Reason and the Imagination,* ed. J. A. Mazzeo (New York, 1962), pp. 231-53.

[34]Advertisement to *Lyrical Ballads, with a Few Other Poems* (London, 1798), p. [i].

3

Donne's "Epithalamion made at Lincoln's Inn": Context and Date

That is some satire keen and critical,
Not sorting with a nuptial ceremony.

—*A Midsummer Night's Dream,* v. i. 54–55

Donne's "Epithalamion made at Lincoln's Inn" differs from his "Epithalamion . . . on the Lady Elizabeth and Count Palatine" and his epithalamion for the Earl of Somerset in that its occasion is not known. It differs from them, too, in that its wit seems more crudely licentious, harsher, less neatly integrated. This peculiarity of tone has not been entirely unnoticed. Grierson implied that the Lincoln's Inn epithalamion was "reprehensible" when he coupled it with "the most reprehensible" of the earlier elegies,[1] and he thought that its third stanza abounded in satire,[2] though some of the satire disappeared when he retracted his original reading of line 26.[3] But Grierson's comments on the poem have been largely neglected despite the fact that it has a number of puzzling elements which disturb the conventional epithalamic attitude.

One of these elements is Donne's reference to death in a marriage poem. This is odd, but the oddness has not disturbed readers unduly, perhaps because Donne refers to death several

[1]Herbert J. C. Grierson, ed., *The Poems of John Donne* (Oxford, 1912), II, lxxxi, n. 2.
[2]Ibid., p. 99.
[3]Idem, "Note on the Text and Canon," *The Poems of John Donne* (Oxford, 1933), p. 1.

times in his other epithalamions. In the "Epithalamion . . . on the Lady Elizabeth," "The Sparrow that neglects his life for love" is conventional and apt for the occasion — St. Valentine's Day — and we are attracted, not repulsed, by so pleasant a way to die. Donne's suggestion that the noble lovers are a pair of phoenixes, that their "motion kindles such fires, as shall give / Yong Phoenixes, and yet the old shall live" is delightful for its ingenious invention. His likening of the bride's jewels to a blazing constellation which signifies "That a Great Princess falls, but does not die" pleases us not so much for the intensity of its visual imagery as for the felicity of its suggestion of the marriage bed. Again, when Donne announces that "A Bride, before a good night could be said, / Should vanish from her cloathes, into her bed, / As Soules from bodies steale, and are not spy'd," we are delighted by the aptness — and the incongruity — of his analogy. Similarly, in the epithalamion for the Earl of Somerset, Donne's introductory statement that the marriage reprieves the old year, due to die in five days, his reference to the "death bed" of the year in a poem celebrating the marriage bed, seems only to enhance the glory of the occasion. In his stanza of benediction, Donne addresses the couple as "Blest payre of Swans," and he wishes that they never sing until "new great heights to trie, / It must serve your ambition, to die." Here the eager desire for heavenly joy is wittily ambiguous; the reference to death is properly improper, and it is followed, properly — and improperly — enough, by the exhortation, "Raise heires." In referring to the death of the swan, Donne makes his swans generate life; they are hardly of the breed of the chaste swans greeted by the Jovelings of Spenser. When Donne in his "good-night" mentions the lamp which burned for fifteen hundred years in Tullia's tomb, it is not the tomb that we remember but the picture of the lovers as everlasting "love-lamps." He suggests that fire ends in ashes, but only to contrast the everlastingness of the love of the couple: "joyes bonfire" burns eternally, for bride and groom are both fuel and fire.

Donne starts the Lincoln's Inn epithalamion by comparing a single bed to a grave: "It nourseth sadnesse," and the body in it

remains in one place. But in his very expression, "your bodies
print / . . . the yielding downe doth dint," Donne looks forward to a "yielding" of another sort, and, indeed, his next line is
"You and your other you meet there anon." Later in the poem
he exploits a like idea: the marriage bed is "onely to virginitie /
A grave, but, to a better state, a cradle." These references to
the grave are somewhat blunter than those in the other epithalamions. They are not so audacious, so witty, so lovingly developed. Donne's further references to death in the poem disturb
us. One of them is not analogical at all; the other is a revolting
analogy. Donne writes

> Thy two-leav'd gates faire Temple unfold,
> And these two in thy sacred bosome hold,
>   Till, mystically joyn'd, but one they bee;
> Then may thy leane and hunger-starved wombe
> Long time expect their bodies and their tombe,
>   Long after their owne parents fatten thee.

It is conceivable that the church in which a marriage takes
place may bring to mind those buried there. It is conceivable,
too, that tombs may be mentioned in a wedding poem, but
even Tennyson does not escape unscathed from a rather inop-
portune morbidity in the Epilogue of *In Memoriam*. But Donne
does more than suggest that the church will receive the bodies
of the lovers. He is hopeful that the lovers' parents will die before they do, and his use of "fatten" expresses an untoward
relish. This seems like bad taste, but the passage is offensive
beyond this. Donne calls the marriage a mystical union, but his
words do not communicate a spiritual idea; they undercut it.
The "sacred bosome" of the church does not bother us, but
when it is conjoined with "leane and hunger-starved wombe,"
we are distressed by the fleshly aspect of the metaphor — all the
more so since, after all, we remember the bride standing by
while Donne addresses the church. "Leane and hunger-starved
wombe" outrages us not only because of its implication that the
church hungers for the death of the bride and groom, but also

because we cannot help applying the words to the bride as well as to the church, and cannot help thinking that Donne wants us to do so. And what shall we make of the "two-leav'd gates"? Our minds withdraw, and not into happiness. We are happier when Donne later compares the bride in her nuptial bed to a pleasing sacrifice on love's altar. But Donne's exploitation of this image is not wittily lascivious; it is grossly cruel. The bride lies like a sacrificial lamb while the bridegroom, like a priest, comes tenderly "on his knees t'embowell her." Tenderly? Is this the tenderness of the boudoir or the abattoir?

In each of the epithalamions, too, Donne refers to riches or money, but once again the references seem crude and tasteless only in the Lincoln's Inn poem. In the "Epithalamion . . . on the Lady Elizabeth," the bride is ablaze with rubies, pearls, and diamonds. Donne's description is hardly startling, and to make it so he must turn the jewels into stars. His description (in stanza vii) of the activities of the wedding bed in terms of a business transaction is discreetly coy. The analogy is conventional enough; its wit lies in Donne's extensive exploitation of the convention. To be in debt, for love, is no more serious than to "die" for love. Lovers' "debts" and their "deaths" are paid in the same stock exchange, but Donne does not pull the occasion down to the level of the marketplace. In the Somerset epithalamion Donne also mentions the bride's jewels, but only to suggest once more that they are stars and that the stars are not so pure as their spheres. So, too, his description of the bride's silk and gold serves to praise and elevate her, for, he says, silk and gold, "the fruits of wormes and dust," are just objects for the sight of the common onlookers at the wedding ("dust, and wormes").

But in the Lincoln's Inn epithalamion, the description of the bride's flowers and jewels does not lead to such elaborate compliment. They are to make her fit fuel for love, "As gay as Flora, and as rich as Inde." If the analogies are conventional, the stanza in which they appear is hardly so. In it, Donne addresses the bridesmaids as "Our Golden Mines, and furnish'd Treasurie." To be sure he calls them "Angels," but his reason follows immediately: they bring with them "Thousands of Angels" on their wedding days. All we are told of the bridesmaids, then, is that they are rich. And the bride? In one line she is "As gay as Flora, and as rich as Inde," and in the next she is "faire, rich, glad, and in nothing lame." The bride, then, is fair. At least she is "in nothing lame." And she, too, is rich. Donne seems preoccupied with this particular virtue. Is there not something a little ungentlemanly, a little crass and vulgar, in his attitude?

In the next stanza of the poem, some of the groom's attendants are called "Sonnes of these Senators, wealths deep oceans," and again the overt reference to wealth seems adventitious and crude. In his last stanza, Donne refers to the bride's desire to exchange virginity for womanhood by talking about her preference for "a mothers rich stile." The emphasis on money in the Lincoln's Inn epithalamion seems far removed from the conventionally witty business of indebtedness in the Valentine epithalamion.

Donne's description of the bride in the Lincoln's Inn epithalamion also seems different from the descriptions in the others. The Princess Elizabeth is a blazing constellation, a phoenix. She and Frederick are two glorious flames which meet one another. The beauty of Lady Frances is so brilliant that she must powder her hair lest its intense luster affect the onlookers as Phaëton, not Phoebus, and, for the same reason, she must have a tear of joy in her inflaming eyes. The Lincoln's Inn bride is conceitedly dressed, adorned with flowers and jewels, and Donne writes of her as she approaches the chapel,

> Loe, in yon path which store of straw'd flowers graceth,
>   The sober virgin paceth;
>   Except my sight faile, 'tis no other thing.

Like the bride in Spenser's *Epithalamion*, this modest bride comes "with portly pace," but Spenser devotes some fifty lines to a description of his bashful bride's charms. Shall we suppose that Donne's bride has both ravished his sight and impaired his speech? Hardly. He says, nor can his blunt meaning be mistaken, "Unless I'm blind, that thing is the bride." This is a strange epithalamion indeed.

It is strange in its refrain. In the "Epithalamion . . . on the Lady Elizabeth," the refrain is an address to Bishop Valentine, and it integrates the bird imagery and stresses all the romantic and holy aspects of the wedding day. In the Somerset epithalamion, the "inflaming eyes" and "loving heart" of the refrain apply equally to the bride and groom. But in the Lincoln's Inn poem, the refrain "*To day put on perfection, and a womans name*" oddly concentrates attention on the occasion as it is important for the bride. The groom seems slighted. The epithalamion is strange, too, in that the wedding guests in their dancing are compared to "toyl'd beasts." Worse than this, the groom's attendants are called "strange Hermaphrodits." In the last stanza the bride is strangely likened to a faithful man who is content to spend this life for a better one.

In Theseus's words (and Dr. Johnson's), How shall we find the concord of this discord?

We shall not find it, I think, merely in assuming that the poem celebrates a less memorable wedding than that of the Princess Elizabeth or of the Earl of Somerset. The mere doffing of the party manners which Donne might have used on those occasions would not lead to a strange indulgence in tone and in wit on a lesser occasion. The crude, scoffing element in the poem makes it unlikely, too, that it was an offering in jest from one smart young man to another smart young man about to marry, even if we take into account the differences in taste between Donne's day and our own. The wit is too close to insult: it has not the cavalier geniality of Donne's other epithalamions, but rather the heavy-handed raillery of his satires. Donne is here crudely utilitarian in a genre which is customarily complimentary. It seems very doubtful, then, that the occasion of Donne's poem is the actual wedding of a rich maid of London and a gentleman of the Inns of Court. There is good reason to believe that Donne is not celebrating a real wedding at all.

The manuscripts of Donne's poems provide us with indistinct clues about the occasion of the "Epithalamion made at Lincoln's Inn," and with more definite ones about its approximate date. Grierson and Gardner agree that the presence of the poem in the Westmoreland manuscript, where it follows the elegies and precedes the verse letters, points to its being the only one of the epithalamions written when the first part of that manuscript was made.[4] Gardner also suggests that since it is there entitled just "Epithalamion," we have further reason to suppose that the other epithalamions were not yet written. Moreover, in the first part of the Westmoreland manuscript, all the verse letters but one belong to the time before Donne's marriage and are addressed to the circle of his friends at the Inns of Court. This part of the manuscript appears to have been copied from a collection of Donne's poems made about 1600. On the basis of the Westmoreland manuscript alone, it seems safe to assume that the epithalamion was "made" at Lincoln's Inn while Donne was a student there.

I. A. Shapiro has admirably summarized Donne's career at Lincoln's Inn from his admission on May 6, 1592.[5] He assumes that since Donne was fined for not acting as Steward of Christmas in 1594 (he had been appointed to the office on November 26) and since he is not mentioned in the *Black Books* of Lincoln's Inn as a student after he had been fined, Donne must have left Lincoln's Inn in December 1594. John Sparrow makes the same assumption and starts Donne on his travels.[6] But R. C. Bald has discovered that on July 20, 1595, Donne agreed to take

---

[4]*The Poems of John Donne* (1912), II, 91; Helen Gardner, ed., *John Donne: The Divine Poems* (Oxford, 1952), p. lxxix; hereafter cited as *Divine Poems*.

[5]I. A. Shapiro, "John Donne and Lincoln's Inn, 1591-1594," *TLS*, Oct. 16, 1930, p. 833, and Oct. 23, 1930, p. 861.

[6]John Sparrow, "The Date of Donne's Travels" in *A Garland for John Donne 1631-1931*, ed. Theodore Spencer (Cambridge, Mass., 1931), pp. 121-51. Sparrow thinks there is a "strong probability" that Donne left London before Christmas (p. 133), but he settles on 1595-96 (p. 134) to reconcile his date with Grierson's suggestion that indications in the Satires and Elegies make it probable that Donne was in London during 1594 and 1595 (*The Poems of John Donne* [1933], p. xvi).

"into his service to instructe and bring upp one Thomas Danbye of the age of fifteene yeres or there aboutes."[7] Here is presumptive evidence that Donne was in England in the middle of 1595. There is no real evidence that he left Lincoln's Inn or England until he joined the Cadiz expedition at the end of May 1596. We may, then, suppose that the Lincoln's Inn epithalamion was written at some time between May 1592 and the middle of 1596.

The manuscripts of Donne's poems seem to show that Donne himself did not consider this epithalamion equal in worth or similar in kind to his others. It is not included in those manuscripts which Grierson and Gardner call Group I (*D, H 49, Lec, C 57,* and *SP*). Gardner argues convincingly that the manuscripts in this group derive from one which Donne himself unwillingly made just before taking orders, in compliance with Somerset's request that he should publish his poems. She suggests that Donne omitted from his collection such poems as he thought not worthy of a volume designed to win the favor of the great.[8] A large number of these were familiar verse letters addressed to the less distinguished circle of his youth, though Donne seems to have included the verse letters which he was particularly proud of—"The Storme," "The Calme," and "To Mr Rowland Woodward" ("Like one who'in her third widdowhood"). We are, I think, forced to conclude that Donne himself considered the Lincoln's Inn epithalamion unworthy of inclusion not only because it was an intimate reminder of his Inns of Court days but also because he felt that it lacked merit. Some of the manuscripts in which the poem does appear, however, may point more precisely to the reason for its exclusion from Group I. In about half of the manuscripts in which the poem appears it is entitled "Epithalamion on a Citizen." This title seems to imply that the occasion Donne celebrates is not a very notable one.

---

[7]Mr. Bald's evidence is based on an action in Chancery which Donne brought in 1598 against one Christopher Danby, a gentleman of Yorkshire (P.R.O., C. 3, 266/93). It was presented in a paper, "Donne's Travels," read before the English VI group of the Modern Language Association in New York on Dec. 29, 1948. I am indebted to Mr. Bald for sending me his manuscript and permitting me to quote from it.

[8]*Divine Poems*, pp. lxiv-lxv.

But it is odd that not one of the manuscripts gives the name of the citizen. It is likely that the use of "Citizen" is generic, and that though some of Donne's contemporaries were unaware of the specific details of the occasion of the poem, their use of "Citizen" in the title of a poem written by a young gentleman indicates their feeling that Donne's intent was not entirely serious. It is hard to believe that in his Lincoln's Inn days Donne could not have written, had he wanted to, an epithalamion, no matter to whom it was addressed, which would merit inclusion in such a collection as he was making in 1614. The manuscripts lead us to conclude that the Lincoln's Inn epithalamion is a *jeu d'esprit* which Donne later cast aside.

The poem, then, may not celebrate a real wedding. Does it celebrate a mock wedding? I think that Donne wrote it for just such an occasion, and I wish to show, though the available materials are scanty, that such an occasion is in harmony with the long tradition of Inns of Court reveling.

Inns of Court reveling is most frequently associated with the production of lavish masques for specific occasions: with the "Masque of Proteus" devised by the gentlemen of Gray's Inn for their extraordinary Christmas festivity in 1594; with the masque composed by George Chapman and designed by Inigo Jones which was performed by the gentlemen of the Middle Temple and of Lincoln's Inn to celebrate the marriage of the Princess Elizabeth in 1613; with the spectacular *Triumph of Peace* of 1634, acted by the four Inns for the King and the Court, with a script by James Shirley, architecture by Inigo Jones, and music by Simon Ives and William Lawes. But the Inns did not need an occasion for a masque. William Browne's dedication of his *Inner Temple Masque*, or *Ulysses and Circe* (1615) is interesting because it reveals that the masque is entirely independent of occasion. Browne reminds the gentlemen of the Inner Temple that "it was done to please ourselves in private," and his reference to "those other the society hath produced" probably indicates that such performances were not uncommon.[9] Masques

---

[9]Cited by A. Wigfall Green in *The Inns of Court and Early English Drama*

were, on the whole, exceptional excrescences which evolved from the normal procedure of reveling in which highly ritualistic "solemn revels," marked by obeisance and stately parade, were followed by "post revels" or informal dancing by the younger gentlemen. Into this standardized form of entertainment the high-spirited young men at the Inns gradually introduced pageantry or a play, buffoonery, and burlesque.[10]

The amount of such reveling must have been remarkable. An entry in 1431 in the *Black Books* of Lincoln's Inn shows the frequency of reveling in an order which restricts such occasions:

> . . . it is accorded by all the felawschip that ther schall be iiij revels in the yeere and no mo, that is to sayyng, in the fest off All Halowen oon, to the wych schall be contributorie as well the persons wych were woned to paye to Seint William ys revell as tho the wych were woned paie to Seynt Hugh is Revell; and in the fest off Seint Arkenewold another, to wych schall be contributorie Seint Edmond is men. Item, the iij^de in the fest off Purificacion off owre Lady, to wych all the remenaunt schall be contributorie savyng Seint Peter and Seint Thomas men. The Ferthe on Midsomer Day, to wych sall be contributorie Seynt Peter and Seint Thomas men.[11]

It is doubtful whether this order was followed to the letter, for in 1448 there is a reference to "the revels at Christmas last."[12]

(New Haven, 1931), p. 113. Browne's words "please ourselves in private" do not imply that his masque was performed exclusively for the members of the Inner Temple. Many guests had been invited to the performance. See J. Bruce Williamson, *The History of the Temple, London*, 2d ed. (London, 1925), p. 314.

[10]Green, p. 12. Williamson says (p. 174) that the Inner Temple records for 1561–62 refer to sums laid out for "maskes, playes, disquysinges [*sic*] or other like."

[11]W. P. Baildon, ed., *The Records of the Honorable Society of Lincoln's Inn. The Black Books* (London, 1897–1902), I, 4; hereafter cited as *Black Books*.

[12]Ibid., p. 18. It is difficult to generalize about the frequency and the occasions of reveling because of the nature of the records in the *Black Books*. These are mainly concerned with promulgations, appointments, fines, and accounts; customary procedures can only be inferred. An entry of Nov. 5,

Attendance at the revels seems to have been compulsory, for there is a record of four men being put out of commons "for goyng out of the Hall on Hallowmas evyn at the tyme of the Revelles."[13] There is some evidence that the ritual of the revels palled on the gentlemen of Lincoln's Inn: on one occasion, one of them was put out of commons because he sang mockingly and irreverently at the revels;[14] on another occasion, all the fellows of the Inn refused to dance before the distinguished guests invited by the Benchers.[15] There is evidence, too, that it was hard to enforce discipline.[16] An entry on November 14, 1608 is illuminating: a committee of three Benchers and three others is appointed "to conferr wth the younge gentlemen towchinge the time, manner and charge of the Revells and sportes intended."[17] It is apparent that the young gentlemen took an active part in the planning of the reveling, and also that the revels were invariably combined with sports. Nor is it strange that the young gentlemen often confused the two. At Midsummer, for instance, ritualistic candles and reeds were ordered for the Inn,[18] and a light erected in the Hall to honor St. John; it is no surprise to find in an entry that "Eldrington, Harrington, and Berners, aboughte Trynyte Sondaye laste, in the nyghte tyme, did take downe the lyghte of Sainte John in the Hall, and did hang in the stede therof a horsehede, in dyspite of the Sainte."[19]

Although Saturday nights at the Inn seem to have been given over to card playing and dicing, there is at least one indication that informal entertainment of other sorts also took place then.

1566, refers to All Saints and Candlemas as "the two principall festes" (I, 353). In 1614, All Saints, Candlemas, and Ascension weeks are called "graund weekes" and Trinity Sunday is called a "graund day," but only when Midsummer Day is not in term. If Midsummer Day fell in Trinity Term, it, rather than Trinity Sunday, was celebrated as a grand day (II, 166). In 1622, reference is made to "the 4 festivall Graund Dayes" (II, 235).

[13]Ibid., I, 291 (*anno* 1549).
[14]Ibid., p. 306 (*anno* 1553).
[15]Ibid., II, xxviii, 131 (*anno* 1610).
[16]Ibid., p. 16; also I, 295; II, 22, 43, 91, 102, etc.
[17]Ibid., II, 115.
[18]Ibid., I, 313, 316, 321, 324.
[19]Ibid., p. 273 (*anno* 1546).

At a Council held on November 2, 1559, it was ordered that "the Butler shall note every Saterdaye at night whoe faylyth at Revells that were at supper that night in the Howse, and that he that faylyth shall forfett iiijd. for every tyme, to be collectid by the Buttler, and therefore the Post Revelles to be agayne used as they have byn before this time."[20] This entry shows the frequency of the informal entertainment put on at the Inn. The spectacular masques that are remembered are a small and unusual part of the playing and the dancing, the music and the buffoonery, the improvisation and the burlesquing in which the young gentlemen of the Inn engaged.

If we view Donne's epithalamion in the context of Inns of Court reveling, the strangeness of its tone and the oddness of its details disappear. We should expect Donne to use broadly discordant effects, not subtly witty ones. The tasteless references to death expressed in the images of the emboweling priest and of the female organs of the church would convulse the young gentlemen of the Inn. They would thoroughly enjoy Donne's jibes at their mundane preoccupation with angels. In a mock-marriage, the part of the bride would be played by one of the "painted courtiers," and the words on the bride's approach — "'tis no other thing" — would be not only fitting but funny. Moreover, under such circumstances, the refrain becomes a jocular device: it serves as a continual reminder that the man playing the part of the bride is literally putting on the name of woman for "today" and "tonight." No wonder, then, that Donne focused attention in it on the bride alone.

In a conventional epithalamion, the reference to the hermaphroditism of the groom's attendants is out of place. But in a mock-epithalamion the reference becomes innocently salacious: the Inns of Court men are "Of study and play made strange Hermaphrodits" because at such performances they must take the female parts. Donne's conceit at the end of the

---

[20]Ibid., p. 329.

poem, which compares the bride to "a faithfull man content, / That this life for a better should be spent," becomes still another device to emphasize the confusion of sex caused by a man's playing the part of the bride. The final reference to the bride as "This Sun" becomes more than a conventional epithet for the bride's transcendent beauty; it, too, takes advantage of the gender of the bride, and Donne uses the stale sun-son pun freshly to call attention once more to his unusual bride. "Wonders are wrought," indeed, "for shee which had no maime," except that "shee" is a "he," "*To night puts on perfection, and a womans name.*"

In the context of an epithalamion "made" or performed at Lincoln's Inn, Donne is free to endow his "Temple" with biological functions, for he is alluding to a temple of the law. Such gross stress on the procreative capacities of a church admits of no allegorical interpretation; to take a serious view of the poem is to say that Donne's canticle here sings a song of sacrilege. But to a group of students at Lincoln's Inn, "Temple" would inevitably call to mind the two rival institutions, and the gentlemen at Lincoln's would be delighted by Donne's irreverence. They would not feel insulted when Donne compared them to "toyl'd beasts"; since they had a superfluity of dancing in their solemn revels, they would enjoy Donne's oblique reference to their "pleasing labours." His lines about the chains and robes "put on / T' adorne the day, not thee" would remind them not only of the vestments which adorned the man-bride but probably also of the ritualistic trappings in which the Inn officials were bedecked. They would appreciate Donne's little professional joke in his mention of "elder claimes," and they would delight in his comparing the naked bride to the naked truth.

Donne's poem is not a serious epithalamion, but neither is it a "satire keen and critical." It is closer to the "palpable-gross play [that] hath well beguil'd / The heavy gait of night." To see it as a broadly satiric entertainment is to rid it of its difficulties and to place it rightly, not with Donne's other epithalamions, but with his satires and love elegies.

I should like to propose, though more tentatively, that Donne wrote his epithalamion for a performance at the Midsummer revels of Lincoln's Inn in 1595. The date is based on three assumptions which I shall try to show to be fairly sound: (1) Donne's poem could have been written only after the publication of Spenser's *Epithalamion*; (2) the Midsummer season is peculiarly fitting for such a performance; (3) Donne was still at Lincoln's Inn in June 1595.

It is difficult to see why Donne should have turned to the epithalamic genre for a revels entertainment. In England the epithalamion was neglected until the 1590s, and it seems strange that Donne should have satirized broadly in a genre with which his audience would not be very well acquainted. George Puttenham's discussion of the epithalamion in *The Arte of English Poesie* conveniently shows us what the genre meant to the cultivated Elizabethan gentleman.[21] For him, epithalamions were essentially "ballades at the bedding of the bride," and his description was based on his familiarity with the lyric epithalamions of Catullus and one made "of late yeares" by Johannes Secundus.[22] Puttenham did not consider the great number of Latin epithalamions of the Renaissance, which were predominantly not lyric, but, following the pattern of Claudian and Statius, essentially narrative and descriptive.[23] The only epithalamion in English printed before Spenser's was Sidney's song of the shepherd Dicus at the marriage of Thyrsis and Kala, written in the early 1580s and first published in the 1593 *Arcadia*. It was neither a bedding ballad nor an "epical" poem modeled after the epithalamions of Claudian and Statius, but a pastoral benediction. Against the background of the epical character of

---

[21]George Puttenham, "The Maner of Rejoysings at Mariages and Weddings," *The Arte of English Poesie*, bk. I, ch. xxvi.

[22]The Latin epithalamion of Secundus is a real bedding ballad that starts at the wedding couch, describes in detail similar to that of Carew's "The Rapture" the amorous combat, and ends with a stanza of hope that the marriage may be fruitful.

[23]See Robert H. Case, *English Epithalamies* (London, 1896), p. xxi, and Cortlandt Van Winkle, *Spenser's Epithalamion* (New York, 1926), pp. 6-7, 19.

the major epithalamic tradition of the Renaissance and the paucity of models in English, the startling originality of Spenser's poem stands out — despite scholars' pointing to sources and analogues for hundreds of particular details.[24] Spenser fused the narration of the events of the bridal day and the description of its many participants and places, typical of the epic or heroic epithalamion, with the bedding ballad and the personal appeal for benediction in a poem glowing with lyricism.

Donne's Lincoln's Inn epithalamion has the same blending of the epic narration of the bridal day with an essentially lyric intent, and this fusion of the traditions was available to him only after the publication of Spenser's poem.[25] If Donne had written his poem before he saw Spenser's, he would probably have satirized in the neo-Latin epical fashion familiar to some in his audience or in the pastoral-benediction fashion of Sidney. Something caused him to satirize in the peculiar form he chose, and that was probably the form recently used by the most highly regarded poet of his day. Spenser's *Amoretti* and *Epithalamion* were entered in the Stationers' Register on November 19, 1594, and the first edition is dated 1595. The volume probably appeared early in that year, though perhaps after March 25. If we assume, as I think we must, that Donne modeled his epithalamion on Spenser's, then Donne's poem was not written earlier than the first part of 1595.

I have implied that Donne turned to the epithalamic genre and to Spenser's design because he could assume that Spenser's poem would be fresh in the minds of his audience. A recent work by a popular writer is always fair game for parody, but more than recency may have drawn Donne to Spenser's *Epithalamion*. In Donne's poem, the line "Hee [the sun] flies in win-

[24]See Van Winkle's edition of the *Epithalamion* and also James A. S. McPeek, "The Major Sources of Spenser's *Epithalamion*," *JEGP*, 35 (1936), 183–213.

[25]Grierson says that Donne comes nearer to Spenser in the epithalamions than in any other kind of poem (*The Poems of John Donne* [1912], II, 91), and Charles G. Osgood thinks that Donne here imitates Spenser's meter and design (*The Works of Edmund Spenser, Variorum Edition; The Minor Poems*, II [Baltimore, 1947], 659).

ter, but he now stands still" seems to indicate a summer date, though conventionally in an epithalamion the sun never sets quickly enough. The most important revels at this time of year were held at Midsummer, and Midsummer seems the most likely occasion for the performance of Donne's epithalamion. If Donne were casting about for a subject for a Midsummer entertainment, he would find special relevance in Spenser's poem. Spenser makes it clear that his marriage took place on the feast of St. Barnabas, and the proverb "Barnaby bright, Barnaby bright, / The longest day and the shortest night" shows that (with the calendar ten days out) the feast of St. Barnabas and Midsummer were frequently associated. I do not wish to suggest that Donne wrote a mock-Anniversary for Spenser, but I think it likely that the date of Spenser's wedding, a lovely detail which Spenser treats most charmingly, must have impressed Donne and tempted him to toy with the idea of Midsummer marriage. In June the newness of Spenser's poem would make Donne's burlesque topical and obvious. Moreover, the customary festivities of the Midsummer season make the Midsummer revels the perfect occasion for a mock-epithalamion.

When Spenser referred to the heavens "In which a thousand torches flaming bright / Doe burne . . . ," he may have been using a common conceit for stars, but his plea for darkness and for quiet has particular significance in the light of Midsummer tradition. The ancient sun-rites were celebrated by the lighting of bonfires, and the lights and reeds mentioned in the *Black Books* reflect a citified version of this.[26] Dekker mentions bonfires and triumphing on Midsummer Night in his *Seven Deadly Sinnes of London* (1606).[27] Although the latest surviving record of a pageant at Midsummer in London is for 1545,[28] provincial towns continued to have Midsummer Shows well into the seven-

[26]See Sir Henry Ellis's revision and enlargement of John Brand's *Observations on the Popular Antiquities of Great Britain* (London, 1877), I, 298-308; hereafter cited as Brand.

[27]Cited in Brand, I, 318. The reference is to Dekker's third day's triumph, "Candle-light, or The Nocturnall Tryumph."

[28]See *Malone Society Collections III* (Oxford, 1954), pp. xxiii, 36.

teenth century.[29] The marching watch of two thousand in London at Midsummer was discontinued by the middle of the sixteenth century, but ensign-bearers still roamed the city at the end of the century.[30] In his *Popular Antiquities,* Brand says that the ritualistic dance around the coal fire in the Inns of Court may be connected with Midsummer festivity,[31] and we have already had an example of the horseplay which some gentlemen of Lincoln's Inn indulged in at this time of year. Brand further shows that at this season other customs were followed: fernseed was esteemed, love divinations of all kinds were popular, and boys dressed in girls' clothes.[32] The Midsummer tradition helped to create the special aura of *A Midsummer Night's Dream,* and Shakespeare's very title was an invitation to a giddy, vertiginous, and sublunary world.[33] The same tradition would make Donne's audience peculiarly susceptible to midsummer madness.

[29]Robert Withington, *English Pageantry,* I (Cambridge, Mass., 1918), 44–47.

[30]Brand, I, 326–28.

[31]Ibid., p. 310.

[32]Ibid., pp. 311, 314–15, 330 ff.

[33]In the light of this tradition, Dr. Johnson's statement, "I know not why Shakespear calls this play a *Midsummer-Night's Dream,* when he so carefully informs us that it happened on the night preceding *May* day," is strangely unperceptive. (See Horace H. Furness, ed., *A Midsommer Nights Dreame,* vol. X of *Variorum Shakespeare* [Philadelphia, 1895], v.) Steevens noticed that Olivia said of Malvolio's seeming frenzy that "it is a very *Midsummer* madness," and he went on to say, "That time of the year, we may therefore suppose, was anciently thought productive of mental vagaries resembling the scheme of Shakespeare's play." The editor of *A Midsummer Night's Dream* in the *Variorum Shakespeare* was even more positive: he says, "To the inheritors of the English tongue the potent sway of fairies on Midsummer Eve is familiar. The very title is in itself a charm, and frames our minds to accept without question any delusion of the night." Shakespeare's exploitation of social customs has become a scholarly commonplace since the publication of C. L. Barber's *Shakespeare's Festive Comedy* (Princeton, 1959).

It would be pleasant to think that Donne had in mind both Spenser's *Epithalamion* and *A Midsummer Night's Dream* when he wrote his epithalamion, but our lack of precise knowledge about the composition and the performance of Shakespeare's play makes this connection tenuous. Dover Wilson's conclusion (in *A Midsummer-Night's Dream* [Cambridge, 1924], p. 100) that the play was "first handled by Shakespeare in 1592 or before, rehan-

I think we may assume that Midsummer revels took place at Lincoln's Inn in 1595 despite the lack of documentary corroboration. They seem to have been customary, and there is no evidence in the *Black Books* that they were not held. In 1595 Trinity Sunday fell on June 15 (O.S.). Trinity Term usually began on the Wednesday after Trinity Sunday;[34] in 1595, then,

---

dled in 1594, and rehandled once again in 1598" gives us the extreme dates and the extreme theory of revision. Most commentators accept 1594-96 or 1595-96 for performance on the public stage and raise the possibility of a private performance at a noble wedding. Wilson's suggestion that Oberon's epithalamion was sung and danced by the fairies accords with what we know about the writing and, possibly, the performance of epithalamions in England, though his suggestion that it was not added until 1596 or 1598 does not recognize its integral and necessary contribution to the spirit of the play (*Shakespeare's Happy Comedies* [Evanston, 1962], p. 206; *MND*, pp. 97-99, 151-53). His shrewd comment that the fairies stream into the hall with rounds of waxen tapers on their heads which they kindle at the hearth as they pass it (*MND*, pp. 98, 151) fits beautifully the custom of Midsummer lights.

It is impossible to say whether Donne saw a performance of *A Midsummer Night's Dream* before he wrote his epithalamion; nor, if he saw a performance, could we tell exactly what version he saw. About all we may say is that it is "of interest" that his mock-marriage at the Revels is an inversion of a high point of Shakespeare's play, the revels at the triple marriage.

Gardner suggests (*John Donne: The Elegies and The Songs and Sonnets* [Oxford, 1965], p. xxxiii) that there may be a reminiscence of *A Midsummer Night's Dream* in "The Perfume," and her suggestion is provocative. In his poems, Donne refers to fairies just three times. In the *First Anniversary* (ll. 142-43), he merely links fairies with pygmies as creatures of fable who may pass as credible since man has lost his original stature. If, in "The Perfume," he had in mind Shakespeare's fairies tripping through the house to bless the lovers, he metamorphosed them; the "Faiery Sprights" in his poem are the "little brethren" of his mistress who "oft skipt" into the lovers' chamber on the sweet nights he is with her, and they are bribed the next day by their father "to tell what they did see." In all three of his epithalamions, Donne mentions the entertainment (banqueting, music, dancing, masquing) that delays the bedding of the bride. Lines 67-68 of the epithalamion for the Princess Elizabeth — "The masquers come too late, and I'thinke, will stay, / Like Fairies, till the Cock crow them away" — may, as W. Milgate's notes suggest (*John Donne: The Epithalamions, Anniversaries and Epicedes* [Oxford, 1978], p. 116), refer to Campion's masque performed on the night of Elizabeth's wedding, in which the last song says, "The cocks alreadie crow," but Donne may have remembered, too, that Theseus called for masque and music to serve as abridgment of the evening and that Oberon ordered the fairies to stray through the house till break of day.

[34]Williamson, p. 119, n. 3.

term began on June 18. Since Midsummer was customarily celebrated in conjunction with St. John's Day, June 24,[35] it fell in
1595 during Trinity Term, and it, rather than Trinity Sunday,
would be celebrated as a "grand" day.

Was Donne at Lincoln's Inn as late as June 1595? Shapiro has
examined in the manuscript *Black Books* of Lincoln's Inn (vol.
v) lists of those who should have kept vacations and either did
or did not, from the Easter vacation of 1589 to the Easter vacation of 1596. In these lists Shapiro has found that Donne's absence at the Easter vacation in 1593 is duly noted; he has found
no record that Donne either kept or failed to keep a vacation after the notice of his keeping the autumn vacation of 1594. But
Donne's being appointed Steward of Christmas on November
26, 1594, shows that he was at Lincoln's Inn at that time. That
he was fined for not performing his duties as Steward, and that
his name does not appear in the vacation lists after October
1594, do not prove that he left Lincoln's Inn between November 26 and December 25, 1594. He may have skipped attendance at a vacation or two while still maintaining his Lincoln's
Inn connection (we know, for example, that his absence at the
Easter vacation in 1593 was no indication of complete sever-
ance). Nor does his defection as Steward indicate that he had
left the Inn. Stewardships in the Inns must have been expensive
and dull, and fines from men refusing to serve as stewards of
various occasions seem to have constituted a staple sum of Inn
income. There is no more frequent entry in the *Black Books*
than that of Mr. So-and-so fined so much for refusing to serve
as steward of this or that[36] (the fines were standardized, and
that for the Steward of Christmas was smaller than most, 26s.
8d.).[37] Donne's defection as Steward need not mean, then, that

[35]For the conjunction of Midsummer with St. John's Day, see Brand, I,
298–305.

[36]For example, at Lincoln's Inn, the appointed Stewards of Christmas were
fined in 1586 and in 1587 (*Black Books*, II, 5, 9). At the Inner Temple it was
customary to reappoint annually for several years the same persons to Christmas offices, and the same persons were repeatedly fined for not appearing
(Williamson, pp. 442–43, 209).

[37]*Black Books*, II, 1, 5.

he was absent from London and from Lincoln's Inn during and after Christmas 1594.[38] Indeed, Shapiro prints the part of the treasurer's record for (November) 1594 to (November) 1595 which shows that the Inn received from Donne the sum of 26*s*. 8*d*. for not acting as Steward of Christmas. Since it is not likely that Donne paid his fine in advance, we have here evidence that he was at the Inn after Christmas 1594. It is even conceivable that the very payment of the fine indicates that Donne planned to remain at the Inn for a time. Had he severed his connection with the Inn before Christmas (or even after), he might not have been fined or felt obliged to pay his fine. The vacation lists inform us, I think, that Donne determined not to study law seriously about or after Christmas 1594, but they do not tell us that he left Lincoln's Inn at that time; in fact, from Bald's evidence that Donne was in London even in July 1595, we may probably assume that he spent Midsummer at Lincoln's Inn.

It is likely, then, that in the "Epithalamion made at Lincoln's Inn" we catch Jack Donne in a carefree midsummer mood after he had decided that the law was not for him. We see in the poem not the serious poet of compliment but the roistering Inns of Court man of three and twenty, "not dissolute, but very neat; a great visiter of Ladies, a great frequenter of Playes, a great writer of conceited Verses."[39]

---

[38]During Donne's residence at Lincoln's Inn, the custom of keeping Christmas in all its ancient grand ceremonial seems to have been largely discontinued. In 1597 some sort of "shew" was presented (ibid., II, 55), but with reference to the omission of a solemn Christmas in 1595 Baildon notes: "This custom of keeping solemn or grand Christmas seems to have been given up" (ibid., p. 44).

It is possible that Donne spent Christmas 1594 frolicking at Gray's Inn, for this was the year that the gentlemen of Gray's kept up their merriment from December 20 until Shrove Tuesday (Green, pp. 73, 99). To be sure, the gentlemen of Gray's had invited only the gentlemen of the Inner Temple to join their festivities, but gentlemen at the other Inns may have been attracted by the noise and have tried to participate.

[39]Sir Richard Baker's description of Donne at Lincoln's Inn, in *A Chronicle of the Kings of England* (London, 1643), p. 156.

4

The Dating of
Donne's *La Corona*

> May all men date Records, from this. . . .
>
> —"An Epithalamion . . . on the Lady
> Elizabeth, and Count Palatine," l. 42

Herbert J. C. Grierson was the first to propose that the *La Corona* sonnets were composed at Mitcham "in or before 1609."[1] His conjecture was based on a three-pronged argument. First, he accepted A. B. Grosart's suggestion that Donne's verse letter "To E. of D. with six holy Sonnets" was sent with a copy of six of the *La Corona* sonnets, but he rejected Grosart's identification of "E. of D." with Doncaster, and instead proposed Richard Sackville. Since Sackville did not become third Earl of Dorset until February 27, 1609, Grierson said that this was the earliest date at which the verse letter could have been addressed to him as "E. of D." Second, the date 1609 was supported by evidence in Harleian MS. 4955 (*H 49*). In this miscellany, some poems by Dr. Francis Andrews are dated "August 14. 1629."[2] Donne's poems follow those of Andrews, and *La Corona* and twelve of Donne's Holy Sonnets are prefaced with the heading "Holy Sonnets: written 20 yeares since." Twenty years before 1629 would bring us to 1609, a date which Grierson assumed to be "quite possibly right" for *La Corona* and "certainly wrong" for the Holy Sonnets.[3] Third, Grierson

---

[1]Herbert J. C. Grierson, ed., *The Poems of John Donne* (Oxford, 1912), II, 226.

[2]Ibid., p. lxxxiii.

[3]Ibid., p. 227.

connected *La Corona* with Donne's sonnet "To Mrs. Magdalen Herbert: of St. Mary Magdalen." This sonnet, Izaak Walton had said in his *Life of Herbert* (1670), was sent with a prose letter which reads in part,

> . . . *by this Messenger, and on this good day, I commit the inclosed* Holy Hymns *and* Sonnets *(which for the matter, not the workmanship, have yet escap'd the fire) to your judgment, and to your protection too, if you think them worthy of it; and I have appointed this inclosed* Sonnet *to usher them to your happy hand.*

Though Walton thought that the hymns were lost, Grierson thought they must be *La Corona*. Since the prose letter sent with the hymns was dated July 11, 1607, and since the date seemed justifiable, Grierson would seem to imply that *La Corona* was composed prior to that date, despite his cautious phrase "in or before 1609." He supposed that the sequence was first sent to Mrs. Herbert and that the same sequence minus one poem was later sent to Richard Sackville (though perhaps before he assumed his earldom, since any later transcript would adopt the title to which he succeeded in 1609).

The first of Grierson's proofs has been greatly weakened, if not vitiated, by Helen Gardner's work on the Holy Sonnets. Gardner accepts Grierson's identification of Dorset with the "E. of D.," but she makes a strong case for identifying the six holy sonnets sent to him with Sonnets 1-6 (*Poems*, 1633).[4] She wisely says that the ingenuity of *La Corona* lies in the seven poems making up an unbreakable circle and that to omit one would be to destroy their point; she reminds us that Donne's friends were a close group, that Dorset was a friend of Edward Herbert, and that it would have been risky for Donne to tell Dorset that he had inspired poems which had been sent to Mrs. Herbert two years before.

The second of Grierson's proofs, tenuous as it is, retains considerable value. To be sure, Gardner has shown that *H 49* is the

---

[4]Helen Gardner, ed., *John Donne: The Divine Poems* (Oxford, 1952), p. xlix; hereafter cited as *Divine Poems*.

least logical of the Group I manuscripts in its arrangement; that its text has far too many careless blunders to be thought of as near the root of the manuscript tradition; and that, for *La Corona*, it alone errs in omitting the end of line 10 and the beginning of line 11 of the first poem.[5] Still, though the copyist was careless, he seems to have known that Donne's holy sonnets were about twenty years old. His "20 yeares," as Gardner says, is probably a round figure, not a precise date. Gardner thinks that it is impossible to say whether his statement is meant to refer to *La Corona* alone, or to include the twelve Holy Sonnets in the manuscript.[6] Since, however, in the Group I manuscripts, *La Corona* precedes the Holy Sonnets under the general title of "Holy Sonnets," it is likely that the copyist of *H 49* meant his date to refer to all the sonnets. His date has considerable validity for the twelve Holy Sonnets if we accept, as I think we must, Gardner's newly proposed date,[7] and it probably has equal validity for *La Corona*.

Grierson's third proof has been accepted by Gardner, though she says that the identification of *La Corona* with the "Holy Hymns *and* Sonnets" in the letter which Walton printed and the consequent dating of *La Corona* by the date of the letter (July 11, 1607) must be regarded as not more than a highly probable conjecture.[8] This date was made suspect by Edmund Gosse, who saw that Walton printed in the Appendix to his *Life of Herbert* another letter from Donne to Mrs. Herbert which bears the same date. Gosse called the date an "impossible" one, but thought that the year was probably right.[9] Grierson, however, accepted Walton's date, for he thought that by July 11 (O.S.) Donne meant July 22 (N.S.) and that *"this good day"*

---

[5] Ibid., pp. lix–lx.

[6] Ibid., p. 57.

[7] Gardner thinks that Sonnets 1–6 (1633) were written between February and August 1609, and that the others (except those in the Westmoreland MS.) were written after August 1609 and before the *First Anniversary* (ibid., pp. xlix–l).

[8] Ibid., pp. 55–56.

[9] Edmund Gosse, *The Life and Letters of John Donne* (London, 1899), I, 166–67.

referred to St. Mary Magdalen's day.[10] Grierson's error in assuming a difference of eleven days between the Julian and Gregorian calendars in the seventeenth century was pointed out by H. W. Garrod.[11] Though Garrod knew that Walton was bad at dates, he thought it hardly likely that his date was wrong in all its parts or even in two of its three parts. Assuming wisely that "*this good day*" referred not to St. Mary Magdalen's day but to the "Sunday" mentioned in the letter, Garrod tried to deduce which of the three parts of the date was incorrect and emended the date to January (Jany) 11, 1607, only to find later that he had overlooked that this Old Style date would mean 1607/8, and that January 11, 1607/8 was not a Sunday but a Monday.[12] I. A. Shapiro informed Gardner that he saw no reason to suspect an error in the month or year of the letter, and that he dates it July 1607.[13]

Walton's date is important, for it is the sole reason for dating *La Corona* in or before July 1607. But Walton's date is wrong in all its parts.

When Walton printed Donne's letter to Mrs. Herbert in the *Life of Herbert*, he also printed three other letters from Donne to Mrs. Herbert in an Appendix. These three letters seem to be the first of a series which Donne wrote when Mrs. Herbert was absent from London. In the first, dated "Michin, *July* 11. 1607," Donne reveals that he has discovered that Mrs. Herbert has left London and that he does not know where she has gone:

> I take the boldness of accusing you, who would draw so dark a Curtain betwixt me and your purposes, as that I had no glimmering, neither of your goings, nor the way which my Letters might haunt. Yet, I have given this Licence to Travel, but I know not whether, nor it. It is therefore rather a Pinnace to discover; and the intire Colony of Letters, of Hundreds and Fifties, must follow.

[10]*The Poems of John Donne*, II, 228.
[11]H. W. Garrod, "Donne and Mrs. Herbert," *RES*, 21 (1945), 165.
[12]See *Divine Poems*, p. 56.
[13]Ibid.

Donne wrote the second time on "*July* 23. 1607"; he wrote from London, where he had called on Mrs. Herbert, only to find that she was still away and that his first letter had not been forwarded:

This is my second Letter. . . . After I knew you were gone (for I must, little less than accusingly tell you, I knew not you would go) I sent my first Letter, like a *Bevis* of *Hampton*, to seek Adventures. This day I came to Town, and to the best part of it, your House; for your memory, is a State-cloth and Presence; which I reverence, though you be away; though I need not seek that there, which I have about and within me. There, though I found my accusation [his first letter], yet any thing to which your hand is, is a pardon; yet I would not burn my first Letter, because as in great destiny no small passage can be omitted or frustrated, so in my resolution of writing almost daily to you, I would have no link of the Chain broke by me, both because my Letters interpret one another, and because only their number can give them weight.

The third letter in Walton's Appendix is dated "*August* 2d. 1607." Donne wrote from London; Mrs. Herbert had not yet returned.

The date of the letter in Walton's text is wrong not only because that letter was written on a Sunday, and July 11, 1607 was a Saturday, but also because it cannot be reconciled with the letters in the Appendix. The letter in the text starts,

Your Favours to me are every where; I use them, and have them. I enjoy them at London, *and leave them there; and yet find them at* Micham: *Such Riddles as these become things unexpressible; and, such is your goodness. I was almost sorry to find your Servant here this day, because I was loth to have any witness of my not coming home last Night, and indeed of my coming this Morning.*

It would appear that Donne had just received favors from Mrs. Herbert in London, and that additional of her favors had arrived at Mitcham even before he had returned home. Not only is this information incompatible with the information in the first letter in the Appendix that Mrs. Herbert has left London, but the date of the latter is unquestionably right in view of its relation to the second letter in the Appendix. In the light of the three letters in the Appendix, we may be sure that the one in the text was not written between July 11 and August 2, 1607.

Our first clue that Walton tampered with the letter in the text comes from comparing his version in the *Life of Herbert*, 1670, with that in the 1675 edition. In 1670, the letter closes,

> Your unworthiest Servant,
> unless your accepting him,
> have mended him.

In 1675, the words "*to be so*" are added after "him" in the second line and a comma is inserted after "unless." The expansion is typical of Walton's attempts to clarify in revising, even when there is nothing to be gained and perhaps something to be lost by a picayune change. Had he tampered with the letter prior to printing it in 1670? When we compare it with the letter in the Appendix which is dated July 11, 1607, we see that not only are the dates identical, but that the closes are similar. The letter in the Appendix ends,

> *Your unworthiest Servant,*
> *Except your accepting*
> *have mended him.*

Even as the date of this letter seems genuine, so does its close. The play on *except* and *accept* seems Donnean; moreover, the play is intrinsic to the letter. Donne's first sentence in it reads, "Every excuse hath in it somewhat of accusation; and since I am innocent, and yet must excuse, how shall I do for that part of accusing." On the other hand, the close of the letter in the text does not seem peculiarly indigenous to the body of the letter; it lacks the singular applicability which the closes of many of

Donne's letters have. Walton, I think, lifted it from its original context and watered it down at the same time that he appropriated the date of the letter.[14]

It is fruitless to speculate about Walton's reason for grafting the close of the letter in the Appendix upon that in the text. The letter in the text appears in the midst of Walton's muddled description of the beginning of the friendship of Donne and Mrs. Herbert, and Walton may have thought that its real date did not adequately support his account. Or, since Walton frequently printed only so much of a letter as was pertinent to his purpose, he may have cut more than its close. R. E. Bennett has shown that in the *Life of Donne,* 1670, Walton appropriated the signature of a letter (*"At my* Micham *Hospitall,* Aug. 10") which had been printed in *Letters to Severall Persons of Honour* and grafted it, with slight change, upon another letter written several years after Donne's residence at Mitcham; again, in 1670, Walton added the date "Sept. 7" to a pastiche of several letters, as Bennett says, "in order to create a pleasing verisimilitude."[15] But why would Walton have used the same date twice? He frequently nodded when he was manipulating dates, and his error here is no stranger than his adding to the *Life of Donne,* 1658, the date of Donne's will (December 13, 1630) after he had meticulously omitted it in 1640 to support his statement that Donne had made his will some time before his last sickness.

Since Walton's date on the letter with which Donne enclosed "Holy Hymns *and* Sonnets" to Mrs. Herbert is worthless, there is no evidence to date *La Corona* in July 1607, even if we accept Grierson's identification of the "Holy Hymns *and* Sonnets" with *La Corona*. The letter itself, stripped of its date, is of little help. Its tone of friendship and domesticity may indicate that it was written later than the three letters in the Appendix, which are

[14]The letter in the Appendix is written from "Michin"; I would suggest that Walton was responsible for regularizing this to "Micham" in the letter in the text.

[15]R. E. Bennett, "Walton's Use of Donne's Letters," PQ, 16 (1937), 30–31.

stiff and ingenious letters of compliment, but, even if this guess has any validity, its sole value is to suggest that *La Corona* is later than August 1607.

How much later? Gardner has noticed that Donne's "Upon the Annunciation and Passion falling upon one day. 1608" is very near to *La Corona* in mood and style.[16] "The poem," she says, "has obvious affinities with '*La Corona*', which was probably written the year before."[17] One of these affinities, though, to be sure, it is hardly peculiar to these two poems, is Donne's dependence on the circle. In *La Corona*, the first line of each sonnet after the first repeats the last line of the preceding sonnet, and the last line of Sonnet 7 repeats the first line of Sonnet 1. In "Upon the Annunciation and Passion falling upon one day. 1608," the coincidence causes Donne to write,

> . . . of them both a circle embleme is,
> Whose first and last concurre; this doubtfull day
> Of feast or fast, Christ came, and went away.

The conjunction Donne celebrates fell on March 25, 1608.[18] If we assume that *La Corona* was written before this date, we must say that Donne was moved, for some reason, to write in circular form a poem celebrating the mysteries of faith and recalling the events in the life of Christ from which the mysteries are derived, and that he later wrote a poem describing a smaller circle on the accident of the Annunciation and the Passion falling on the same day. I find it easier to believe that the coincidence of the Annunciation and the Passion in 1608, an event which took place only one other time in Donne's life, provoked him to describe Christ's human life, and that he later composed the fuller circle of *La Corona*.

I must return to the copyist of *H 49*, who "makes me end, where I begunne." His statement in 1629 that *La Corona* and

[16]*Divine Poems*, p. xxxiii.

[17]Ibid., p. 95. [Changed in 2d ed., 1978, to "probably written in the same year."]

[18]Ibid.

twelve of the Holy Sonnets were written "20 yeares since" remains the only unaltered proof in Grierson's proposals. Though the figure was probably a round one, it coincides remarkably with Gardner's suggestion, based on other evidence, that the Holy Sonnets were largely written in 1609. I suspect that he is right in dating the *La Corona* sonnets also, and that they were written shortly before the Holy Sonnets, that is, late in 1608 or early in 1609.

5

Two Flamens:
The Poems of Dr. Donne

> With God, and with the Muses I conferre.
>
> —"Satyre I," l. 48

At no time in his life did John Donne look upon the writing of poetry as a vocation. Still, his poems were for him far more than "the recreations of his youth,"[1] and long after he had made the Church his vocation there were times when verse alone could serve his purpose. Most of his poems he wrote in the twenty-five years before he took orders. During his first ten years in orders, he wrote no more than thirteen poems; he wrote only one verse in the last six years of his life. As poet, he was not a prolific writer; his poems do not number two hundred. The *Songs and Sonets* make up somewhat more than a quarter of these; their average length is about thirty lines, and altogether they are about 80 percent as long as Shakespeare's *Sonnets*. Another quarter of the poems, the epigrams and sonnets, are very short. His longest work on one subject is not one poem, but three, the *Anniversaries* and the funeral elegy for Elizabeth Drury, and together these are about as long as Book X of *Paradise Lost*; his other poem of length, "Metempsychosis," is about a quarter as long as *Paradise Regained*. After he was ordained, Donne wrote about seven hundred lines of verse, more than half of these as one poem, his only versification of Scripture; but among them are, perhaps, three of his most extraordinary sonnets and, certainly, his three hymns.

---

[1]The phrase is Izaak Walton's. *The Life and Death of Dr Donne* in *LXXX Sermons preached by . . . John Donne* (London, 1640), sig. B4^r.

Donne was a careerist from the start. His fortune was such that he needed an occupation, and he wrote much of his poetry in order to further his career. The love elegies and the satires, the early verse letters and the prose paradoxes were meant to make him shine, to call attention to his sprightly mind, to afford him the kind of distinction for wit and sophistication as an Inns of Court man that would get him on the courtly ladder. The poems to the Countess of Bedford and to other noble ladies, the epicedes, the *Anniversaries*, the later epithalamions were intended to win him patronage, not so that, like Jonson, he could pursue a career as writer, but to gain for him a place in the Queen's household, a secretaryship in Ireland or with the Virginia Company, or the ambassadorship to Venice.[2] R. C. Bald points out that "during the Mitcham years Donne was nearer to being a professional author than at any other period of his life."[3] During those years, from 1606 through 1611, Donne was desperate to rehabilitate and advance his reputation at Court, and it is not hard to understand why he addressed poems to the Countess of Huntingdon and to Magdalen and Edward Herbert, why in 1609 "he acted almost as if he were Lady Bedford's officially appointed laureate,"[4] why he wrote "An Anatomy of the World" for Sir Robert Drury, why he wrote *Pseudo-Martyr* and *Ignatius his Conclave*. Nor is it hard to perceive the same motive behind the poems of the next three years — the second *Anniversary*, the elegy on Prince Henry, the epithalamions for the Princess Elizabeth and the Earl of Somerset, and the "Obsequies to the Lord Harrington." But even before the Mitcham years, and during them, Donne was writing verse that was more private: the songs and sonnets were largely unknown to most of his contemporaries.[5] The Mitcham years were the years, also, of "A Litanie"; "Upon the Annunciation and

[2]R. C. Bald, *John Donne: A Life* (Oxford, 1970), pp. 160-62, 289-92; hereafter cited as Bald.

[3]Ibid., p. 200.

[4]Ibid., p. 177.

[5]Alan MacColl, "The Circulation of Donne's Poems in Manuscript," in A. J. Smith, ed., *John Donne: Essays in Celebration* (London, 1972), pp. 28-46; Helen Gardner, ed., *John Donne: The Elegies and the Songs and Sonnets* (Oxford, 1965), pp. xlix-l.

Passion falling upon one day. 1608"; the *La Corona* sonnets; the Holy Sonnets; and of *Biathanatos*, which had been sent only to "some particular friends in both Universities."[6] In the next years, Donne wrote "Goodfriday, 1613. Riding Westward" and he continued to work on the *Essays in Divinity*, which seems to have been unknown even to Walton in 1640, though he had access to many of Donne's manuscripts,[7] and which was in 1651 first "printed from an exact Copy, under the Authors own hand."[8] Much that Donne wrote, much of his poetry, he wrote for self-advancement, but he never "utterly delivered" himself from what he called "this intemperance of scribling."[9] Though he said of his scribbling to his friend, Sir Henry Goodere, "I thank God my accesses are lesse and lesse vehement," he says in the same letter that "in that solitarinesse and arraignment of my self, [I] digested some meditations of mine," and through all his life he wrote from time to time not to shine but to give shape to his private meditations.

Donne was not content, however, merely to cultivate his own garden or to spend all his "little stock of knowledge upon matter of delight."[10] "The primitive Monkes," he said "were excusable in their retirings and enclosures of themselves: for even of them every one cultivated his own garden and orchard, that is, his soul and body, by meditation, and manufactures; and they ought the world no more since they consumed none of her sweetnesse, nor begot others to burden her."[11] But he thought that "to be no part of any body, is to be nothing." "At most," he said, "the greatest persons, are but great wens, and excrescences; men of wit and delightfull conversation, but as moales

---

[6]*Letters to Severall Persons of Honour* (London, 1651), p. 21; hereafter cited as *Letters*.

[7]See *The Life and Death of Dr Donne*, sig. B4^v; "*The Copy of a Letter writ to Mr.* Walton *by Dr.* King, *Lord Bishop of* Chichester" in Izaak Walton, *The Life of Mr. Rich. Hooker* (London, 1665), sig. A2^v; David Novarr, *The Making of Walton's* Lives (Ithaca, 1958), pp. 24–28.

[8]"To the Reader," *Essays in Divinity by John Donne*, ed. Evelyn M. Simpson (Oxford, 1952), p. 4.

[9]*Letters*, p. 228. For addressee, see Roger E. Bennett, "Donne's *Letters to Severall Persons of Honour*," *PMLA*, 56 (1941), 136–37.

[10]*Letters*, p. 228.

[11]Ibid., p. 48. The following quotations are from the same letter, p. 51.

for ornament, except they be so incorporated into the body of the world, that they contribute something to the sustentation of the whole." He felt a pull to indulge himself in humane learning and languages, but both his social and economic position and his conception of man as a social being led him to believe that such indulgence, though a beautiful ornament to a great fortune, was for him "the worst voluptuousnes." Even a letter sent to a friend, he thought, ought not be a self-centered meditation or rumination: "When Letters have a convenient handsome body of news," he said, "they are Letters; but when they are spun out of nothing, they are nothing, or but apparitions, and ghosts. . . . [The] materialls and fuell of them should be a confident and mutuall communicating of those things which we know."[12] Still, there were times when he could not restrain his private sentiments, and he is forced to say, "I mean[t] to write a Letter, and I am fallen into a discourse"[13] or to admit that a letter has "extended and strayed into a Homilie."[14] Indeed, he confesses to Goodere what the "two ordinary forges" of his letters to him are in a letter which does not depend on them: "I write not to you out of my poor Library, where to cast mine eye upon good Authors kindles or refreshes sometimes meditations not unfit to communicate to near friends; nor from the high way, where I am contracted, and inverted into my self."[15] The intensity of Donne's reliance on his writing is clear in a letter to Goodere in which his news, the birth of his fourth child, Francis, is buried in his description of how he occupied his time during his wife's labor. Goodere had sent him some papers, and he sends one in return. He writes,

> It is (I cannot say the waightyest, but truly) the saddest lucubration and nights passage that ever I had. For it exercised those hours, which, with extreme danger of her, whom I should hardly have abstained from recompensing for her company in this

[12] Ibid., p. 121.
[13] Ibid., p. 72.
[14] Ibid., p. 112.
[15] Ibid., p. 137. For addressee, see I. A. Shapiro, "The Text of Donne's *Letters to Severall Persons*," *RES*, 7 (1931), 293. Bald (p. 158) identifies the "high way" as the road between Mitcham and London.

world, with accompanying her out of it, encreased my poor family with a son. Though her anguish, and my fears, and hopes, seem divers and wild distractions from this small businesse of your papers, yet because they all narrowed themselves, and met in *Via regia*, which is the consideration of our selves, and God, I thought it time not unfit for this dispatch.[16]

We do not know what paper Donne sent Goodere,[17] but, in the act of writing, "all narrowed themselves" for him; his whole world came to a focus in his writing. He may call rhetoric an empty thing, yet, he says, "Rhetorique will make absent and remote things present to your understanding." He may call poetry a weak thing, yet, he says, "Poetry is a counterfait Creation, and makes things that are not, as though they were."[18]

Joan Webber has beautifully demonstrated the degree to which the whole state of the world was for Donne as preacher subsumed into rhetoric, how he viewed word and world, form and content, sign and thing as almost synonymous.[19] She shows Donne's tendency to minimize the distinction between the printed word and the natural world as he exploits in numerous metaphors the implications of the Book of Creatures to suggest that "man is a word speaking words, a book within a book,"[20] as he uses rhetorical and grammatical terms as the vehicles of his metaphors. She shows how nearly Donne identified life and art, how much at home he was in a literary universe. She goes so far as to say that Donne achieved his fullest artistic expression in the pulpit, and she is right. It was the sermon that provided

---

[16]*Letters*, p. 147. See Bald, pp. 156–57.

[17]Was "the saddest lucubration and nights passage" in which "all narrowed themselves" "A Nocturnall upon S. Lucies Day, being the shortest day"? This suggestion of Louis L. Martz (*The Poetry of Meditation* [New Haven, 1954], p. 215) has more merit than those, his own alternative among them, which would date the poem after Ann Donne's death. The date of Francis Donne's birth is not known; he was baptized on January 8, 1607 (Bald, p. 555).

[18]G. R. Potter and Evelyn M. Simpson, eds., *The Sermons of John Donne* (Berkeley, 1953–62), IV, 87; hereafter cited as *Sermons*.

[19]Joan Webber, *Contrary Music: The Prose Style of John Donne* (Madison, 1963). See, mainly, ch. 5.

[20]Ibid., p. 125.

him with the opportunity to manipulate and exploit his verbal tools most fully. Paradoxical as it may seem, the universe of Donne the preacher was more literary and aesthetic than it had been before he took orders. It is as if he could in the sermons multiply his exploration of possibilities, his recognition of alternatives, his invention of ingenuities because he had arrived at settled convictions about the relation between man and God. But it is true, too, that he had earlier, as a poet, tried by means of verbal tools to control a universe which was rather more unruly, to move not toward long-accepted truths but toward new-found land. After he took orders, he turned to verse infrequently and for a variety of reasons, but some of the poems reveal the persistence of his old habit of using verse to focus a world more tumultuous than that of the sermons.

Alan MacColl says rightly at the conclusion of his study of the circulation of Donne's poems in manuscript that Donne "seems increasingly to have come to regard a reputation for writing poetry as unsuitable for a man seeking or occupying a public position." MacColl is right, too, when he says, "It would be wrong to conclude from this that he never took his verse seriously. . . ."[21] Whatever Donne's own view of the place and purpose of poetry may have been, he had as a careerist to be sensitive to the view of the world that mattered to him; and that world, though it tolerated, even applauded, the youthful demonstration of skill in versifying, thought that too long and too great a preoccupation with verse indicated a fundamental lack of seriousness. When, in 1609, Goodere informed Donne that the Countess of Huntingdon might welcome some verses, Donne, who had known her in 1600, when he was one of the secretaries of her stepfather, Sir Thomas Egerton, the Lord Keeper and Master of the Rolls, was uncertain of her attitude toward poetry and

---

[21]MacColl, p. 45. His sentence continues, "though in his later years he seems to have felt something of the sober Christian remorse for ill-spent time and talents voiced by other great poets before him." Certainly these words cannot characterize the Donne who wrote "Hymne to God my God, in my sicknesse" at the end of 1623, but certainly, too, Donne gave up the writing of poetry in 1625, after he could not refuse to write a poem he had no wish to write.

fearful that the making of verses might diminish his stature in her eyes. When he wrote, "that knowledge which she hath of me, was in the beginning of a graver course, then of a Poet, into which (that I may also keep my dignity) I would not seem to relapse. The Spanish proverb informes me, that he is a fool which cannot make one Sonnet, and he is mad which makes two," he does not express his own view of poetry but he pays pragmatic homage to the prevailing view of the world. He has another reason for declining to write; he knows that the Countess of Bedford is properly appreciative of his verse, that she does not feel his writing to be incompatible with his dignity and with his pursuit of a graver course, and he would not jeopardize his integrity: "for her delight (since she descends to them) I had reserved not only all the verses, which I should make, but all the thoughts of womens worthinesse." He does, however, send Goodere some verses for the Countess of Huntingdon, with instructions to use his discretion in presenting them to her, entreating him first "that by this occasion of versifying, I be not traduced, nor esteemed light in that Tribe, and that house where I have lived," and then that he judge whether "these verses be too bad, or too good, over or under her understanding, and not fit."[22] This last shows, of course, Donne's concern to fit his verse to his audience, but it hardly demeans the nature of poetry that he states that it may be beyond the understanding of a reader. When, a few years later, Donne compromised his integrity to the Countess of Bedford, and not only expressed his thoughts of women's worthiness in the *Anniversaries* but allowed them to be printed for a new patron, he was forced to admit that his praise of Elizabeth Drury and his publication had damaged his reputation with noble patronesses, but he offered a double defense of poetry itself. "Of my Anniversaries," he wrote to George Garrard, "the fault that I acknowledge in my self, is to have descended to print any thing in verse, which though it have excuse even in our times, by men who professe,

---

[22]*Letters,* pp. 103–4. For the date of the letter, see Bald, p. 111, n. 1, and p. 180, n. 1.

and practise much gravitie; yet I confesse I wonder how I declined to it, and do not pardon my self." He admits his error, but he insists, too, that poetry has not only been written but published, and in his own day, by men of gravity. "But," he says, "for the other part of the imputation of having said too much, my defĕce is, that my purpose was to say as well as I could: for since I never saw the Gentlewoman, I cannot be understood to have bound my self to have spoken just truths, but I would not be thought to have gone about to praise her, or any other in rime; except I took such a person, as might be capable of all that I could say. If any of those Ladies think that Mistris *Drewry* was not so, let that Lady make her self fit for all those praises in the book, and they shall be hers."[23] If Donne's poem does not contain "just truths," neither does it contain falsehoods; he is as aware as Sidney was of the golden domain that poetry occupies.

It is hard to imagine Donne, or, for that matter, anyone else in 1607/8, writing the dedication to the sister Universities with which Jonson prefaced the publication of *Volpone*, but, after all, he descended to have his Latin commendatory verses printed with the play. Nor is it likely that he told Jonson only what Jonson wanted to hear; if he himself would not have considered it the highest of compliments to be addressed as "POETA," he was too much of a poet to speak lightly of the poet's daring and skill, his genius and his industry, and even of his function as lawgiver. Donne was already in orders when Jonson published, several years later, the epigrams addressed to him, and it is hardly likely that he had any objection to compliments paid to him as poet and judicious critic, especially since Jonson referred to his "most earely wit." Donne could not, would not, deny that he was poet; he did not wish to be considered "mere poet." He was not averse to recalling, when he preached to a sympathetic and familiar audience, his days as poet. He starts a sermon at Lincoln's Inn by acknowledging his particular love for the Psalms of David and the Epistles of St. Paul. He might

---

[23]*Letters*, pp. 238-39.

justify his affection for them, he says, by Augustine's predilection for the Psalms and Chrysostom's for the Epistles, but he admits that he loves them because they are "written in such forms, as I have been most accustomed to; Saint *Pauls* being Letters, and *Davids* being Poems." He continues, "Therefore is Gods will delivered to us in *Psalms*, that we might have it the more cheerfully, and that we might have it the more certainly, because where all the words are numbred, and measured, and weighed, the whole work is the lesse subject to falsification, either by substraction or addition."[24] Donne is here making a case for the accuracy of the text of the Psalms, not a case for the "truth" in poetry, but his words are a more faithful reflection of his attitude toward verse than his later ones that he did his best in verse when he had least truth for his subject.[25]

Several months after the death of young John Harrington on February 27, 1614, Donne bid his farewell to poetry. The "Obsequies to the Lord Harrington, brother to the Lady Lucy, Countesse of Bedford" was not a spontaneous expression of grief. In its last lines, Donne explains that his Muse has been "cast / Behind hand" by the greatness of his grief, but it seems clear that he decided to write the poem only after he had decided to enter orders. His poem was calculated to move Lady Bedford "to so much compassion"[26] that she would offer to pay his debts: not only does its length seem intended to demonstrate that he would lavish on Harrington the effort he had expended on Elizabeth Drury, but he says, too, that he inters his Muse in Harrington's grave — she "hath spoke, and spoke her last." He meant the words seriously. When he wrote Goodere on December 20, 1614, that he was "brought to a necessity of printing" his poems and addressing them to the Earl of Somerset, he saw the "incongruities" in his decision, which made him "a Rhapsoder of [his] own rags," and he thought that the printing of his

[24]*Sermons*, II, 49–50.

[25]See p. 195.

[26]The words are Donne's, in a letter to Sir Henry Goodere in which he expresses his disappointment that the Countess, who had been so touched by his elegy that she offered to pay his debts, sent him only £30 when he explained to her that he wished to enter the ministry free of debt (*Letters*, p. 219).

poems before he took orders would expose him to "many interpretations." Although he felt obliged to descend into print, he
meant to publish "not for much publique view, but at mine
own cost, a few Copies." He wrote, too, "I would be just to my
written words to my L. *Harrington*, to write nothing after
that"; he obviously looked upon the printing of some of his
poems "as a valediction to the world, before I take Orders."[27]

Despite his renunciation of verse, despite his cognizance of
widespread opinion that to be a rhymer clashed with the gravity
of the priesthood, despite his having in sermons an outlet for
self-expression and self-examination, Donne did, occasionally,
write poems after his ordination. My purpose here is to try to
understand why he did so, what occasions or circumstances
made him violate his intention to write nothing in verse after his
elegy on Lord Harrington — not so much to probe the motive of
verse, as to see what the contexts of a poem, if they are recover-
able, tell us about the poem and about Donne. Some of the
poems I deal with can be dated readily; others have been generally accepted as having been written after Donne's ordination,
and these, too, I shall discuss in order to examine in detail the
nature of the evidence on which the conventional date is based.
All are worth looking at very closely, though several have been
abundantly scrutinized. Some of the poems resemble in intent
and technique what Donne had written earlier, but others differ radically as he breaks new ground. To look carefully at what
he wrote, to see what circumstances prompted him to write, to
speculate about his aims will show, I think, how deeply in-
grained in him was the habit of verse and how much it continued to matter to him.

"To Mr. George Herbert, with my Seal, of the Anchor and Christ"

Although Donne worked hard to assemble his poems at the
end of 1614 — he wrote Goodere that it cost him "more dili-

---

[27]Ibid., pp. 196–98.

gence, to seek them, then it did to make them"[28] — the pressure he felt to publish subsided, and they remained in manuscript. Still, several weeks after he told Goodere that he would write no more verse, probably a few days after he had been ordained deacon and priest, he wrote a poem, "To Mr. George Herbert, with my Seal, of the Anchor and Christ."[29]

Donne's intimate friends and the people from whom he had sought patronage had for some time known of his plans to enter the Church.[30] When he was ordained on January 23, 1615, he sent his news to friends who were not in London, perhaps to Sir Henry Wotton at The Hague[31] and to Sir Edward Herbert, who had been on the continent since the spring of 1614. His letter to Sir Edward has survived: it is succinct, witty, modestly self-aggrandizing but, withal, deferential, and its close makes it clear that it was written on "the very day wherein I took orders."[32] The letter did not bear Donne's old seal of entwined snakes but a new one of Christ crucified to an anchor, which Donne had devised in anticipation of his new career.[33] It is hardly surprising that Donne should have written to Sir Edward. He had perhaps met him (and his mother) in 1599;[34] there is evidence of Donne's friendship with Magdalen Herbert

[28]Ibid., p. 197.

[29]This title is Helen Gardner's emendation of the one used in Donne's *Poems*, 1650. See her discussion in *John Donne: The Divine Poems* (Oxford, 1952), pp. 141–43; hereafter cited as *Divine Poems*. She predicates a Latin title, but such a one, if it existed, would have been scribal or editorial; Donne would not normally have given a title to a poem sent as an epistle.

[30]See, for instance, Donne's letters to Viscount Rochester (later Earl of Somerset) and to James, Lord Hay, in *A Collection of Letters, made by Sr Tobie Mathews K^t* (London, 1660), pp. 319–22; hereafter cited as *Mathew Collection*.

[31]See Bald, p. 305. His evidence is based on a letter in the Burley MS., printed in Evelyn M. Simpson, *A Study of the Prose Works of John Donne*, 2d ed. (Oxford, 1948), pp. 333–34; hereafter cited as *Prose Works*.

[32]John Hayward, ed., *John Donne: Complete Poetry and Selected Prose* (London, 1930), pp. 465–66.

[33]Bald, p. 305.

[34]Mario M. Rossi, *La vita, le opere, i tempi di Edoardo Herbert di Chirbury* (Florence, 1947), I, 39.

in several letters of 1607,[35] and of his familiarity with Sir Edward in poems dated 1608-10;[36] in the spring of 1613, Donne spent several weeks with Sir Edward at Montgomery Castle in Wales;[37] and he had close ties to the Herbert family to the day he died.[38] It is rather more surprising that he should have written at greater length to Sir Edward's brother George, a young man of twenty-one, who had recently been made a Minor Fellow at Trinity College, Cambridge.[39]

Donne's lines to George Herbert show "no signs of great intimacy," Helen Gardner says; she finds them "formal and impersonal," and she thinks the poem "a natural one for Donne to send to a rising young scholar, who was the son and brother of close friends."[40] Still, there is no question that Donne informed young Herbert that he had taken orders in a way that he thought Herbert must appreciate and that he went to some trouble to do so in twenty-two lines of ingeniously conceited verse. Only in oblique fashion, in a participial phrase, does he indicate that he has been admitted to or adopted in God's family; his emphasis is on the significance of his new crest and his old, on what it means that he has substituted an anchor for the cross on which Christ was crucified and that he has not had to renounce his old crest of serpents (adherence to the cross implies a crucifixion of nature which makes the serpent effect not just his death but his cure). Both the nature of his wit and his transmutation of the cross remind of his earlier poem "The Crosse." Toward the close of that poem, Donne's advice, "So

[35]See Chapter 4.
[36]Bald, p. 185.
[37]Ibid., p. 183, n. 1, and pp. 270-71.
[38]To avoid the plague in London, Donne spent the summer and autumn of 1625 at Sir John Danvers's house in Chelsea (ibid., pp. 472-80). He preached a memorial sermon for Lady Danvers in 1627 (*Sermons*, VIII, No. 2). He bequeathed a picture to Sir John Danvers in his will, and he refers there to an annuity he received from monies he had placed with Danvers (Bald, pp. 566-67).
[39]Amy M. Charles, *A Life of George Herbert* (Ithaca, 1977), pp. 71-72; hereafter cited as Charles.
[40]*Divine Poems*, pp. 141, 146.

when thy braine workes, ere thou utter it, / Crosse and correct concupiscence of witt," works ironically and reflexively to point up his own witty performance, and he did not heed the advice either in that poem or in the poem for Herbert. He seems to have taken it for granted when he informed young Herbert of his ordination that Herbert would relish an epistle in verse and one which demonstrated his customary wit.

To be sure, Donne seems to distance himself some from his old wit by applying it to a sacred subject and, moreover, by writing in Latin. He probably turned to Latin not in tactful self-protection but out of his awareness of the interests and capacities of Herbert. Although Donne attests to his own interest in languages,[41] he had not, except for a couple of epigrams and for poems to Ben Jonson and to a Dr. Andrews, written in Latin verse. He used Latin here because he knew that Herbert was, even at nineteen, an accomplished — and published — Latinist.[42]

But Donne's verses to Herbert are tailored for their recipient beyond their wit and their Latin. Having exploited the significance of his seals for himself, he tells Herbert that he sends under his new seal his pledges of friendship, his good wishes, and his prayers, and he expresses his hope that St. George, whose image appears on the Great Seal of Britain, may heap even more on Herbert by way of royal gifts. This last is not unambiguous,[43] but it appears that Donne was familiar with Herbert's ambitions for a career at court and recognized in Herbert a younger version of himself and of the ambitions and pulls he still felt, though, as a last resort, he had taken orders. Even as he spoke of the security of the anchor which he had provided

---

[41]*Letters*, p. 51.

[42]His two Latin poems on Prince Henry, in *Epicedium Cantabrigiense* (Cambridge, 1612), preceded the English poems that his brother Edward and Donne himself wrote for the third edition of Joshua Sylvester's *Lachrymae Lachrymarum* (London, 1613). Before many years, Herbert would be appointed Praelector in Rhetoric (in 1618) and University Orator (in 1620).

[43]Donne's last lines are

> Mitto, nec exigua, exiguâ sub imagine, dona,
> Pignora amicitiae, et munera; Vota, preces.
> Plura tibi accumulet, sanctus cognominis, Ille
> Regia qui flavo Dona sigillat Equo.

for himself, he wished something else for his young friend. It is likely not only that Donne knew of Herbert's desires, but also that Herbert was acquainted with Donne's long-standing ambitions, that he was aware that Donne's entrance into the Church represented the frustration of those ambitions, a realization by Donne that his service must be directly to his God and only indirectly to his King. If Herbert read the poem as a statement in which Donne indicated the rightness of his own choice for himself, Herbert must have seen, too, that Donne still wished for him what Donne had once wanted for himself.

The very existence of the poem is evidence that Donne's familiarity with Herbert and his affection for him are greater than has customarily been assumed. If the conceits in the poem are frigid, the poem itself is far more than a cold announcement of a step taken. It is a private epistle made for a special recipient; Donne knew that George Herbert would appreciate a *verse* letter, a Latin letter, a witty letter, one that conveyed the announcement of his ordination hieroglyphically, through the exploitation of the new seal on the letter itself.[44] He saw fit to break his vow to write no more verse because he was aware of what his ordination would mean to a young friend who shared his love of poetry and his secular ambition. He must have felt that Herbert had sensitivity and tact enough to keep so personal a poem for his eyes alone, and his feeling was right. It is not surprising that no manuscript of the poem has survived or that it was not printed with Donne's poems until 1650.

The English which follows in Donne's *Poems*, 1650, translates the last two lines: "And may that Saint which rides in our great Seal, / To you, who bear his name, great bounties deal." John T. Shawcross says that the translator misreads, that "cognominis" refers to Herbert's surname, and that the last line alludes to the white horse of Rev. 19:11-12. His own translation is not right, I think: "May He heap more upon you, sainted of surname, / who seals his princely gifts with a glittering steed" (*The Complete Poetry of John Donne* [Garden City, N.Y., 1967], pp. 369-70). Donne's sense is, rather: "May he, sainted with the same name you have, heap more upon you — he who seals with a bright horse [who is on the Great Seal which authorizes] royal gifts."

[44]For Herbert's reply to Donne's poem, see *Divine Poems*, pp. 143-47, and Novarr, *The Making of Walton's* Lives, pp. 503-6.

"To Mr. Tilman after he had taken orders"

In light of the paucity of poetry Donne wrote after he was ordained, it is hard to understand why he was moved to write a
poem to a Mr. Edward Tilman after Tilman had written a
poem about "his motives not to take orders" and had then taken
them. Although Helen Gardner explored the possibility that
Tilman might have been related, through his wife, to the
Brooke family with whom Donne was familiar, she found no
evidence that Donne was personally acquainted with Tilman.[45]
R. C. Bald found that a Mr. Tyllman lived in the parish of St.
Clement Danes between 1610 and 1618, speculated that he
might have been a kinsman of Edward Tilman's who brought
him to Donne's attention, but could not prove that Donne knew
either of the Tilmans.[46] Gardner's and Bald's discussions of the
poem make its very existence even more puzzling. Although
Gardner speaks of the accent of warm sincerity in Donne's glori-
fication of the priest's calling, she finds Donne's response to Tilman's poem very strange in that Donne seems to ascribe Tilman's
reluctance to take orders to the same motive which influenced
him—"the unattractiveness of the clerical profession from a
worldly point of view."[47] Bald emphasizes the lines in the poem
in which Donne asks Tilman whether he is aware of changes in
himself now that he has entered orders, and he thinks that
"Donne seems to be reflecting his own feelings rather than those
of Tilman; he himself was only too conscious of the meagre
social prestige which attached to his new profession, and it was

[45]*Divine Poems*, pp. 128–29.
[46]Bald, p. 303.
[47]*Divine Poems*, pp. 132, 129. Gardner provides some evidence for the
"Lay-scornings of the Ministry," the contempt in which the profession was
held in the seventeenth century (pp. 130–31). That attitude received much
comment in the century, and in his *Life of Herbert* (1670), Walton made Herbert the exemplar of the thesis that the clerical life is worthy of men of family,
education, and talent. Gardner's phrase "worldly point of view" includes
monetary considerations. The remuneration of a parish priest was often, to be
sure, no more than a pittance, but Donne seems to have been certain from the
day he entered orders that the King and his other patrons had other, more lu-
crative arrangements in mind for him.

he who had been disappointed to find that, in spite of his new calling, he was still the same sinner he had always been."[48] Both Gardner and Bald focus, then, on Donne's responding in the poem to matters which troubled him, not Tilman. Although it is probable enough that the motivation behind a poem may be found in what a poet unconsciously reveals of himself, the epistolary form of Donne's poem to Tilman makes it likely that Donne was responding to more than his own inner needs, that some immediate and external circumstances or events called forth the poem. Even Bald feels, despite his focus on Donne's self-revelation, that Donne wrote his poem with Tilman's poem in mind, and Gardner considers it a "reply" (though a "very odd" one) to Tilman's poem.[49]

Tilman's emphasis in the mediocre lines of "Mr. Tilman of Pembroke Hall in Cambridge his motives not to take orders"[50] is on his sense of personal unworthiness, his "Concupiscence," his passionate temperament ("gall" and "wrath"), his ambition and envy. He does not refer to the "Lay-scornings of the Ministry" which Donne uses as the main organizing principle of his poem, but in his next-to-last stanza, he contrasts ambition and humility, and much as he makes the stanza work to show the higher glory of men of God, he sees this higher glory as concomitant with lowly place in the world. He addresses ambition as "Gyant Vice," and though he says it is "naught," he adds "and mine," for he repines at every great man. The "Refined Faculty" teaches men to aspire by way of a paradox — "Friend sitt lower, that thou maist sitt higher" — but when Tilman asks whether he is himself familiar with "Supple Humility," he must say no. We do not know exactly when Tilman made his self-assessment or how he managed to overcome his reluctance to take orders. He was, however, ordained deacon on December 20, 1618.[51]

---

[48]Bald, pp. 303-4.

[49]Ibid., p. 303; *Divine Poems*, p. 129.

[50]First printed by H. Harvey Wood in "A Seventeenth-Century Manuscript of Poems by Donne and Others," *Essays and Studies by Members of the English Association*, 16 (1931), 179-90.

[51]Gardner summarizes much of what is known of Tilman in *Divine Poems*,

The three surviving complete manuscripts of Donne's poem entitle it, with negligible variation, "To Mr. Tilman after he had taken orders." If the title is to be trusted, Donne knew when he wrote "To Mr. Tilman" that Tilman had changed his mind. His poem is not an argument addressed to one of the chief of God's sinners; it is not advisory, but neither is it, except by indirection, congratulatory. It is a poem welcoming Tilman to his new profession, in which Donne, remembering Tilman's poem, implies that Tilman has changed and in which he asserts the glory of the priesthood. Donne's opening lines, "Thou, whose diviner soule hath caus'd thee now / To put thy hand unto the holy Plough," may be a reminiscence of Tilman's lines in which he says that he could clasp the "unrepented Plough, eternall Yoke," "Could I dare / To thinke my selfe as fitt as Thou art good" (ll. 10–13). Donne starts by announcing that Tilman has made the scorn of the laity for the ministry into a victory rather than an impediment, and, though the bulk of the poem takes the form of a number of rhetorical questions, he makes a number of assertions. For all his questioning, in lines 1–22, the nature of the change Tilman feels in himself, Donne implies that Tilman has found new thoughts and stirrings in himself, new riches, now that he is "new feather'd with coelestiall love," and he assumes that Tilman's "gayning" "surmount[s] expression." The rest of the poem answers the question, "Why doth the foolish world scorne that profession, / Whose joyes passe speech," by a series of questions in which Donne clearly shows the nobility of ministers, who are ambassadors of God, links between heaven and earth. There is wit in Donne's rhetoric. If the wit in his images is a little stale — he had made prior use of the loadstone, Indian voyages, the King's stamp, the properties of angels, and a new-found star — his last image, which culminates in his calling a priest a "blest Hermaphrodite," is particularly effective:[52]

---

p. 128. See, too, Allan Pritchard, "Donne's Mr. Tilman," *RES*, ns 24 (1973), 38–42.

[52]Even this image, however, Donne had used before. See "Epithalamion made at Lincoln's Inn," l. 30.

> These are thy titles and preheminences,
> In whom must meet Gods graces, mens offences,
> And so the heavens which beget all things here,
> And th'earth our mother, which these things doth beare,
> Both these in thee, are in thy Calling knit,
> And make thee now a blest Hermaphrodite.

Throughout the poem, Donne depresses secular rank and place below religious: he plays kingly coronation against the crown of Christ, royal honors against the heavenly kingdom, earthly privileges against the heavenly prerogatives of Mary and of preachers, civil titles against godly preeminence. The whole tenor of his poem is antithetical to the last line of his poem to George Herbert, with its wish that Herbert may achieve worldly prosperity, "Regia . . . dona."

The poem to Mr. Tilman does, however, have an interesting relation to Herbert. Lines 29–30 read:

> Would they thinke it well if the day were spent[53]
> In dressing, Mistressing and complement?

In lines 79–80 of "The Church-Porch," Herbert advises,

> Flie idlenesse, which yet thou canst not flie
> By dressing, mistressing, and complement.

We must assume either that Herbert had seen Donne's poem in manuscript or that Donne had seen a draft of "The Church-Porch" and had taken over one of its lines, a procedure so foreign to the way he worked that it is not likely he would have adopted it unless he expected Herbert to see what he had done. F. E. Hutchinson thought it "likely enough" that Herbert began writing "The Church-Porch" and others of his English poems in

[53]This is the reading of the Dobell and O'Flaherty MSS.; the first three words appear also in the Welbeck MS. Gardner followed the MSS. in the first edition of *Divine Poems*, but she decided, as it is likely the editor of *Poems*, 1635, did, that the line was "hopelessly unmetrical" and printed his version, "As if their day were onely to be spent," in her 2d ed. (1978), pp. 32, 101.

the first few years after he took his B.A. at Cambridge in 1613, but he thought, too, that Herbert had borrowed Donne's line.[54] Amy M. Charles makes a persuasive case in her recent biography that Herbert may have begun "The Church-Porch" as early as 1613 and that he probably addressed the poem to his younger brother Henry, shortly after Henry first went to France early in 1614.[55] The line in "The Church-Porch" almost identical with Donne's appears in the Williams manuscript of Herbert's poems, and Charles thinks that Herbert copied some or all of his English poems into that manuscript before March 1618, perhaps as early as 1613-14 and 1616-17.[56] It would seem, then, that Herbert composed his line long before Tilman took orders, and that Donne incorporated it into "To Mr. Tilman."[57] He may have seen Herbert's poem when he went to Cambridge within two months of his own ordination,[58] or he may have been sent a copy by Herbert later, in the three and a half years or more that elapsed before he wrote "To Mr. Tilman."

There is no evidence that Herbert knew Tilman, but they must have met at Cambridge. Tilman had matriculated from Pembroke Hall in 1609, Herbert from Trinity on December 18, 1609; both had taken the B.A. in 1613 and the M.A. in 1616. Tilman became a Fellow in 1613; Herbert was made a Minor Fellow on October 3, 1614, and a Major Fellow on March 15, 1616.[59] Both had ambitions for high civil office; both felt the pull of the Church, either from religious temper or because the University statutes stipulated that a Fellow must take orders within a set period if he was to retain his office.[60] Legalistically, at least, civil office was incompatible with orders: the diaconate

[54]F. E. Hutchinson, ed., *The Works of George Herbert* (Oxford, 1941), pp. xxvi, 477; hereafter cited as Hutchinson.

[55]Charles, pp. 77-78, 83-84.

[56]Ibid., p. 87.

[57]This is my conclusion, not Charles's. See her n. 54, p. 84.

[58]Bald, pp. 307-8.

[59]*Divine Poems*, p. 128; Charles, pp. 66, 71-72.

[60]See "Walton on Herbert's Resignation of His Fellowship," Appendix F in my *The Making of Walton's* Lives, pp. 516-20.

did not commit its holder to the parochial life, but it did debar him from civil employment. For Tilman, the evidence that he was both ambitious for high place and attracted to the Church is in his own poem. For Herbert, there is ample documentation. His letters from Cambridge contain such sentiments as "after I enter'd into a Benefice"[61] and "I am now setting foot into Divinity, to lay the platform of my future life."[62] Still, from the middle of September 1619, he used all the means at his disposal to become University Orator,[63] and it is likely that he wished to emulate the career of the incumbent. Francis Nethersole had become one of the secretaries of Viscount Doncaster, special ambassador to the princes of Germany; he carried dispatches between England and Germany, and he was knighted, during the course of his service, on September 19, 1619. When, on October 21, 1619, the University Senate approved a leave of absence for Nethersole as Orator, it appointed Herbert his deputy. Nethersole resigned the Oratorship on January 18, 1620, and Herbert was appointed in his place three days later.[64]

By January 21, 1620, Herbert was on the road toward those royal gifts which, five years before, Donne had wished for him out of his awareness that Herbert must eventually choose between State and Church as he had. In the intervening years, Herbert must have been severely troubled by the necessity of a choice; and, regardless of Donne's good wishes, he was cognizant that Donne, despite his own preference, had settled for the Church. I would suggest that it was Herbert who called Donne's attention to Tilman's problem and to his poem, with his own situation very much in mind.

Donne's poem to Tilman was certainly written after December 20, 1618, when Tilman became deacon, and almost certainly before May 12, 1619, when Donne left for Germany as Viscount Doncaster's chaplain. It was written, then, at about

[61]Hutchinson, p. 367, dates Letter V "[1618]." Charles thinks it is earlier, but her discussion is not entirely clear; see pp. 75, 77–78, 86, 88.

[62]Letter III, in Hutchinson, pp. 364–65; dated "*March* 18. 1617 [18]."

[63]Ibid., pp. xxvii–xxviii, 369–70, 580; Charles, pp. 98–99.

[64]Bald, p. 344; Hutchinson, pp. xxviii–xxix, 580.

the time he wrote "A Hymne to Christ, at the Authors last going into Germany," after he had been Divinity Reader at Lincoln's Inn for two and a half years. During his several months on the Continent, Donne wrote very few letters and probably only one poem.[65] If I am right that Donne's poem to Tilman was intended for Herbert as well as for Tilman, he would not have written it after mid-September of 1619, for he would have known from Herbert or from Sir John Danvers or from Sir Francis Nethersole (whom they had tried to influence) of Herbert's lively efforts to become Orator. We may be sure that the "after he had taken orders" in the title of the poem refers to Tilman's having been ordained deacon; he was not ordained priest until March 12, 1620, almost two months after Herbert had been appointed Orator.

Donne's lines to Tilman were, then, I think, written with Herbert in mind, about four years after Donne had, on the occasion of his own ordination, expressed his hope that Herbert might not have to take orders, that he might receive the royal gifts he wanted. It is likely that the poem reflects Donne's considered view of Herbert's chances for a court career in early 1619 and that it is also a reflection on his own career in the Church. The concern of the poem with the degree to which Tilman is aware of a change in himself may, as Bald says, reflect Donne's own self-questioning, but its assumption that Tilman feels new thoughts, stirrings, and rewards probably reflects like changes which Donne recognizes in himself. His concern to counter the contempt in which the Church was held by the worldly-wise may indicate his awareness that the matter of earthly preferment and its relation to a career in the Church was very much on Herbert's mind. Donne makes clear his own belief in the nobility and dignity of his position, and we may assume that in 1619 he was not averse to advocating the Church as a career for Herbert. Nor was he averse to doing so in a poem. Given his subject matter and his stance, no one was likely

[65]Bald, p. 345; see, below, my discussion of Donne's version of Gazet's *"Vota Amico facta."*

to accuse him of playing with toys. It is, nonetheless, interesting that young George Herbert, a poet, a man faced with the same problem which had exacerbated Donne, should have overcome Donne's reluctance to write poetry—and not once, but twice. Donne broke his resolution when he knew that verse was the decorous and tactful way to demonstrate his understanding, his sympathy, and the warmth of his feeling.

The Dating of the Sonnets in the Westmoreland Manuscript

The poems to Herbert and to Tilman are occasional poems. Donne's epithalamions, his epicedes, some of his verse letters indicate that he frequently used an occasion as the springboard for poetry. Our interest in such poetry is usually commensurate with the degree to which Donne moved beyond the occasion and used his verse as a means of self-expression. Much of Donne's poetry is, however, independent of occasion, what Walton would have called a free-will-offering. But even here we can distinguish poetry of two kinds. The love elegies, the satires, some of the verse letters are independent of occasion, but are, on the whole, public rather than private verse. They are voluntary, not occasional, but their primary motive is not a compulsive need to explore and express for one's own sake: they were intended to circulate and to enhance Donne's reputation. Many of the songs and sonnets, however, Donne seems to have written for himself; he appears to have restricted their circulation. After his ordination, too, he turned to verse from time to time in order to work out private concerns. Three of the Holy Sonnets seem, in Gardner's words, "inspired by what appear to have been casual moods."[66]

Walton said that Donne's "many divine Sonnets" had been written "in his declining age."[67] His statement received support

---

[66]*Divine Poems*, p. 78.
[67]*The Life and Death of Dr Donne*, sig. B4^r; not changed in later editions of the *Life*.

in the 1890s, with Edmund Gosse's discovery that the West-moreland manuscript contained three sonnets which appeared nowhere else. Gosse thought that the first of these, "Since she whome I lovd, hath payd her last debt," must have been written after the death of Ann Donne on August 15, 1617; he assumed that all nineteen of the Holy Sonnets were written at the same time and that to date one was to date all.[68] Grierson agreed,[69] and it remained for Gardner to demonstrate brilliantly and conclusively that twelve of the sonnets must have been written in 1609 and to suggest that four "penitential" sonnets were probably written between the second half of 1609 and the writing of the *First Anniversary* in 1611.[70] Gardner thinks that the three sonnets preserved only in the Westmoreland manuscript are "entirely unconnected with each other," that they are "'separate ejaculations.'"[71] She suggests that they were written after Donne's ordination (and she provides external evidence to date "Since she whome I lovd, hath payd her last debt" and "Show me deare Christ, thy spouse, so bright and cleare") and thinks they did not circulate because Donne suppressed them in his anxiety "not to be thought of as a versifier."[72]

It is natural and seems logical to try to account for the omission of some poems in some manuscripts on the basis of their having been written late in Donne's career or of their deliberate suppression.[73] But frequently such arguments get us into additional problems; for instance, if the four "penitential" sonnets were written before 1612, we must assume, since they do not

[68]Edmund Gosse, *The Life and Letters of John Donne* (London, 1899), II, 106.

[69]Herbert J. C. Grierson, ed., *The Poems of John Donne* (Oxford, 1912), II, 225.

[70]*Divine Poems*, pp. xliii-l.

[71]Ibid., p. xli. Although Gardner theorizes about the order and relation of sixteen of the Holy Sonnets, she preserves for these three the term which Grierson had used to characterize all of them since he could not find a definite significance in any order (*The Poems of John Donne*, II, 231).

[72]*Divine Poems*, pp. 77-78.

[73]See *The Making of Walton's* Lives, pp. 100-101, n. 22.

appear in the Group I and Group II manuscripts, that Donne deliberately suppressed them, and it is difficult to understand why he should have wanted to do so. It is particularly difficult to explain the absence and presence of poems in the Westmoreland manuscript.

Gardner describes the Westmoreland manuscript (*W*) as written throughout in the hand of Donne's friend Rowland Woodward, but she finds that it falls clearly into three parts. The first of these contains the five accepted satires, thirteen elegies, the Lincoln's Inn epithalamion, and a large group of verse letters addressed mainly to Donne's friends at the Inns of Court. None of these poems dates after 1598, except for the verse letter "To L. of D.," which Gardner would place between February and August 1609.[74] The second part has the nineteen Holy Sonnets, followed by the *La Corona* sonnets. The third contains the Paradoxes and Problems (some of the latter probably written as late as 1607 or 1609),[75] the epigrams, and one lyric, "A Jeat Ring Sent." Gardner thinks that *W* is very close to Donne's own papers, that its text is very good and its extrinsic authority high.[76] Still, *W* does not contain, for whatever reason, the songs and sonnets, the two later epithalamions, the verse epistles to ladies, and the other religious poems which Donne wrote prior to his ordination. As a matter of fact, except for the three unique sonnets it does not contain anything that can be dated after the publication of *Pseudo-Martyr* in January 1610, a very fine copy of which, inscribed by Donne to Woodward, was attached to *W* when the library of the Earls of Westmoreland was sold in 1892.[77] Except for these sonnets, then, there is nothing in *W* to suggest a date later than 1610. But Grierson, who thought that portions of *W* might have been collected early, felt that the manuscript might have been transcribed as late as

[74]*Divine Poems*, pp. xlviii–xlix.
[75]Simpson, *Prose Works*, pp. 146–48; Bald, p. 200.
[76]*Divine Poems*, pp. lxxviii–lxxxi; *The Elegies and the Songs and Sonnets*, p. lxxii.
[77]*The Poems of John Donne*, II, lxxxi.

1625, and Gardner maintains that it could not have been written before 1617.[78]

How strong is the extrinsic evidence that the three sonnets unique in *W* were written not in 1609 (or a year or two later), when all the others were written, but after Donne's ordination? The argument for the later composition of "Since she whome I lovd, hath payd her last debt" rests on two bases. First, Gosse's assumption that the "she" of this sonnet must be Ann Donne has seemed so right and natural and inevitable that it has never been challenged. It has no more or no less to commend it than has Walton's guess that the woman in "A Valediction: forbidding Mourning" must be Ann Donne. Both are attempts to connect biography and poetry; both are attractive, and unsupported. The "she" of this sonnet may refer to any one of Donne's real or imagined "prophane" loves; it may refer to Cecilia Bulstrode, who died on August 4, 1609, and whose death Donne and many others noticed in verse. Second, Gardner assumes, from the tone of resignation which she finds in the poem, that Donne did not write it immediately after the death of his wife. Since she thinks the sonnet reads "like a first working-out of an idea more powerfully expressed" in Donne's "A Hymne to Christ, at the Authors last going into Germany," she is inclined to date it just before Donne's journey in May 1619. That idea — that God manifests his love to man by depriving man of earthly happiness — she finds also in a letter of Donne's written a year or two *before* Ann's death;[79] and, we may suggest, it is not so fresh and idiosyncratic an idea that Donne could not have used it earlier.

Only one persuasive argument has been advanced for dating "Show me deare Christ, thy spouse, so bright and cleare" after

---

[78]Ibid., pp. lxxx–lxxxi; *Divine Poems*, p. lxxix (2d ed., p. lxxx). Both assume 1617 as *terminus a quo* since they assume that "Since she whome I lovd" is about the death of Ann Donne; Grierson refers also to the scribal hand. W. Milgate dates the manuscript "about 1620" on the basis of Gardner's argument regarding the composition of "Since she whome I lovd" (*John Donne: The Satires, Epigrams and Verse Letters* [Oxford, 1967], p. xlvi).

[79]*Divine Poems*, p. 78; Bald, p. 316.

Donne took orders. Gardner agrees with Evelyn Simpson[80] that the sonnet is a plea for the reunion of Christendom, for a Universal Church. She argues, moreover, that its first lines express Donne's distress at the condition of Christendom at the beginning of the Thirty Years' War; that the primary image of the poem, the woman who, "rob'd and tore / Laments and mournes in Germany and here," represents the Jerusalem of Lamentations; and she suggests that Donne saw a parallel between the captivity of Israel and the collapse of the Protestants after the defeat of the Elector in the battle of Weisser Berg on November 8, 1620 (N.S.). Because news of the defeat reached England a month or more later, Gardner thinks that Donne wrote his sonnet at the end of 1620 or early in 1621.[81] Plausible as her suggestion is, however, Donne was interested in the condition of Protestantism abroad, and particularly in Germany, long before 1621, and it is plausible, too, that he might have written the poem even before he went to France and Germany with Sir Robert Drury in 1611.

The only extrinsic evidence that "Oh, to vex me, contraryes meete in one" was written after Donne took orders is, simply, this: it appears only in *W*, in conjunction with two other sonnets which appear only there and which *may* have been written after Donne took orders. Nor is the internal evidence any more convincing. Perhaps the sonnet, in its emphasis on Donne's inability to be constant in vows, devotion, and contrition, differs a little from the other Holy Sonnets, with their stress on sin and unworthiness, but the difference is likely to persuade only the reader who is anxious to find one. Donne does say, "Inconstancy unnaturally hath begott / A constant habit," and it is tempting to see a pun in "habit," but when Donne uses this pun in the sermons he does not so suppress it.[82] There is, then, even less evidence that this sonnet is late than there is for the other

---

[80]*Prose Works*, p. 101.
[81]*Divine Poems*, pp. 121–27.
[82]See Webber, *Contrary Music*, p. 138.

two. If they are late, however, and we cannot rule out that possibility, they are the most personal, the most intimately self-expressive poems Donne wrote after his ordination. No others are so private, so out of keeping with Donne's image of himself as priest that he would have felt it necessary to suppress them. If they are late, they indicate that at least in the first half-dozen years after his ordination Donne felt at times impelled to poetry in order to probe his inner being and express the depths of his belief, times when he was moved to allay his pain by drawing it through "Rimes vexation," when he sought to tame and mollify his emotions by fettering them in verse; he did not do this so undisguisedly during the last decade of his life. Interesting as the three sonnets are in themselves, the possibility that Donne may have written them after he had renounced poetry makes them even more interesting. And, slight as the evidence is that they are late, it is about as strong as that for earlier composition; until new evidence is brought forward, we must still consider them in a discussion of Donne's last years as poet.

"Oh, to vex me, contraryes meete in one"

In "Oh, to vex me," Donne's concern is his inconstancy in vows, in devotion, and in contrition, a concern not limited to a man of the cloth, but—if we date the poem after 1617—one closely related to a subject of Donne's in his poem to Tilman: the nature of Tilman's change, or lack of it, after he had committed himself to orders. In that poem, Donne had asked whether Tilman had experienced new thoughts and stirrings, whether he had attained more "noble goods" in less time and with less pain, whether he had changed only in external attributes, not in substance (and he had implied that Tilman had indeed changed). In the sonnet, Donne is distressed because he has not changed: he is as inconstant in his attitude toward heavenly things as he was when his concerns were secular, and he is vexed that his behavior is full of contradictions. The paradox at the heart of the poem is not very fresh or striking; it is the old idea of immutable-in-mutability; he is constant in his inconstancy. Its development is rather more interesting, since Donne compares his attitude toward devotion to his "prophane love" and to a "fantastique Ague." If some of the earlier Holy Sonnets get their power from Donne's conjunction or juxtaposition of the religious and the erotic, that is doubly true here, for we do not expect a man in orders to admit to an indulgence in profane love, and Donne not only does so but admits, too, his fickleness. Moreover, his use of "prophane love" masks only slightly a Petrarchan attitude toward women. He says that he is as "humourous," as subject to changes of mood, in his religious devotion as he is in his love; his contrition, like his love, is sometimes full of petitions and sometimes wordless; it is sometimes infinite and sometimes nothing. His devotion, he continues, is subject to the paroxysms characteristic of an ague: his "devout fitts come and go away." One day he deliberately puts God out of his mind; the next, he self-consciously and obsequiously courts Him; the day following, cognizant of God's wrath, he shakes with fear. The poem ends quickly, with Donne's recognition of the difference between his religious condition and an ague; his best days, he announces, are those when his awareness of the power of God makes him quake.

The impact of Donne's recognition and acknowledgement of his inconstancy, his awareness that he has not fundamentally changed, is heightened for us if we think that he wrote this sonnet after his ordination. And the vexation he expresses at the contraries he finds in himself perhaps lends credence to a late date for the sonnet. He had not always felt so about contradictions and paradoxes; there had been a time when he had joyfully exploited them in prose and in verse. His attitude toward change itself underwent change. As a young man he had chosen for a swashbuckling portrait of himself the motto "Antes muerto que mudado," and "Sooner dead than changed" expresses his steadfastness as well as his proud resolution and defiance.[83] Just as defiantly, he celebrated variety and change in

[83]See the early portrait engraved by William Marshall for *Poems, By J. D.*, 1635.

the love elegies and in some of his lyrics. Later, he explored with ingenuity and equanimity the inevitability of change even where the ideals of beauty and virtue are concerned.[84] In one of the early sermons, however, he expresses no surprise that "the Prophets, and other Secretaries of the holy Ghost in penning the books of Scriptures, do for the most part retain, and express in their writings some impressions, and some air of their former professions; . . . ever inserting into their writings some phrases, some metaphors, some allusions, taken from that profession which they had exercised before," and he asserts that the soul "that hath been transported upon any particular worldly pleasure, when it is intirely turn'd to God . . . , doth find in God fit subject, and just occasion to exercise the same affection piously, and religiously, which had before so sinfully transported, and possest it."[85] Despite his assumption here that a prophet's soul is turned entirely to God, he sees fit to admit his own wavering in another sermon, for he recognizes that "certainely is there nothing, nothing in spirituall things, perfect in this world."[86] In the sonnet, Donne's distress stems from his disappointment that he is far from the perfection which he thinks to be characteristic of the truly spiritual life. He is vexed that he finds something of his old secular self in his attitude toward God, and the sonnet itself reveals that his interest in verse, his penchant for paradox, his compulsion toward self-examination and self-expression are still an intrinsic part of himself.

"Since she whome I lovd, hath payd her last debt"

The sonnet "Since she whome I lovd, hath payd her last debt" is like "Oh, to vex me" in that it, too, is concerned with the discreteness of the secular and the holy and seems to have been written by a man who scrutinizes his behavior because new cir-

---

[84]See the *Second Anniversary*, ll. 387–400, and "Obsequies to the Lord Harrington," ll. 41–52.

[85]*Sermons*, I, No. 5 (preached Dec. 14, 1617), p. 236.

[86]Ibid., VII, No. 10 (preached Dec. 12, 1626), pp. 264–65.

cumstances have not changed him as he expected they would or because he has not changed himself as he thought he must, given his new circumstances. The sense of distinguished and divided worlds is so vivid that we must remind ourselves it is not in these poems alone that Donne's ability to project a scene imaginatively, to render a situation realistically and dramatically, is so strong that we are constantly tempted to assume an immediate, personal experience, a biographical reference. Once the idea enters our heads that the poem was written after the death of Ann Donne, its relation to life, its dependence on direct experience, makes it seem more pathetic and more intense to us. But of course the pathos and intensity are there regardless of when Donne wrote the poem and regardless of whether the situation is real or imagined.

That situation focuses on the poet's response to the death of the woman he loved, and he announces in the first quatrain that since her soul has been "early'into heaven ravished," his mind is wholly set "in heavenly things." Despite the surface of calmness and acceptance, there is a discordant rub in the lines. The orthodoxy of "[she] hath payd her last debt / To Nature" is undermined by the almost parenthetical idea which follows: "and to hers, and my good is dead." Gardner glosses this correctly, I think, when she reads it to mean, "Death ends the possibility of doing good to oneself or to another," though she thinks the reading "strained."[87] It is not strained; it is, given the direction of the rest of the quatrain, a blunt, pragmatic, earth-focused intrusion. The woman's good and her good to him are in this life, not the next; there is no vestige of the idea Donne expresses elsewhere that the saintly dead may be God's factors for the living.[88]

The second quatrain starts, "Here the admyring her my

[87]*Divine Poems*, p. 79. In her 2d ed., Gardner deletes her comment on this interpretation, but she now seems to prefer an alternative one: "Her death is for her good, since by it she enters heaven early, and it is for his good, since now all his affections are set on 'heavenly things'" (pp. 153-54).

[88]For instance, in "The Canonization" and in the epistle to the Countess of Bedford, "Reason is our Soules left h; .1d, Faith her right."

mind did whett / To seeke thee God," and the "here" is ambiguous. The referent for "here" may be "heaven" and "heavenly
things"; Donne's admiration of her, now that she is in heaven,
may direct his attention to God. But "here" may refer to earth.
In the last line of the first quatrain, Donne had stated that his
mind is "Wholy" set in heavenly things. Though it is possible to
read "admyring her my mind did whett / To seeke thee God"
as explaining why his mind is wholly set in heavenly things, it is
equally possible that Donne is saying, first, "her death has focused my attention *entirely* on heaven," and then, "when she
was alive, it was my admiration of her that led me to love of
God." Regardless of how we read the first two lines of the quatrain, its main idea is unchanged: the poet has found God; God
has "fed" his thirst, has provided sustenance for the parching
void the woman's death has created; but, for all the waters of
comfort he has received, his thirst (like the dropsy) is unquenchable and the heat of his desire for love still melts him.

The sestet is unusual; its conclusion is more fully expressed in
the first two lines than in the last couplet. These lines contain a
question and a statement: Donne asks why he should find it
necessary to beg for even more love than God has given him,
and he states that God has already offered all His love to him in
compensation for the love of the mistress he has been deprived
of. The last four lines are in the form of a statement which develops the extent of God's demonstrated love, but at the same
time they explain why God has exerted himself to show His love
and they imply why it is that Donne is unsatisfied despite his
recognition of God's exertion. God fears lest Donne direct some
of his love to others than God, to "saints and Angels"; He is so
jealous in His love that He fears lest Donne show affection for
the world, the flesh, and the devil. Donne implies that he needs
more love than God has thus far showered on him because
God's love has thus far been an insufficient substitute for his
earthly love and for the love he still has for a woman who has
become a saint and an angel.

It is only in the first quatrain of the sonnet that the tone
seems to be one of resignation, but even there the bluntness and

finality of "to hers, and my good is dead" introduces an overtone of disaffection into the seeming acceptance. The rest of
the sonnet projects the note of unhappiness, turmoil, and distress. Donne does not say, perhaps cannot get himself to say,
that God has ravished his earthly love *because* He so loves
Donne that he would direct Donne's love toward Himself alone;
he undercuts the directness of God's intervention by suggesting
the voluntariness of his mistress's action in paying her debt to
Nature and also by his use of the passive "her soule early into
heaven [is] ravished" rather than the active "God ravished her."
He does not find a manifestation of God's love for him in His
ravishing of the mistress but in His attempt to demonstrate His
love after his mistress has been ravished. He sees that he should
be content since God exerts Himself in wooing his soul, but he
makes clear how hard a job God has, how much He must exert
Himself, since He is aware that Donne's love is so attached to an
earthly subject that even when he directs his love to heaven it
may come to rest not in God Himself, but in the heavenly transmutation of his earthly love. The only referent *within* the poem
for "the World, fleshe, yea Devill" is Donne's love for his mistress. For all that she may have whetted his mind to seek God, it
is she who represents his joys, his good in this world. God's love
seems an insufficient replacement for her love, and Donne feels
the pull of fleshly desire, of affection for the things of this
world, of sin rather than virtue. The idea is very close to one
which Donne explored in several of the Holy Sonnets: there,
Donne's sense of his own unworthiness is so great that he insists
God must make a peculiarly strenuous effort to save him; here,
Donne has already found God, and God has, indeed, fed his
thirst, but he still remains subject to temptation, and God must
work still harder. It is, perhaps, this difference which tempts us
to think the sonnet may be a late one. And two other aspects of
the poem lend some credence to a late date.

Although Donne says that love of his mistress has led him to
love of God, the thrust of the sonnet is to suggest that earthly
love is, largely, profane. It dichotomizes earthly love and heavenly; it sets up a competition between them. To be sure, in the

epistle to the Countess of Huntingdon, "That unripe side of earth," Donne censures a love which is excessively earthly ("He much profanes whom violent heats doe move / To stile his wandring rage of passion, *Love*"), and in the Holy Sonnet "What if this present were the worlds last night?" he connects "profane mistresses" to his days of idolatry, but his usual attitude in the lyrics is to see love as a harmony of the physical and the spiritual. His customary attitude is to insist on the sanctification of love, as he does in "The Canonization," to see small change between bodily love and ecstatic love, to emphasize a love so refined that earth and heaven are seamless. Even in "A Litanie," he asks the Lord to deliver us from thinking that "this earth / Is only for our prison fram'd" or that God is "covetous" toward those whom He loves or that those who seek God "are maim'd / From reaching this worlds sweet" (stanza 15). We sense a change in the sonnet. There is something of the world, the flesh, and the devil about the love of a woman, something in opposition to love of God, something which reminds us of the "prophane love" of "Oh, to vex me." That secular love has a place inferior to that of heavenly love may be indicative of a later perspective, the perspective of a man in holy orders.

But, if the place of secular love in the total scheme of things is depressed, Donne's attachment to it remains undiminished. The sonnet is an astonishing confession of how much his love for a woman means to him and an extraordinarily passionate expression of how her death has affected him. This sonnet, unlike the others, is elegiac. Unlike Ben Jonson, Donne did not write elegiac poetry for those closest to him; his elegies and epicedes are characterized by his intellectual agility and his erudition, not by a sense of personal loss. The emotional violence of this elegiac sonnet is similar to that of "A Nocturnall upon S. Lucies Day" and of the Holy Sonnets, and it is, again, tempting to think that only the death of Donne's wife, two and a half years after he had committed himself to the greater love of God, could have caused emotion of this kind. But the very comparison of the emotion here with that of the early Holy Sonnets and the conjunction of that emotion with death in "A Nocturnall" serve to remind us that Donne had expressed such emotion earlier. All we can say is that Donne may have written "Since she whome I lovd" after his ordination, and, if he did, it is evidence not only that he had retained his old poetic power but also that a crucial personal crisis made him re-utilize that power.

"A Hymne to Christ, at the Authors last going into Germany"

If we must be tentative about the dates of the two sonnets I have discussed and about that of "Show me deare Christ, thy spouse" (which I shall examine a little later, at a place where it *may* belong chronologically), we can date with some precision one of the three hymns which Donne wrote. Its title in the edition of 1633, "A Hymne to Christ, at the Authors last going into Germany," accurately reflects the title in the manuscripts, both in its reference to "hymn" and to the occasion for which it was composed. Donne was informed of his appointment as chaplain to Viscount Doncaster's special embassy to Germany shortly before March 9, 1619, and he left England on May 12;[89] he probably wrote the hymn in March or April, and he may have included a copy of it with the poems and the manuscript of *Biathanatos* he sent Sir Robert Ker before his departure.[90]

Donne was forty-six when he received the King's "commandment" to accompany his old friend and patron to Germany; both the King and Doncaster had long known of his earlier desire for a position abroad in the service of the Crown and they must have thought that Donne would relish the opportunity

[89]Bald, pp. 340, 347.

[90]*Letters*, pp. 21–22. The hymn appears in all the manuscripts of Group II. Although Alan MacColl suggests that the poems sent to Ker in 1619 make up the Group II collection, he thinks that "A Hymne to Christ" was among the poems added after 1619 to produce *Y*, the Group II manuscript used by the editor of *Poems*, 1633 ("The New Edition of Donne's Love Poems," *EIC*, 17 [1967], 259). The fact is that we do not know what poems Donne sent to Ker in 1619, and, as Mark Roberts says in his response to MacColl's suggestion, it is hard to prove that the poems sent to him were the basis for *Y* (p. 265).

and the honor granted him. Far from being elated, Donne seems to have been worried and insecure. He fretted about leaving behind "a scattered flock of wretched children," the youngest not yet three; his health was not good ("I carry an infirme and valetudinary body," he wrote Goodere); he seems to have worried about interrupting his tenure at Lincoln's Inn; he was fearful even of how he might be received by the Jesuits, whom he had earlier attacked.[91] It was not just a normal traveler's foresight and efficiency which made him survey and empty his "Cabinet of Letters" and send *Biathanatos* to Ker with the direction, "Reserve it for me, if I live";[92] if the mood of his letters at the time seems somewhat melodramatic and overwrought, if his expressions of anxiety seem somewhat overdone for a man on an official visit to the Continent, his apprehensiveness, extending even to thoughts of death, seems deep-rooted and genuine.

That apprehensiveness Donne expressed in letters to his friends and when he made a public pronouncement of his impending departure at the close of a valedictory sermon preached at Lincoln's Inn on April 18, 1619.[93] Troubled though he was, he did not on this occasion seek to work out his private problems or express his private qualms in a sonnet. Those problems and qualms may lie behind the hymn which he wrote, but he had resolved them before he wrote. The hymn is a powerful poem in which Donne asserts his faith in God's mercy, prays that he may be so totally consumed in God's love that he may be forgetful of worldly ties, and welcomes the everlasting night of death as an escape from the stormy days of life. Gardner says, rightly, that the hymn is like the sonnet "Since she whome I lovd" in its dependence on the idea of God as a jealous lover,[94] but there are crucial differences between the poems, both of them filled with intense passion, which point up how private

[91]*Letters*, p. 174; Bald, p. 361.
[92]*Letters*, pp. 224, 22.
[93]*Sermons*, II, No. 11, pp. 248–49, 388–90.
[94]Donne had, of course, memorably exploited the idea earlier in the sonnet "Batter my heart."

the sonnet is. In the sonnet, Donne emphasizes the idea that God must be a more ardent wooer in order to compensate for the death of his loved one; the hymn is dominated by Donne's focus on the possibility of his own impending death and by his own willingness to put aside the things of this world. The sonnet, despite its reference to the world, the flesh, and the devil, mainly pits the love of God against love for a woman; in the hymn, Donne's secular love is far more general, diffuse, and abstract: passionate love of one woman is replaced by the "fainter beames" of human affection in "all whom I lov'd . . . , and who lov'd mee" and by the love of fame, of wit, of worldly hopes. Not only are these called "false mistresses," but Donne also distances them by suggesting that they are more characteristic of youth than of maturity. The sonnet gets its force from its emphasis on what God must overcome since Donne's earthly love is so great that his thirst is unquenchable; though he asks, "Why should I begg more love" when God has offered all, his very way of putting the question suggests that the effort God makes is provoked by His awareness of the magnitude of the threat which Donne's secular love poses. In the hymn, on the other hand, the stress is not on the resistance God must overcome; Donne is more than willing to welcome God's love, is more than ready to surrender to it. The sonnet focuses constantly on opposition; the hymn prayerfully requests intervention. The sonnet is more idiosyncratic in its highly individualized and narrowly limited situation, more private in its almost heretical obstinacy. The hymn is far more conventional in its situation and attitude: it is less eccentric, more public, in that its situation is common to all men traversing the sea of life, and its sentiment is devotional. "We" could be substituted for "I" in the poem without doing violence to its situation and attitude.

There is no indication in Donne's verse after his ordination that he felt under any extrinsic obligation to use his ability as a poet in the service of the Church. It is possible to see the hymn as a public prayer written, fittingly, by a man conscious of his laureatelike position as the chaplain to an embassy, but that view is, I think, simplistic. Certainly Donne had felt no similar compulsion in the four years he had been in orders. To be sure, there had been times in his secular career when he had written poems because he felt under some obligation to write them or when he thought it would advance him to do so.[95] He was under no such obligation when he willingly used his pen to write controversial prose in support of the Church, and he wrote religious verse voluntarily prior to his ordination. He had, indeed, before his ordination, written "A Litanie," but even here it is his independence which is evident. He defended his right as "a Lay man, and a private" to use "such divine and publique names" as *litany* and *meditation* to describe "his own little thoughts," and he made it clear that his poem was not intended for public service in the Church but for his friends.[96] It is likely that he voluntarily wrote the hymn partly to express for himself and to dramatize for others the resolution of his apprehensions about departing for Germany and partly out of a feeling that it was entirely fitting that, in his role as chaplain, he give public expression to an attitude, unexceptional and orthodox but still stamped with his own characteristic mark, which he considered proper to inculcate in those for whose religious guidance he was responsible. The widespread availability of the hymn in manuscript is an indication that Donne was not averse to its being known.

The hymn provided the challenge of a new genre, and Donne seems to have been delighted with the opportunity for a bravura performance. For the occasion he carved out a stanza he had never used before, two pentameter couplets, mainly closed, followed by a triplet made up of two pentameters and a fourteener. The first of his four stanzas is more timid, more overtly explicatory, than we expect of him, but the tameness of the opening gives way to a series of striking antitheses in the rest of the poem. Donne develops powerfully his main figure of God as a lover who is yet not jealous enough for him since He does not

---

[95]For instance, the elegies for those in the Countess of Bedford's circle, two of the epithalamions, the elegy on Prince Henry.

[96]*Letters*, p. 33.

put limits on man's freedom of will to love as he sees fit; who does not free his soul from loving others than Himself; who in giving Donne the liberty to love where he will deprives him of true liberty, which inheres in directing one's love toward God; who does not truly love Donne if He does not care whom Donne loves. Donne concludes with a show of his old rhetorical ability as he uses an image of divorce and marriage and as he exploits the paradox that those "Churches are best for Prayer, that have least light," and he does more. The hymn differs from most of his verse in the regularity of its rhythmic beat and in the resonance of his diction, and its musicality shows clearly that he intended it to be sung. He uses forms of the word "love" ten times in the last three stanzas, and the word reverberates through the poem, reinforced by the liberal use of *l*'s. The consonance in the poem is matched by a flamboyant use of assonance and an extravagant amount of internal rhyme.[97] Donne had always been sensitive to the modulations of speech and skillful and subtle in exploiting them. His adaptation here to the requirements of choral performance is equally brilliant.

"Translated out of *Gazaeus, Vota Amico facta. fol.* 160"

At some time during his several months on the Continent, Donne translated from the Latin a twelve-line prayer written by the Belgian Jesuit, Angelin Gazet (1568-1653), as part of his volume *Pia Hilaria Variaque Carmina*. The fact that he chose to do so is almost more interesting than his little poem, however accomplished and charming that is. For all his early interest in Ovid and for all that he learned from Ovid's elegies, Donne never saw fit, so far as we know, to put an Augustan poet into English. Except for a translation made "at Sea," long lost when

---

[97]See, for instance, his use of the "I" sound in stanza 1, as it relates to the *c* rhyme; his use in ll. 3 and 4 of that stanza of *sea, mee, be, mee,* and their relation to the *a* rhyme of four lines of stanza 2, which uses, internally, *seas, sea, trees,* and *seeke.* Note, too, such juxtapositions as *thou* and *clouds* in l. 5, *thee* and *th'Eternall* in l. 14, and the use of the *r* sound in ll. 15-16.

he redid it for Lady Bedford in 1608, and lost to us,[98] and his translation of the Lamentations of Jeremiah (which I shall discuss shortly), he Englished only the little poem made by a Jesuit. The choice may seem a strange one for a man who had recently written, "I goe into the mouth of such adversaries, as I cannot blame for hating me, the Jesuits,"[99] but Donne's familiarity with the work of Catholic writers (including Jesuits) long preceded the specific reading he did when he would controvert their arguments, nor was he at all backward in consulting a great many Catholic commentators when he was preparing his sermons. Simpson has indicated Donne's particular indebtedness to the work of two Jesuits, Benedictus Pererius and Cornelius à Lapide, and she says that from 1614 on Donne secured copies of the commentaries of à Lapide and used them almost as soon as they were published.[100]

Like Donne's poem to Herbert, his translation of Gazet's prayer appears in none of the manuscripts; it was first published in *Poems*, 1650, but there is little reason to doubt its authenticity. The 1650 edition of the *Poems* is the first over which the younger John Donne exerted control, and he swept together a number of items not previously published or not published before with Donne's *Poems*, which were then printed on sheets inserted at the end of the volume. Most of the new pieces are authentic, and, misleading as the additional words on the title page, "To which / Is added divers Copies under his own hand / never before in print," may be, it is likely that Donne's son found copies of the "Catalogus Librorum" and of the prayer in Donne's own hand. The prayer is entitled "Translated out of *Gazaeus, Vota Amico facta. fol.* 160," and the younger Donne may have found the translation in a volume of *Pia Hilaria Variaque Carmina* which had belonged to his father[101] or among some of his loose papers.

---

[98]Bald, p. 176; *Letters*, pp. 207-8.

[99]*Letters*, p. 174.

[100]*Sermons*, X, 367-74.

[101]The book is not among those definitely known to have been in Donne's library. Sir Geoffrey Keynes thinks that Donne may have bought fewer books

In *Pia Hilaria Variaque Carmina*, Gazet put together a volume of pious recreations for the amusement and instruction of Latinists and prospective Latinists (it has a glossary of obscure words). It contains various poems of his own making, some on serious subjects, and one of these, "Angelo Custodi," had been printed as early as 1606. These are far outnumbered by his versifications of diverting episodes and anecdotes drawn from the lives of the saints and other sources. The first edition was published at Douay in 1618, and the book immediately became very popular: in 1618, an edition was published at Rheims; another, without date, was probably published in that year at Trier; and, too, a pirated edition appeared at Rheims. Three more editions appeared in 1619, one at Trier and two (with the addition of ten poems) at Douay.[102]

---

after he took orders than he had done before, but we know little about books published after 1616 which Donne purchased or was given. See Keynes, *A Bibliography of Dr. John Donne*, 4th ed. (Oxford, 1973), pp. 258-79, esp. 258, 261-62, 272 (item L123), and Bald, pp. 394-95, 443, 531-32. Many of the books known to have been in Donne's library with publication dates between 1614 and 1616 were published in Germany.

[102]Grierson referred only to the Dillingen edition of 1623 (*The Poems of John Donne*, II, 263) and Milgate to that edition and a revised one of 1629 (*John Donne: The Satires, Epigrams and Verse Letters*, p. 280), though Gosse thought that Donne had used the Douay edition of 1618 (*The Life and Letters of John Donne*, II, 118). My statements are based on information about Angelin Gazet in Arthur Dinaux's *Archives historiques et littéraires du nord de la France et du midi de la Belgique*, ns 2 (Valenciennes, 1838), 455-57; Carlos Sommervogel's new edition of Aloys de Backer's *Bibliothèque de la Compagnie de Jésus*, 10 vols. (Brussels and Paris, 1890-1909), III, cols. 1297-98, and IX, col. 403; *Bibliotheca Belgica: Bibliographie Générale des Pays-Bas*, ed. Marie-Thérèse Lenger (Brussels, 1964); *National Union Catalog: Pre-1956 Imprints*; and *Catalogue Général des livres imprimés de la Bibliothèque Nationale*.

Sommervogel probably predicated an edition in 1617 because Dinaux cited one and because the Douay edition of 1618 has a "Privilegium" dated October 20, 1617, but he places a question mark after his entry.

Many editions followed those of 1619: 1621, Poitiers; 1623, Dillingen, Lyon, and La Flèche; 1624, La Flèche; 1625, Pont-à-Mousson; 1627, Cologne; 1629, Antwerp (by Plantin); 1631, Cologne; a second volume was added to the work in the Lille edition of 1638. A translation into French appeared in 1628 and was reprinted several times. The Latin was first printed in London in 1657.

Only the "*fol.* 160" in the title of Donne's translation provides a clue to the copy he saw or owned. In the Douay edition of 1618, "*Vota Amico facta*" is printed on page 98. The last poem ends on page 151, and the pages which follow are not numbered. The "Onomasticon vocum obscuriorum" preempts six pages, a "Censura" is on the following page, and a "Privilegium" on the page after that. If Donne owned a copy of this edition and put numbers on the unnumbered pages, "*fol.* 160" may mean that he wrote his translation of "*Vota Amico facta*" on the blank page which is the verso of the last printed page. In the Trier edition published in 1618 and reprinted in 1619 with a revised title page, "*Vota Amico facta*" is printed on page 101. Page 160 contains the last of the text proper, and there is not enough space at the bottom for Donne to have placed his translation of "*Vota*" there. Page 160 is followed by five unnumbered pages containing the "Onomasticon" and by three blank pages. If Donne's "*fol.* 160" refers to a Trier edition, it merely means that he made a notation on the paper he used to write his translation that the edition of *Pia Hilaria* he saw had 160 pages of poems.[103]

We do not know very much about Donne's activities on the Continent, but Bald has reconstructed the progress of the embassy in detail, and between the end of May and the end of September in 1619 Donne spent much of his time in cities which were a hundred or a hundred and fifty miles from Trier, in the area where the Trier editions of Gazet would have circulated. How arduous his duties were we cannot tell: there is evidence

[103]The text of "*Vota Amico facta*" in Douay 1618 and in the Trier editions differs substantively from that printed by Grierson (*The Poems of John Donne*, II, 262) only at line 3, where Grierson prints "semper" and they have "saepe."

I am indebted to Dr. Hans Henning of the Zentralbibliothek der Deutschen Klassik in Weimar for information about and some Xerox pages of the undated Trier edition, and to Marie-Thérèse Lenger of the Bibliothèque Royale Albert Ier in Brussels for information about and some Xerox pages of the Trier edition of 1619. Columbia University Libraries kindly made available to me microfilm of pages in the Douay edition of 1618 (a copy once owned by Augustus Jessupp).

that he preached twice in Heidelberg before the Prince and Princess Palatine, the Frederick and Elizabeth of his Valentine epithalamion, and that he preached at The Hague on December 19, 1619. He may have preached regularly for Doncaster's entourage; on one occasion, at least, he helped Doncaster with his correspondence.[104] It would seem that he found time to keep abreast not only of political events, but also of what was being published on the Continent, and that he found time, too, to read an amusing best-seller and to translate into verse which displays all his customary skill a pleasant little prayer which appealed to him.

"Show me deare Christ, thy spouse, so bright and cleare"

Although Donne's little prayer was the only poem he wrote while in Germany, Gardner finds in both the sonnet "Show me deare Christ, thy spouse, so bright and cleare" and in "The Lamentations of Jeremy, for the most part according to Tremelius" indications that the state of Protestantism in Germany continued to concern him, and she dates these poems within a year or so after his return. She suggests that Donne identified the distress of German Protestantism in 1620 with the biblical image of the Church as a woman in distress, the desolate Jerusalem of Lamentations.[105] Her evidence is not compelling, but no one has made a better suggestion. We can be sure that Donne did not write the sonnet during his stay in Germany.[106] We cannot be sure that it does not, in fact, long predate his ordination, though perhaps Donne would have had more reason to suppress it if he wrote it after he took orders.

"Show me deare Christ" is a petition that God reveal to Donne His true Church and allow him to participate in it, but it

---

[104]Bald, pp. 348-64. See, too, P. R. Sellin's attempt to define Donne's role in "John Donne: The Poet as Diplomat and Divine," *HLQ*, 39 (1976), 267-75.

[105]*Divine Poems*, pp. 104, 124-25.

[106]Line 4 has the phrase "in Germany and here," and "here" is obviously England.

is a petition in which he exposes with wit and with scorn the claims of contending theological and ecclesiastical factions whose arguments and behavior have rent the fabric of the Church and in which he states that the true Church is one "open to most men," the Church Universal. The question of the true Church had long exercised Donne. In the preface to *Pseudo-Martyr*, he admits to his long "irresolution" in choosing a religion. He had refused to make *"any violent and sudden determination"* until he had, he says, *"to the measure of my poore wit and judgement, survayed and digested the whole body of Divinity, controverted betweene ours and the Romane Church."*[107] Many years before, he had ridiculed in "Satyre III" the methods by which Catholics, Calvinists, and Anglicans had arrived at their support of a "true" Church, and he had ridiculed equally the man who rejected all creeds and the man who accepted all because he found them fundamentally alike. He did not identify the true Church in the satire. His purpose was to show the necessity of anti-authoritarianism; the burden of his argument is that it is right to "doubt wisely," since the search for truth is long, arduous, and indirect. In the satire, Donne had personified each church or position as a woman, and his contempt is not nearly so much directed at each woman as it is at her lover. He attacks Graccus, for instance, for his indifference and his self-indulgence, for a lack of discrimination caused by the cavalier profligacy of his affection:

> Graccus loves all as one, and thinkes that so
> As women do in divers countries goe
> In divers habits, yet are still one kinde,
> So doth, so is Religion; and this blind-
> nesse too much light breeds.

Donne had no use for a self-serving, indiscriminatory latitudinarianism, though tolerance and latitude, as well as a quintessential purity, are implied in the Church Universal he envisions in "Show me deare Christ."

---

[107] *Pseudo-Martyr* (London, 1610), sig. B3^r.

In discussing Donne's theology, Simpson emphasizes his "wider vision," his passionate longing for the reunion of Christendom, his ready admission that Canterbury, Geneva, and Rome were branches of the One Church, and she says that "this was perfectly compatible with loyalty to the Church of England."[108] Gardner says that the sonnet "Show me deare Christ" is "not merely 'compatible with loyalty to the Church of England'; it could hardly have been written by anyone but an Anglican." She suggests that if Donne deliberately withheld it from publication, he did so not because of the doctrine he advocated but because he thought it was not fitting for a clergyman to indulge in the wit of his opening images, the mockery of his middle lines, the daring conceit of his conclusion.[109] We may grant that Gardner's description of Anglican tolerance and comprehensiveness truly characterizes some liberal Anglicans, but we must remember, too, that others of them thought that a wise and godly reformation called for an assertive claim for exclusivity and a doctrinal and ecclesiastical dogmatism very different from Hooker's stance in the *Laws of Ecclesiastical Polity*. We may grant, also, that Donne was a liberal Anglican. In the *Essays in Divinity*, written prior to his ordination and, it appears, without a view toward publication, Donne states that the unity of the Church does not lie in uniformity, in "one precise forme of exterior worship, and Ecclesiastick policie," and he wishes that "the whole catholick Church, were reduced to such Unity and agreement, in the form and profession Established, in any one of these Churches (though ours were principally to be wished) which have not by any additions destroyed the foundation and possibility of salvation in Christ Jesus."[110] Donne expresses the same wish in a number of the sermons. Even in the sermon he preached at The Hague on December 19, 1619, when the resolutions of the Synod of Dort were still fresh in men's minds, he spoke of the danger of that narrow unity which leads to separation and he said:

[108]*Prose Works*, pp. 111, 101.
[109]*Divine Poems*, pp. 122–23.
[110]*Essays in Divinity*, ed. Simpson, pp. 49, 51–52.

The Church loves the name of Catholique; and it is a glorious, and an harmonious name; Love thou those things wherein she is Catholique, and wherein she is harmonious, that is, *Quod ubique, quod semper*, Those universall, and fundamentall doctrines, which in all Christian ages, and in all Christian Churches, have beene agreed by all to be necessary to salvation; and then thou art a true Catholique.[111]

In the following paragraph, he must have made some of his audience aware of an impediment to a Universal Church at the same time that he advocated a unity which is both spiritual and civil. "God," he said, "saw a better likelihood of avoyding Schisme and dissention, when those whom hee called to a new spirituall brotherhood in one Religion, were . . . tied in civill bands, as well as spirituall." If Donne pleaded for a Universal Church, he was also a strong believer in a state church, and, moreover, in strict adherence to the laws of the state. Even in the first sermon preached to King Charles, on April 3, 1625, Donne distinguished between what was essential to a Universal Church ("the *foundation* of the first *House*, the *Church*") and what impeded it:

Bee not apt to call *Super-Edifications, Foundations*; Collaterall Divinitie, Fundamentall Divinitie; Problematicall, Disputable, Controvertible poynts, poynts Essentiall, and Articles of Faith. Call not *Super-Edifications, Foundations*, nor call not the *furniture* of the *House, Foundations*; Call not *Ceremoniall*, and *Rituall* things, *Essentiall* parts of Religion, and of the worship of God. . . .[112]

He qualified his last statement by adding "otherwise then as they imply *Disobedience*: for *Obedience* to lawfull Authoritie, is alwayes an *Essentiall* part of Religion," and there is no mistaking what he meant by "lawfull Authoritie": "*God* hath commended our Spirits, not onely our civill peace, but our Religion

---

[111]*Sermons*, II, 280.
[112]Ibid., VI, 258.

too, into the *hand* of the *Magistrate*."[113] Clearly, Donne yearned for a Universal Church and made known his wish when he preached, but he supported, too, the lawful civil authority which customarily fettered and imprisoned the word *religion* and immured it "in a *Rome*, or a *Wittemberg*, or a *Geneva*."[114] He must have been aware that one of his firm beliefs tended to frustrate the other.

He was aware, too, that to voice his support for a Universal Church was to expose himself to detractors. In a sermon preached at Lincoln's Inn, probably in 1618, he says,

> Let a man be zealous, and fervent in reprehension of sin, and there flies out an arrow, that gives him the wound of a *Puritan*. Let a man be zealous of the house of God, and say any thing by way of moderation, for the *repairing* of the *ruines* of that house, and *making up the differences* of the Church of God, and there flies out an arrow, that gives him the wound of a *Papist*.[115]

In his next sermon, he considers it "a lamentable thing, when ceremoniall things in matter of discipline, or problematicall things in matter of doctrine, come so farre, as to separate us from one another . . . ," and the close of his sentence emphasizes the extent of the separation: "in giving ill names to one another."[116] A few years before, in a letter to Sir Henry Goodere in which he had stated that it was a "sound true opinion, that in all Christian professions there is way to salvation," he had warned that Goodere had perhaps voiced his support for the opinion too "incommodiously or intempestively" and that his friendship with people of "all the impressions of Religion" had made him a mark "for every sophister in Religion to work on." "It hath hurt very many, " he said, "not in their conscience, nor

---

[113]Ibid., p. 245.

[114]The words are Donne's in a letter to Goodere which is often quoted to demonstrate his belief that all churches are "virtuall beams of one Sun" (*Letters*, p. 29).

[115]*Sermons*, II, 58.

[116]Ibid., p. 111.

ends, but in their reputation, and ways, that others have thought them fit to be wrought upon."[117] Donne was careful even in his private correspondence to make sure that his opinions would not be open to misinterpretation and that he would not be subject to the charge of scandal.

In both his public and private statements, then, Donne's yearning for a Universal Church was customarily tempered by his political pragmatism and by his sensitivity to the opinion of those who were easily scandalized.[118] If "Show me deare Christ" was written after his ordination, Donne had good reason to restrict its circulation. Clearly, however, he felt so strongly about the doctrine of One Church that there was a time when he was impelled to express his feeling in the privacy of a sonnet. He did so in his own idiosyncratic way, and he probably thought that the way, too, would scandalize. Neither the wit of the contrasted images of the Church as brazen whore and as mournful ravished virgin nor the mockery of the pretensions of Geneva and Rome would have given scandal to Anglican readers, but such readers would have been troubled by his daring exploitation of the main image, introduced in the first line of the sonnet. The line, "Show me deare Christ, thy spouse, so bright and cleare," is unexceptional in its doctrine, and hymnlike in its musicality and emphasis: the *r* sound rings through the line, the sound of "Christ" resounds in "bright," "cleare" repeats the sound of "deare," and the focus of the line is at its precise midpoint in "thy spouse." Donne prepares for the shocking eroticism of the last four lines by asking about the "spouse," "Dwells she with us, or like adventuring knights / First travaile we to seeke and then make love?" Gardner paraphrases the last lines thus: "Lord, do not thus hide thy Bride from our sight, but let me woo the gentle spouse of thy marriage song, who is most faithful to thy will and most pleasing to thee, when the greatest

---

[117]*Letters*, pp. 100–103.

[118]See his letter to Goodere, written in the late spring of 1609 or shortly after, in which he twice says that he writes as he does because he knows that Goodere is "not easily scandalized" (ibid., pp. 160–63). Bald calls attention to Donne's "discretion" in the letter (p. 217, n. 1).

number of men seek and receive her embraces."[119] She gets Donne's intent right, but not his tone. He plays down typological interpretation of the imagery of the Song of Solomon and, taking advantage of the stereotype of the earthly jealous husband, startles us with a Christ-as-husband whose magnanimity and generosity extend to sharing his wife. Donne's word "Betray" is closer to "expose" than it is to "do not thus hide"; the "mild Dove" is not only gentle but a turtledove who is amenable and unresisting; "When she'is embrac'd and open to most men" means, literally, "when she is available to and can be penetrated by the greatest number." The physical passion in the language is an index of the passionateness of Donne's emotion, of the depth of his feeling and the intensity of his appeal, of his awareness of the extraordinary nature of God's love for man. The sonnet is a daring and moving poem, regardless of when Donne wrote it. If, indeed, it was provoked by recent events in Germany, it indicates, once again, Donne's compulsion to express himself in verse at a time when he could not adequately express his deepest feelings in a more public form. It indicates, too, that his poetic power had in no way diminished.

"The Lamentations of Jeremy, for the most part according to Tremelius"

The poems I have discussed thus far show that in the half-dozen years after his ordination Donne's impulse toward poetry was occasionally strong enough to overcome his renunciation of 1614. The hymn of 1619 shows that the idea of using his ability in verse to enhance the worship of the Church must have occurred to him. It may, indeed, have occurred to him long before his ordination, when he wrote "A Litanie," but the composition of that poem may also have made him aware that he could write poetry intended for public service only at the expense of curbing his own individuality, and he had been unwilling to do that in "A Litanie." Gardner rightly calls it "an elaborate private

[119]*Divine Poems*, p. 127.

prayer, rather incongruously cast into a liturgical form" and she points out that Donne's litany, far from being suitable for general use, "could hardly be prayed by anyone but himself."[120] His affection for the Psalms was so great that more than a fifth of his extant sermons take their text from the one book.[121] Many of his friends and contemporaries had attempted translation of the Psalms. He himself said in the poem of praise he wrote about Sir Philip Sidney and his sister, the Countess of Pembroke, that he could scarcely call the English Church reformed until the Psalms were fitly garbed in English, but not one psalm did he put into verse. Except for the hymn of 1619, and one of his other two hymns, only one of Donne's later poems indicates that he was interested in writing "high, holy, and harmonious composures"[122] for the Church. That poem, "The Lamentations of Jeremy, for the most part according to Tremelius," is his longest except for the "Metempsychosis" and the two *Anniversaries*; it is his only translation of Scripture; and there is no question that he intended it for public singing in the Church. We do not know whether Donne's sole motive in writing it was to enrich the service of the Church, whether he wrote it to call attention to himself in order to further his advancement in the Church, whether he turned to translation as an exercise to while away a dull time. It seems likeliest that he wrote the poem during the first months of 1621, but the date is far from certain.

"The Lamentations of Jeremy" was first printed in *Poems*, 1633, from a Group II manuscript.[123] It does not appear in any manuscript of Group I. Since the Group I manuscripts stem from a collection made by Donne himself at the end of 1614 with a view toward publication, the absence of the poem in the Group I manuscripts almost certainly means that it had not been written by the end of 1614. To be sure, Donne suppressed some early poems which he thought unsuitable (verse letters to undistinguished young friends and a *jeu d'esprit* like the Lin-

[120]Ibid., p. xxviii.
[121]*Sermons*, X, 295.
[122]Walton's phrase in *The Life and Death of D*ʳ *Donne*, sig. B4ʳ.
[123]*Divine Poems*, p. 103.

coln's Inn epithalamion); it is possible that he saw fit to exclude "The Lamentations of Jeremy" because it was a translation, but it is more likely that he would have included it gladly as a counterweight to some of the "profane" poems had it been written by 1614. It appears in only two manuscripts of Group II (Trinity College, Dublin [*TCD*]; and its derivative, Norton [*N*]), and in a manuscript that has affinities with Group II, Dolau Cothi (*DC*);[124] of the Group III manuscripts, it is present only in O'Flaherty (*O'F*); it appears, too, in the Bridgewater (*B*) and Osborn (*O 2*) manuscripts. The poem's appearance in *DC* is puzzling. Like *TCD* and *N*, *DC* contains "The Lamentations" and "Upon the Annunciation and Passion falling upon one day. 1608," both of which are missing in the other Group II manuscripts, Trinity College, Cambridge, and *A 18* (British Library, Add. MS. 18647). Unlike all the Group II manuscripts, *DC* does not contain the hymn of 1619 and "A Hymne to God the Father." It is a remarkably complete manuscript of the poems Donne wrote prior to his ordination, and though it does not contain the satires, it contains poems written in 1613 and 1614, "Goodfriday, 1613," the verse letter to the Countess of Salisbury, and the Harrington elegy. If "The Lamentations" was written after 1614, it is the only late poem in *DC*. Its appearance in *B* does not preclude the possibility of a date of composition somewhat earlier than that normally assumed, though not so early as that suggested by its appearance in *DC*. *B* is a manuscript which obviously aims at completeness, but it does not contain "A Hymne to God the Father," "Hymne to God my God, in my sicknesse," and the Hamilton elegy of 1625. The last datable poem it contains is the hymn of 1619, but it is generally described as having been transcribed "about 1620" in order to account for the presence of "The Lamentations." The manuscripts, then, indicate that the poem did not circulate widely. If its absence in the Group I manuscripts points to a date later than Donne's ordination, its presence in *DC* may indicate a

---

[124]*DC* is described by Gardner in *The Elegies and the Songs and Sonnets*, pp. lxx–lxxi, lxxxviii.

date of composition earlier than that of the hymn of 1619, and
the fact that both it and the hymn of 1619 are present in *B* does
not undermine that supposition. All we can say of *B* with certainty is that it was transcribed after the composition of the
hymn of 1619 and almost certainly before the composition of "A
Hymne to God the Father."[125]

The length of "The Lamentations of Jeremy," Donne's obvious care for an authoritative rendering of his text (indicated in
"for the most part according to Tremelius"), his close attention
to the sound of each line, to say nothing of the customary problems posed by all translation into verse, lead us to ask when
Donne may have had time to undertake such a work. Between
1608 and 1611, Donne's energies were almost totally directed
toward writing, and it is not impossible that he wrote "The
Lamentations" at this time, when he turned to religious verse.
But if the *DC* manuscript seems to support such a date, the
Group I manuscripts do not. Although Donne was appointed
Chaplain-in-Ordinary to the King shortly after his ordination,
he was one of forty-eight such chaplains, and his duties were
not arduous.[126] Although he was granted the rectory of Keyston
in Huntingdon in January 1616, and that of Sevenoaks in Kent
the following July, these were sinecures; Donne had no Church
position which demanded his time until he was chosen Reader
in Divinity at Lincoln's Inn on October 24, 1616.[127] He may,
then, have written "The Lamentations" some time in his first
twenty months as priest, perhaps in an attempt to call attention
to himself, but if that was his purpose it is hard to understand
why the poem did not circulate more widely. Again, Donne
must have been a little bored and restless from the beginning of
1620, when he returned from the excitement and stimulation of
the embassy to Germany to the routine at Lincoln's Inn. For
about a year and a half, he seems to have expected that his service under Doncaster would be rewarded by promotion to a
higher office in the Church, and it is possible that when he saw

[125]See Appendix.
[126]Bald, pp. 307, 312–13.
[127]Ibid., pp. 317–18.

himself passed over he turned to "The Lamentations," either to distract himself, or to provide further evidence of his talents. From August 1621, Donne worked aggressively to secure the deanery of St. Paul's, and though he knew by September 13 that the King had chosen him to be the new Dean, he remained apprehensive until his election was formalized on November 22.[128] If he wrote "The Lamentations" in the weeks or months before August 1621, it is possible that he put it aside instead of circulating it widely when he threw himself into seeking active support wherever he might find it.

It is as puzzling to try to account for Donne's decision to English Lamentations rather than, say, some of the Psalms or the Song of Solomon or parts of Isaiah as it is to try to establish its date. His sermons do not show any peculiar interest in or affection for the book. He seems to have preached just two sermons on texts in Lamentations, one on 4:20 at St. Paul's in 1622 to commemorate the Gunpowder Plot, and another on 3:1, "I am the man, that hath seen affliction, by the rod of his wrath," in or after 1624, if its heading in *Fifty Sermons*, "Preached at St. Dunstans," is accurate.[129] Walton added to his life of Donne in 1658 the information that Donne preached a sermon on 3:1 at St. Clement Danes shortly after the death of his wife; he may be right, but that sermon has not survived.[130] Undoubtedly the marriage in 1613 of the Princess Elizabeth to the Elector Palatine whetted his interest in the state of Protestantism in Germany; it is possible that either then or after his participation in

---

[128]Ibid., pp. 370-82.

[129]*Sermons*, IV, No. 9, and X, No. 9.

[130]Bald assumes that Walton's story is accurate, and he explains why Donne would have been able to preach at his parish church (pp. 327-28).

On most occasions when Donne preached more than one sermon on the same text, he preached the sermons successively; what he had to say about a text was too long for the time allotted a single sermon. On four occasions, he seems to have used the same text for sermons which he did not preach consecutively. He used one text for Whitsunday sermons at St. Paul's in 1625 and 1626 (see *Sermons*, VII, 16, for the dates) and another for Whitsunday sermons at St. Paul's in 1627 and 1628. Twice he preached three sermons on one text at St. Paul's within a period of a few months, but either he conceived these as a series or developed them into a series. See ibid., X, 418-21.

the embassy to Germany he saw a parallel between the distress of German Protestants and the Jerusalem of Lamentations, and this may have made the book especially relevant to him. Perhaps, too, the publication in 1621 of a commentary on Jeremiah and Lamentations by Cornelius à Lapide drew his attention to the book.

The title of the poem, however, calls attention not to Donne's debt to à Lapide but to John Immanuel Tremellius; its specificity points to its authenticity and it is clear that Donne wanted to make public his special dependency on Tremellius. But this knowledge does not help to determine the date of the poem or Donne's purpose. Tremellius's translation of the Old Testament was the authorized Latin version of Protestants; it had been published in Frankfort in 1575-79, and three editions were published in London in the 1580s. There is no doubt that Donne used this text for some nuances of approach and meaning, but his translation would not have been very much different had he gone directly to the Geneva Bible and to the King James Bible, which was, of course, in part based on Tremellius.[131] Why, then, did he think it important to put Tremellius's name in his title? It would seem that Donne wanted to add the weight of authority to his translation, to call attention to his care for scholarship. Such a consideration may have concerned him more after his ordination than before, to indicate the seriousness of his intent, but we cannot be sure.[132] His reference to Tremellius is even a little misleading, for though he made his translation as accurate as possible, he was equally concerned with the musicality of his verse. The Sidnean psalms which he

[131]In "Donne's 'Lamentations of Jeremy' and the Geneva Bible," *ES*, 55 (1974), 513-15, John J. Pollock says that Donne relied more heavily on Geneva, but he finds enough dependence on the Authorized Version to suggest that Donne wrote the poem after 1611.

[132]Tremellius's Latin version of the Old Testament was, of course, available to Donne throughout his life. According to Simpson's findings, the first reference to Tremellius in a sermon of Donne's which can be dated tentatively or precisely is in the spring of 1620, and the references continue to the end of his life. See *Sermons*, X, 454 ("Tremellius," under the heading "Bible"), and esp. 322-23; III, 7, 101, 105-6; and IX, 226-27.

praised so highly in a poem written late in 1621 are not scholarly,[133] and Donne would have known this; his praise is based
on their poetic merit. His own purpose in "The Lamentations"
was to use his artistry in the service of the Church. Perhaps his
translation of Gazet's little prayer induced him to try his hand
at something larger. Conceivably, too, the frequent appearance of the hymn of 1619 is an indication of its successful recep-
tion, and Donne may have wished to try his hand at something
similar but more ambitious; certainly, he used in "The Lamentations" the techniques he had used there.

Perhaps it is mere coincidence, but both in the prayer of
Gazet and in Lamentations, Donne translated works which
forced him to write within severe constraints. Gazet's prayer is
mainly structured as a series of parallel clauses, and here Donne
imitated the original. The Hebrew of Lamentations is very in-
tricately structured. The first four of its five chapters are alpha-
betic acrostics, with a stanza for each of the twenty-two letters
of the Hebrew alphabet. The third chapter has sixty-six verses
in English translations because each Hebrew stanza is in three
parts, each of which starts with the same letter. The fifth chapter is not an acrostic, but it, too, has twenty-two stanzas. Tremellius placed the appropriate Hebrew letter before each of his
verses, but he made no attempt to imitate the acrostic in Latin.
Donne disregards the acrostic and does not bother to retain the
Hebrew letters. He uses throughout his poem a four-line stanza
made up of two loose pentameter couplets. In Chapters 1 and
2, he regularly uses one stanza for each of the twenty-two biblical stanzas, and each of his stanzas is end-stopped. In Chapter
3, he mainly uses a four-line stanza for each three-part Hebrew
stanza, but he writes twenty-three stanzas for the twenty-two
Hebrew ones. Sometimes he renders one of the sixty-six biblical

---

[133]William A. Ringler, Jr., says that Sidney and the Countess of Pembroke
modeled their translations on those of Marot and Beza (1562) and that they
depended mainly on Coverdale's version in the Book of Common Prayer.
They consulted the Geneva Bible and Beza's commentary, but neither the
Vulgate nor Tremellius. *The Poems of Sir Philip Sidney* (Oxford, 1962),
p. 505.

verses in part of a line; sometimes he gives it as much as two full lines. One of his stanzas compresses four biblical verses; sometimes only two biblical verses preempt a stanza. On five occasions he starts a biblical verse in the fourth line of a stanza and enjambs it to the next. In Chapter 4 he once again devotes, in the main, a stanza to each of the twenty-two biblical stanzas, but his chapter has eighty lines rather than eighty-eight. No biblical stanza gets more than four lines, but three of them get only two lines and two get three lines, and Donne enjambs three consecutive stanzas. Donne renders the twenty-two shorter biblical stanzas of Chapter 5 in forty-two lines: he generally gives a couplet to each biblical stanza, but occasionally he condenses two biblical stanzas to a couplet. This chapter has no enjambment between its stanzas; not only does Donne end-stop most of his lines, but his last stanza contains only one couplet. His very management of the gross structure of the text is itself a technical accomplishment, and, especially from Chapter 3 on, there is nothing mechanical about his rendering of the original.

It is not possible here to demonstrate fully Donne's preoccupation with the sound of "The Lamentations." One need only open the poem at random and look at the frequent patterns of the end rhyme, the quality of the internal rhyme, the amount of parallel expression with word repetition, the overwhelming emphasis on consonance and assonance. I shall merely point out a few of the extraordinary effects which Donne achieves. Note that he concludes Chapter 1 by repeating the *a* rhyme in the last three stanzas. The word "bee" in l. 137 sets the rhyme for an entire stanza; the rhyme is used internally in ll. 139 and 140, and it is exploited both at the end of a line and internally in the next five stanzas. In l. 161, "Arise, cry in the night, poure, for thy sinnes," Donne not only relies on the echoing sound of *i*, but "cry" and "thy" introduce a rhyme which he uses and reuses both at the end of a line and internally for the last four stanzas of Chapter 2. The *b* rhyme, "heare," of stanza 20 of Chapter 3 (ll. 255–56) becomes the *a* rhyme of stanza 21; the sound of "my" in the first line of stanza 20 carries through the stanza to culminate in "Oh from my sigh, and crye, stop not thine eare," and in stanza 21 the words "thee" and "mee" echo the end rhyme of "nere" and "feare." Part of the effect of the last three stanzas of Chapter 4 stems from the repetition of the sound of the *a* rhyme "hee" (l. 337) throughout the passage. Note the way in which Donne delicately adjusts the sound in lines like "Who honor'd, scorne her, for her foulnesse they / Have seene; her selfe doth groane, and turne away" (ll. 31–32), and the way in which the central words, "O Lord," of l. 44, "How cheape I'am growne, O Lord, behold, and weigh," are enhanced by the sounds of "growne" (which repeats "groane" in l. 41) and "behold." Frequently his effects are blatant, power-ful, and extensive, as in ll. 238–41:

> Thou pardon'st not; Usest no clemencie;
> Pursuest us, kill'st us, coverest us with wrath,
> Cover'st thy selfe with clouds, that our prayer hath

> No power to passe.[134]

Sometimes he will use a dominant sound for a line, as in "They'are darker now then blacknes, none can know" (l. 297), but he will let a *d* thud through an entire stanza (ll. 153–56) or a sighing and sorrowing *s* wander through several stanzas (l. 269ff.). The effects continue to the very last lines:

> Restore us Lord to thee, that so we may
> Returne, and as of old, renew our day.

> For oughtest thou, O Lord, despise us thus,
> And to be utterly enrag'd at us?[135]

---

[134]See, too, ll. 319–21: "Would cry aloud, depart defiled men, / Depart, depart, and touch us not; and then / They fled, and strayd."

[135]Donne's preoccupation with consonance, in conjunction with his depen-dence on Tremellius, can sometimes help us decide what he wrote. In *Divine Poems*, Gardner printed at l. 342: "Those which inhabitst *Huz*, for unto thee"; "Huz" is the reading in *B*, "Hus" in *TCD* and *N*, "Uz" in *O'F*, "her" in *Poems*, 1633. In her 2d ed., Gardner prints "*Uz*"; her note says, "Since both Geneva and *A.V.* have this form I now adopt it, although 'her' (*1633*) suggests 'Huz' or 'Hus' may be Donne's form." Donne's form was almost certainly

So much has been made of the harshness of Donne's diction and of his breaking accent that some critics have thought he was insensitive to sound. His customary numbers are a perfect vehicle for the dramatic lyric and the satiric or ironic attitude he so frequently utilizes. They are not the result of incapacity, and just how exquisitely attuned his ear was is evident in a lyric like "A Valediction: forbidding Mourning," where the smooth and regular numbers reflect marvelously the tones of a sad, thoughtful, and controlled speaker. The chiming quality of "The Lamentations," the resonance of the lines, the way in which the sounds reverberate are not so subtle as this nor are they so stridently orchestral as Dryden's in *Alexander's Feast*. Only in the hymn of 1619 had Donne strived for the kinds of effects he uses here. That Donne saw fit to harmonize his numbers with his intent should not surprise us; he had always done so. But his intent and his numbers in "The Lamentations" are so different from his customary ones that both these surprise us. "The Lamentations" provides the best evidence for Walton's statements about Donne's interest in Church music, and it demonstrates that even when he was in orders he undertook to master a new form and that he did so with remarkable virtuosity.

> "Upon the translation of the Psalmes
> by Sir Philip Sydney, and the
> Countesse of Pembroke his Sister"

In the context of Donne's translation of Lamentations and of the prayer of Gazet, there would seem to be nothing untoward

---

"Huz," and he probably wanted it pronounced "Hutz" to repeat the sounds of "inhabitst." Tremellius (London, 1585) transliterates the Hebrew of Lam. 4:21 as "Hhutzi" (the word is a genitive), repeats this spelling in his marginal note, and uses it wherever the word appears in the OT. His spellings of "Hhutz," "Hhelam" (for AV "Elam" at Gen. 10:22), "Hhebero" (for AV "Eber" at Gen. 10:25) indicate that he rendered the Hebrew ayin as "Hh" (though he used "Hh" for the Hebrew aleph in "Hhobalem" at Gen. 10:28, where AV reads "Abimael"). His "tz" in "Hhutz" accurately transliterates the Hebrew tsadhe.

in his writing a poem "Upon the translation of the Psalmes by Sir Philip Sydney, and the Countesse of Pembroke his Sister" after September 25, 1621. (The *terminus a quo* is readily fixed, since the Countess died on that day and Donne's poem refers to her presence in heaven.) His purpose seems clear, for he writes, "We thy Sydnean Psalmes shall celebrate." The poem is, then, an encomium; its subject is a fit one for a man in orders, and its sentiments are unexceptional. Donne starts by saying that it is supererogatory to seek "new expressions" for God since His "blessed Spirit" so inspired the Psalms of David and the Sidnean translations that they present "the highest matter in the noblest forme." In "Now let the Iles rejoyce," Sidney and his sister have both translated a psalm and applied its doctrine for Englishmen; they have "both told us what, and taught us how to doe," have told us why to sing and taught us how to sing. "In formes of joy and art," they have re-revealed God, and their rendition of the Psalms in English, which has hitherto had translations "more hoarse, more harsh than any other" language, has finally provided Englishmen with a song that so attunes them spiritually that they are properly prepared to sing their part when they join the heavenly choir.

The poem is, however, hardly so bland as I have made it appear. Its expression has the wit and the learning which are reminiscent of Donne's verse letters to noble ladies. Donne's first words are "Eternall God," and his apostrophe is followed by a four-line parenthesis:

> . . . (for whom who ever dare
> Seeke new expressions, doe the Circle square,
> And thrust into strait corners of poore wit
> Thee, who art cornerlesse and infinite).

Except for his translation of Lamentations, all of Donne's religious verse had sought for "new expressions," and the parenthesis itself depends on a new expression even as he condemns the procedure. He wittily compares the futility of new attempts to encompass the perfection of God to the impossibility of squaring the circle. Even though he states that his purpose is to bless the "Name" of God, not to "name" him, he newly names the attributes of God as "cornerlesse and infinite." In another parenthesis, he says that God's gifts are as infinite as He is and that he will fix his praises on just one of them, the Psalms. That one is not, however, simply one and indivisible, and for the next twenty lines Donne exploits the ideas of two-in-one and three-in-one. God's spirit, he says, first fell upon David "in a cloven tongue," and he explains what he means in the poem's third parenthesis: "(For 'twas a double power by which he sung / The highest matter in the noblest forme)." Now God has "cleft that spirit" so that it has worked again upon "Two, by their bloods, and by Thy Spirit one," upon Sidney and the Countess of Pembroke. The brother and sister are "made by thee / The Organ, where thou art the Harmony." They are also "Two that make one *John Baptists* holy voyce," Donne says, and then he builds on his earlier idea that the Psalms represent the conjunction of heaven and earth. He has not thus far taken into consideration the music of the spheres, a third choir, and he would show that the Psalms embrace all three realms. The spheres, he says, "have Musick, but they have no tongue, / Their harmony is rather danc'd than sung," but, he continues, since angels (which he assumes to be the intelligences which govern the spheres) "learne by what the Church does here," all three realms are in harmony. Here, in the compression, complexity, and interconnection of ideas, Donne's wit and ingenuity come through, and there is more. He writes:

> . . . I must not rejoyce as I would doe
> When I behold that these Psalmes are become
> So well attyr'd abroad, so ill at home,
> So well in Chambers, in thy Church so ill,
> As I can scarce call that reform'd untill
> This be reform'd.

"Well attyr'd abroad" and "ill at home" seem to refer to the difference between translations in other vernaculars and in English, but the next line, as Gardner says, gives us the right meaning: "'Abroad,' that is in 'chambers,' the Psalms can be found in this admirable version: 'at home,' that is in Churches, they are sung in a bad version."[136] But Donne still intends the ambiguity of "abroad" and "at home," for, shortly after, he develops the idea that English versions, with the exception of the Sidnean one, are inferior to foreign ones. His repetition of "re-form'd" depends for its impact on our stereotyped reaction to the idea of a reformed Church and to his pointing up the radical meaning of the word, "re-formed," "formed anew," or "re-shaped." At the end of the poem, Donne uses the same technique in his statement (in still another parenthesis) that God has "translated these translators," where the primary meaning of the verb is motional—the translators have been moved from earth to heaven. But God's translation of the translators has a second meaning. Donne refers to "th'Extemporall song" sung by the blessed in heaven, which is "Learn'd the first hower" that they see God. His definition of "th'Extemporall song" undercuts its extemporal quality: it has to be learned (though it is learned quickly), and it is not essentially different from the Psalms but a translation of the songs of the translators. His purpose is, of course, to conclude the poem by emphasizing the "sweet learned labours" of the translators, which tune men so that they can sing their part when they are themselves translated into heaven and join the translators. Donne's subject in the poem is a fitting thanksgiving, but if he has not quite sought to square the circle, he has, at the least, blessed the Name of God with "new expressions" in his praise of the old ones.

The poem presents two main problems. If Donne's purpose was to bless the Name of God, his blessing remained a private and quiet one. The poem appears only in the O'Flaherty manuscript, which provided the text first printed in *Poems*, 1635.[137] Why did it not circulate more widely? Again, Sir Philip Sidney seems to have translated the first forty-three Psalms shortly be-

---

[136]*Divine Poems*, p. 103.
[137]Ibid., pp. lxxxvii–lxxxix.

fore his death; his most recent editor says that the Countess of Pembroke may have finished a first draft by 1593 and that she had completed her work by 1599.[138] Why did Donne wait so long to celebrate their achievement? It is, of course, possible that he did not see a manuscript until shortly before he wrote, but a number of manuscripts were available and it seems proper to assume that the Pembrokes or the Herberts would have brought the translation to Donne's attention long before he wrote his poem. The answers to the questions lie, I think, in the nature of Donne's relation to the Pembrokes and in his own personal circumstances at the time of the death of the Countess.

Donne was not so closely associated with the Sidney-Pembroke circle as Ben Jonson was, but he was closer to them than has been generally recognized. The evidence for Jonson's familiarity is overwhelming and obvious: it is clear in a dozen poems and in several dedications; not only did Jonson tell Drummond that Sir Philip Sidney had translated some of the psalms that were circulating in manuscript under the name of the Countess of Pembroke but he told him, too, that the Countess's eldest son, William Herbert, who became the third earl in 1601, sent him an annual New Year's gift of twenty pounds.[139] It is more difficult to document the extent of Donne's familiarity. Donne's father-in-law, Sir George More, *may* have "travelled with Sir Philip Sidney as his kinsman and companion all over France, Italy and Germany."[140] Donne may have known Sir Philip's nephew, Robert Sidney, the second son of his brother, for Robert was the brother-in-law of Viscount Doncaster (both had married daughters of the Earl of Northumberland, an old friend of Donne and Sir George More) and had accompanied Doncaster on his German embassy.[141] But there is far more spe-

---

[138]Ringler, *The Poems of Sir Philip Sidney*, pp. 500-501.

[139]C. H. Herford and Percy Simpson, eds., *Ben Jonson,* I (Oxford, 1925; rpt. 1954), 138, 141.

[140]Bald cites the words of Donne's brother-in-law, Sir John Oglander (pp. 129-30). There is no evidence that Oglander is right, but he must have had some reason to believe that his father-in-law had known Sidney.

[141]Ibid., pp. 331-32, 344. (Bald seems to confuse Robert with his elder brother, William, who died in 1613; see "Leicester" in *Complete Peerage*.)

cific evidence than this. William, 3d Earl of Pembroke, sent a letter to Doncaster very shortly after his departure from England on May 12, 1619, and he added in a postscript, "I beseech yo[u]r Lo[rdshi]p com[m]end my best loue to Mr Doctor Dunn."[142] A few months earlier, Donne had preached a sermon at The Cockpit, a group of apartments near Whitehall occupied by William's brother, Philip, and his wife, Susan, the Earl and Countess of Montgomery; the Countess had asked him to transcribe it for her and he did so not long before he left for Germany.[143] Donne may indeed have been distantly related to the Herbert family; it is not mere coincidence that the younger John Donne edited in 1660 an edition of the poems of the 3d Earl of Pembroke, and he may be repeating what his father had told him when he states in his dedicatory epistle that he was "obliged to that Honorable Family . . . by descent."[144] Sir Edward Herbert and George Herbert were fourth cousins of William and Philip and had received occasional favors from them;[145] Donne may have become acquainted with the Pembrokes through them.

Grierson stated that the occasion on which Donne wrote "Upon the translation of the Psalmes" was not known, and he thought that Donne might have composed the poem for the Countess of Montgomery.[146] It is more likely that Donne wrote the poem for the 3d Earl of Pembroke. Himself a poet and a patron of poets, Chancellor to the University of Oxford from 1617, he was one of the wealthiest and most influential noblemen in England. In 1614, he and the Countess of Bedford had introduced young George Villiers, the future Duke of Buckingham, to the King and to the Court in an attempt to undermine

[142]Cited by Bald, p. 351.

[143]*Sermons*, II, No. 8, and pp. 23–25.

[144]Bald, pp. 20–21.

[145]See ibid., p. 183, n. 1, for Philip's treatment of Sir Edward when the King granted him Montgomery Castle in 1607; Joseph Summers says that William and Philip were almost certainly influential in George Herbert's election as Member of Parliament for Montgomery in 1624 (*George Herbert: His Religion and Art* [London, 1954], p. 33).

[146]*The Poems of John Donne*, II, 242.

the influence of the Earl of Somerset;[147] he is one of the several people who could have introduced Donne to Buckingham.

When Donne returned from the Continent at the beginning of 1620, both he and his contemporaries thought that he had achieved sufficient distinction to put him in line for a deanery, and Donne pinned his hopes on Buckingham's help. He did not get Salisbury early in 1620, though Buckingham had almost certainly promised it to him, and he was disappointed again a year later when the prospect of a vacancy at Gloucester never materialized. On August 26, 1621, the Bishop of Exeter died; it was known almost immediately that he was to be succeeded by Valentine Cary, Dean of St. Paul's, and Donne knew by September 13, perhaps from the King himself, that he was to have Cary's place at Paul's. All the summer before, Donne seems to have done whatever he could to keep himself in the eyes of those who might help him. He tried to see the Countess of Bedford when she was briefly in London; he knew that Sir Edward Herbert thought to return from his ambassadorship in Paris; he was aware of Doncaster's circumstances, and even those of Bacon, who had recently lost his Chancellorship; he seems to have kept in touch with John Williams, who had not long before been made both Bishop of London and Keeper of the Great Seal. He visited George Abbot, Archbishop of Canterbury, who was under suspension from his ecclesiastical functions pending an investigation into his accidental killing of a man while he had been hunting; he visited Sir Henry Hobart, Lord Chief Justice of Common Pleas, and Sir Julius Caesar, Master of the Rolls. Even though Donne probably knew by mid-September that the King had signed an order for his election to St. Paul's, he expressed his apprehensions and uncertainties in a letter to Goodere, dated October 11. The inquiry into Archbishop Abbot's misadventure delayed Cary's consecration as Bishop of Exeter until November 18; on the next day, the King's letter commanding Donne's election to the deanship of St. Paul's was issued, and Donne was, finally, installed on November 22.[148]

[147]Bald, p. 294.
[148]This paragraph is based on Bald, pp. 370–81.

I think it is likely that Donne wrote his poem "Upon the translation of the Psalmes" within a few days after the death of the Countess of Pembroke and, almost certainly, before he became Dean of St. Paul's. Throughout the summer of 1621 he had left no stone unturned in his effort to procure a deanship, and the death of the Countess gave him an opportunity to call himself to the attention of Pembroke in the hope that he might see fit to support him. R. C. Bald has written that Donne "seems to have owed his deanery largely to the successful employment of the courtier's arts which he had cultivated, and persisted with in spite of heart-breaking disappointments, during the decade preceding his ordination."[149] His statement explains why, almost despite the conventionality of its subject and the conventional sentiments which it contains, "Upon the translation of the Psalmes" seems so similar in its wit and in its learned ingenuity to Donne's earlier poetry of patronage. It was no accident that Donne waited until after the death of the Countess to praise her work and that of her brother. The poem is not a disinterested tribute to work done long before. Donne's quest for the deanery led him to seize the occasion of the Countess's death to communicate a private tribute to Pembroke. The poem he wrote is more a verse epistle than it is eulogy or elegy,[150] and that explains its limited availability and circulation. Here, more than in any other poem that he wrote after his ordination, Donne's motive was the motive behind his earlier poetry of patronage—self-advancement.

The "Ignatii Loyolae ἀποθέωσις" Attributed to Donne

After he became Dean of St. Paul's, Donne turned to poetry even less frequently than he had in the years before. He wrote

[149]Ibid., p. 376.

[150]Why did Donne not write an elegy? I suspect he thought it would be improper, somewhat intrusive to do so, unless he had been asked for one, and that he could not be faulted for writing a poem which, though it referred to the Countess's death, did so discreetly and indirectly while it focused mainly on the worth of the Psalms themselves and on the merit of the Sidney-Pembroke translation.

perhaps nine poems in the seven years after his ordination; in the next nine years he wrote only three or four. He seems to have wanted to avoid being known as a "pleasant poeticall" dean,[151] and he must have been chagrined when the *Anniversaries* were reprinted in 1621, probably by a stationer who thought to profit by Donne's recent appointment. His duties as Dean were multitudinous and time consuming, and it is hard to imagine that he found time to write verse, especially during his first year. From November 22, 1621, he had to familiarize himself with the numerous administrative responsibilities having to do with the personnel and property of the Chapter. For several months he was involved in a lawsuit concerning his resignation of the rectory of Keyston.[152] He had to move his family into the deanery from the house he had rented for some years off Drury Lane, and Walton tells us that "immediately after he came to his Deanry, he imployed workmen to repair the Chappel belonging to his house."[153] In the spring of 1622, he was instituted in the rectory of Blunham in Bedfordshire, the gift of the Earl of Kent, and he probably preached there the following summer; he was made a Justice of the Peace for Kent and Bedford, and may have sat on the bench from time to time. He served occasionally in the Court of Delegates, and his position as Dean probably exposed him to a variety of public duties. In addition to preaching at St. Paul's and still, occasionally, at Lincoln's Inn, Donne, as a new Dean, received numerous invitations to preach elsewhere, and he did not refuse. In July, he gave a sermon at Camberwell; in August, he preached at Hanworth at the request of Viscount Doncaster, before a distinguished company which included the Marquess of Buckingham and the Earl of Northumberland; in September, he delivered a sermon at Paul's Cross in defense of the King's recent "Directions to Preachers," a sermon important enough that the King asked that it be printed; in November, he preached at St. Michael's Cornhill before the Virginia Company, which had made him a

[151]*The Letters of John Chamberlain*, ed. Norman E. McClure (Philadelphia, 1939), II, 407–8.
[152]Bald, pp. 386–88.
[153]*The Life and Death of Dr Donne*, sig. B3^r.

member some months before, and this sermon, too, was printed by request.[154] Donne's activities as a new Dean and his relish in conforming to public expectations of him in his office make it unlikely that he had any time for or any inclination toward poetry in 1622 and make suspect the recent attribution to him of a Latin poem on the apotheosis of Loyola.[155]

The strongest evidence that the poem may be Donne's is internal; the content and style remind us of some of his earlier work. Its subject is Loyola's canonization. Ignatius, the poet says, finally got his Feast Day in the Calendar by ousting St. Germanus of Auxerre from July 31. This led to a hot contention: the interloper refused to go away; the first claimant would not budge; the two did not wish to share. The Holy Father exercises his cleverness anew; he orders them to share quietly, as Simon and Jude do, or, he says, Loyola can have his own day— the one added to Leap Year. The poet's attitude toward Loyola is like Donne's in his *Conclave Ignati: Sive eius in nuperis inferni comitiis Inthronisatio*, of 1611, which was also published in an English translation in the same year. Paul Stanwood finds "no actual echo" of this work in the poem, but he says, rightly, that the poem is Donnean in its satiric tone and in its irreverence and wittiness, and T. S. Healy points out that the dramatic and outrageous situation, the technical accuracy, and the good-humored wit are reminiscent of *Ignatius his Conclave* and of Donne's general manner.[156] Still, the infelicity of making way for Loyola by scratching Germanus from the Calendar must have appealed to widespread anti-Jesuitical sentiment, and the joke about granting Loyola a day during Leap Year seems to have been in the air. Middleton used it in the Induction to *A Game at Chess*, which was on the stage in 1624 and went through four editions in 1625.[157]

The external evidence linking the poem to Donne is very

[154]This paragraph is largely based on Bald, pp. 412–16, 423, 432–38, 499.
[155]P. G. Stanwood, "A Donne Discovery," *TLS*, Oct. 19, 1967, p. 984. The poem is available in Shawcross, *Complete Poetry,* pp. 505–6.
[156]T. S. Healy, ed., *John Donne: Ignatius His Conclave* (Oxford, 1969), p. 175.
[157]Joel H. Kaplan, "The Feast Day of Middleton's Loyola," *N&Q*, 216 (1971), 27–28.

weak. The unique copy, which its scribe attributes to "Dr Dun. Deane of Paules," is among a group of letters and poems in the fourth section of a miscellaneous collection, Volume 27 of the Hunter manuscripts in the Durham Cathedral Library. Twenty of the twenty-four pages of this section, including the poem, are in a hand which Stanwood has identified as that of a Thomas Carre, and he thinks that most of the items in Carre's hand were copied at about the same time, "perhaps in the early 1630s." Carre received his Cambridge B.A. in 1611 and was a fellow of Jesus College until 1618, the year he took orders. He seems to have been preferred in 1620 to the rectory of Hemsworth, in the East Riding, by "my L. Danvers," who, Stanwood says, is perhaps the same Sir John Danvers who was a friend of Donne's; his other preferments include the rectory of Huggate in Yorkshire in 1621, a prebendal stall at Durham in 1631, and the vicarage of Aycliffe in county Durham in 1632. There is no evidence that he knew Donne. His closest connection to the Court seems to have been John Cosin, who was in 1632 Archdeacon of the East Riding and who many years later became Bishop of Durham. There is no evidence of closeness between Cosin and Donne. It is difficult to imagine how Carre may have got a copy of a poem by Donne otherwise unknown. It is easier to imagine that any man faced with an anonymous satiric poem on the subject of Loyola's apotheosis might have guessed that the poem was Donne's, especially if he made his attribution in the early 1630s. *Poems, by J. D.* had been published in 1633 and 1635, and it was no secret that Donne was the author. Even when *Ignatius his Conclave* was published anonymously in 1611, it was an open secret that Donne had written it;[158] when it was republished in 1634 and in 1635, the title page read "By John Donne, Doctor of Divinitie, and late Deane of Saint Pauls." Carre's attribution is as inevitable as it is unimaginative.

Loyola was canonized on March 12, 1622,[159] and the depen-

---

[158]Keynes, *A Bibliography of Dr. John Donne*, p. 13.

[159]Francis Thompson, *Saint Ignatius Loyola*, ed. John H. Pollen (London, 1913), p. 318.

dence of the poem on this occasion points to a date of composition shortly after that date. The satiric attitude that we associate with Donne is present in some of the poems which he wrote after his ordination, but he had not written a "satire" since his poem "Upon Mr Thomas Coryats *Crudities*" in 1611. Before 1622, Donne had written only three poems in Latin.[160] Each of these is addressed to a man who would have particularly relished receiving a personal communication in the language of learning — Ben Jonson ("*Amicissimo et meritissimo Ben. Jonson. In Vulponem*," 1607), Dr. Richard Andrews ("*De Libro cum Mutuaretur Impresso: Domi a pueris frustatim lacerato; et post reddito Manuscripto*," 1612),[161] and George Herbert. If Donne had seen fit in 1622 to write a poem on the apotheosis of Loyola, it is entirely possible that he would have written it in Latin, even as he had written *Conclave Ignati* for an international audience, but he had not so used Latin verse before nor was he to do so again. Donne could have tossed off such a poem, and in Latin, in 1622, and it is fun to think of his writing a second and different "Canonization," but it is most unlikely that the newly appointed Dean of St. Paul's had either the time or the inclination to write such a poem at such a time.

The "Stationes" in *Devotions upon Emergent Occasions*

From the time of his ordination, Donne's literary energy went into his sermons, and the sermon became for him a natural mode of thought and expression. Some 160 sermons are extant; the total number that Donne preached far exceeded the number of his poems. As Reader in Divinity at Lincoln's Inn, he was obliged to preach about fifty a year;[162] after he became Dean of St. Paul's, he was "under a necessitie of Preaching twelve or fourteen solemn Sermons every year, to great Auditories, at

[160]His strange Latin poem of 1623 I shall discuss below.
[161]See Bald, pp. 250-51.
[162]Augustus Jessopp, *John Donne, Sometime Dean of St. Paul's* (London, 1897), p. 113.

Paules, and to the Judges, and at Court";[163] and after 1624 he preached from time to time at St. Dunstan's. Walton's description of the degree to which the sermons preempted Donne's time and care may be inaccurate in its particulars, but its spirit is certainly right.[164] Donne was well aware of "the ticklishnesse of *London*-Pulpits,"[165] and he took pride in his preaching. Even when a sermon was fairly fresh in his mind, it apparently took him about eight hours to produce a polished written version from his original notes,[166] and he was too busy to transcribe his notes with any regularity. But the value he put on his sermons is evident in the way he used his time when he was unable to preach: when in 1625 the plague drove him from London to Chelsea, he wrote out eighty of his sermons in five months.[167]

Donne did no preaching from the end of November 1623, until March 28, 1624.[168] He had been Dean of St. Paul's for two years before an interruption in his busy life forced him to turn from preaching to other modes of expression: in December 1623, he wrote his *Devotions upon Emergent Occasions, and severall steps in my Sicknes*, and in that month, or shortly after, he wrote two or three poems. On the last or next-to-last day of November, Donne fell victim to the "spotted fever" which was epidemic in London, an illness characterized by sudden and violent distress, by prostration and sleeplessness, and sometimes by a rash of spots; a crisis is reached in five to seven days, but the patient is so weakened that the fever may recur, and he needs a long convalescence.[169] Donne was out of danger by December 6, but even a month later he complained, "Though I

---

[163]*Mathew Collection*, p. 354.

[164]Izaak Walton, *The Lives of Dr John Donne . . .* (London, 1675), p. 59.

[165]*Mathew Collection*, p. 355.

[166]*Letters*, p. 154.

[167]Bald, pp. 479-80. Bald identifies Sir Thomas Roe as the addressee of a letter which contains this information; the letter is in Gosse, *The Life and Letters of John Donne*, II, 222-25, and in Hayward, *John Donne*, pp. 486-89.

[168]The last sermon he is known to have preached in 1623 is one on October 23 at St. Paul's, on the occasion of a feast of the Law Sergeants. Bald, pp. 448, 455.

[169]Ibid., p. 450; I. A. Shapiro, "Walton and the Occasion of Donne's *Devotions*," *RES*, ns 9 (1958), 18-21.

have left my bed, I have not left my bed-side," nor had his physicians lifted their prohibition against his reading by February 1.[170] His mind seems to have worked restlessly whenever he was forced to rest his body; writing was, for him, "another part of Physick."[171] Some fifteen years earlier during an "imprisonment" in his bed, he had written the 252 lines of "A Litanie."[172] Now, unable to preach and to read, he wrote the forty-five thousand words of the *Devotions* and made arrangements for its publication within a period of three or four weeks.[173]

The little volume has, between a dedicatory epistle to Prince Charles and the text itself, what seems to be a Latin table of contents, entitled "Stationes, *sive* Periodi *in* Morbo, *ad quas referuntur* Meditationes sequentes":

> 1 Insultus *Morbi primus*;
>   2 *Post*, Actio laesa;
> 3 Decubitus *sequitur tandē*;
>   4 Medicusq; *vocatur*;
> 5 Solus *adest*; 6 Metuit;
>   7 Socios *sibi iungier instat*;
> 8 *Et* Rex *ipse suum mittit*;
>   9 Medicamina scribunt;
> 10 Lentè *&* Serpenti sata-
>   gunt occurrere *Morbo*.
> 11 *Nobilibusq; trahunt*,
>   *a cincto corde, venenum*.
> Succis, *&* Gemmis; *&*
>   *quae Generosa, ministrant*
> Ars, *&* Natura, *instillant*;
>   12 *Spirante* Columbâ,
> *Suppositâ pedibus, revocan-*
>   *tur ad ima* vapores;

---

[170]Bald, pp. 450–51, cites Donne's letter to Sir Robert Ker (*Letters*, p. 249) and another letter in *Mathew Collection*, pp. 302–3.

[171]*Mathew Collection*, p. 303.

[172]*Letters*, pp. 32–33.

[173]Bald, p. 451; the book was entered in the Stationers' Register on January 9, 1624.

13 *Atq;* Malum Genium,
       numeroso stigmate, *fassus,*
Pellitur ad pectus, Morbiq;
       Suburbia, Morbus:
14 *Idq; notant* Criticis,
       Medici, evenisse diebus.
15 *Interea* insomnes *Noctes*
       ego duco, Diesq;:
16 *Et properare* meum, *cla-*
       mant, e turre propinqua
Obstreperae Campanae, alio-
       rum *in funere, funus.*
17 *Nunc* lento sonitu *dicunt,*
       Morieris; 18 *At inde,*
Mortuus *es, sonitu* celeri,
       pulsuq; agitato.
19 Oceano *tandem emenso,*
       aspicienda resurgit
Terra; *vident, iustis,* Medici,
       iam cocta *mederi*
Se posse, indiciis; 20 Id agunt;
       21 *Atq; annuit* Ille,
Qui per eos *clamat, linquas*
       iam Lazare *lectum*;
22 *Sit* Morbi Fomes *tibi*
       Cura; 23 Metusq; Relabi.

The words following each number become the titles of the twenty-three sections into which the *Devotions* is divided,[174] and each section, made up of a meditation, an expostulation, and a prayer, is also preceded by an English paraphrase of the Latin title. The forty-four short lines of the "Stationes" make up twenty-two hexameters, and Joan Webber is right in saying that the verse would be entirely unremarkable if it were not so entirely unexpected.[175]

[174]With one minor change: the first words of the title of Devotion 13 were changed to "Ingeniumq; malum."

[175]Joan Webber, *The Eloquent "I": Style and Self in Seventeenth-Century Prose* (Madison, 1968), p. 20.

Walton says of the *Devotions* that Donne was imitating "the holy Patriarchs, who were wont in that place to build their Altars where they had received their blessing."[176] In fact, Donne writes in Expostulation 13, "*My God, my God,* thou hast made this sick bed thine *Altar,* and I have no other *Sacrifice* to offer, but my self; and wilt thou accept *no spotted sacrifice?*" But he sees, in the following prayer, that "these *spots* are but the *letters,* in which thou hast written thine owne *Name,* and conveyed thy selfe to mee." The spots made by God are examples of God's writing which, properly interpreted by Donne, lead to his spiritual rebirth. This is the "preter-naturall *Birth*" to which he refers in the dedicatory epistle, and he says, "*In this* last Birth, *I my selfe am borne a* Father: *This* Child *of mine, this* Booke, *comes into the world,* from *mee, and* with *mee.*" The implied analogy with God as creator is a daring one; nowhere else in his writing does Donne seem so self-consciously aware of himself as Maker.

In the dedication of the *Devotions,* Donne likens himself to King Hezekiah, who "*writt the* Meditations *of his* Sicknesse, *after his* Sicknesse," but neither in the "Stationes" nor in the *Devotions* is Donne writing a royal hymn. The "Stationes" seems hardly to be a poem at all. It has a metrical design; its words have some sonority — the first syllable of "Morbo" in the title occurs seven times in the poem, *m* and *n* sounds move hauntingly through almost every line, and some consonantal pattern is used. But "Stationes" is a singularly bare enumeration of the stages in Donne's illness, more an arid outline of his sickness than a narrative, from the first symptoms through the appearance of spots, their successful treatment by purging, and the physicians' warning of possible relapse. The poem has none of Donne's customary wit, drama, and imagination. It has little sustained rhetoric: not only are the words broken by numbers, but some of the expression is fragmentary. We get emphasis, but not coherence; "Stationes" strikes us as a group of tags, some very short, some longer.

[176]*The Life and Death of D[r] Donne,* sig. B3[v].

What was Donne up to in creating these tags, these spots of time, these stations or periods? The "Stationes" provides an outline of his illness, but he is not interested in presenting a precise, accurate, day-by-day case history of his sickness and recovery during twenty-three days or stages: as we have seen, his illness and recovery stretched over two months; the critical days came early. In the "Stationes" and *Devotions*, the critical days appear in the fourteenth section; in Meditation 14, Donne undercuts the reality of chronological time ("this *Imaginary halfe-nothing, Tyme*"), and in Expostulation 14 he not only complicates chronological time and his own twenty-three stages by introducing a catalog of the seven critical days of his spirit but he even questions the propriety of thinking in terms of critical days. God, he says, may have reprehended the Galatians for their too precise observation of days, months, times, and years, and He may have forbidden the Colossians all critical and indicatory days, but He did not mean to take away "all Consideration, all destinction of *dayes*": "Though thou remove them from being of the *Essence* of our *Salvation*, thou leavest them for *assistances*, and for the *Exaltation* of our *Devotion*, to fix our selves, at certaine *periodicall*, & *stationary times* [*periodi, stationes*], upon the consideration of those things, which thou hast done for us, and the *Crisis*, the *triall*, the *judgment*, how those things have wrought upon us, and disposed us to a spirituall recovery, and convalescence." Donne states, in Expostulation 16, "I know I cannot have any better *Image* of *thee*, than thy *Sonne*, nor any better *Image* of *him*, than his *Gospell*," but he thinks, too, that man cannot have too many helps for the performance of his religious duties. If it was not necessary for the Church to avail itself of external aids made by Jew or Gentile for thanksgiving and devotion, God is yet pleased to continue toward Christians those assistances which worked upon the affections of natural men before they became Christians. "Must not I, with thanks confesse to thee," Donne asks, "that some *historicall pictures* of [Jesus], have sometimes put mee upon better *Meditations* than otherwise I should have fallen upon?"

Donne's "*historicall pictures*" are the Stations of the Cross, a series of fourteen sculptures or pictures set up in churches, showing various events in the passion of Christ, not all of them explicitly mentioned in the Gospels: (1) Jesus is condemned to death; (2) Jesus is burdened with the cross; (3) Jesus falls under the cross; (4) Jesus meets His mother; (5) Simon of Cyrene helps Jesus carry the cross; (6) Veronica wipes Jesus' face with her veil; (7) Jesus falls a second time; (8) Jesus comforts the women of Jerusalem; (9) Jesus falls a third time; (10) Jesus is stripped of his clothes; (11) Jesus is nailed to the cross; (12) Jesus dies upon the cross; (13) Jesus is taken down from the cross and is placed in Mary's arms; (14) Jesus is laid in the sepulcher. The Stations were intended to stimulate the devotion of worshipers who could not go to the sacred places in the Holy Land. The vivid pictorial representation made it unnecessary for a worshiper to conjure up a place or event imaginatively in order to meditate upon it; he had only to focus his eyes. Donne's twenty-three stations are his own imitation of the fourteen events in the passion of Christ, a selection of the "letters" in which God had written His name, the verbal spots concretized by him in Latin as pictures of his own sufferings for the purpose of his own devotion.[177]

In the very creation of his own "Stationes," there is indication that Donne read his illness metaphorically as evidence of the sickness of his soul. Somewhat later, in a sermon probably preached during the reign of Charles, he cited with approbation Hilary's definition of a healthy soul, "then thou art well, when thou satisfiest thy self with those things, which God hath vouchsafed to manifest in the *Scriptures*," and, he continued,

---

[177]It is possible that one of the *"historicall pictures"* was in Donne's mind when he wrote, in the Holy Sonnet "What if this present were the worlds last night?" the lines, "Marke in my heart, O Soule, where thou dost dwell, / The picture of Christ crucified," but he images the crucifixion vividly elsewhere. In "Goodfriday, 1613," he pictures the crucifixion in detail and follows his description with the memory of a second picture: "If on these things I durst not looke, durst I / Upon his miserable mother cast mine eye." In *Deaths Duell*, he conjures up for his auditors in eight stages "the *whole day* from the *houre* that *Christ received* the *passeover* upon *Thursday, unto* the *houre* in which hee *dyed* the *next* day," and he asks them whether they have lived their last day in conformity with Christ (*Sermons*, x, 245–48).

"if any man will speake a new language, otherwise then God hath spoken, and present new Scriptures, (as he does that makes traditions equall to them) . . . either he understands not himself, or I may very well be content not to understand him, if I understand God without him."[178] Here, to be sure, Donne's main purpose is to denigrate Catholic emphasis on tradition; still, in the "Stationes" he spoke a new language, presented a new Scripture, wrote his own Vulgate, and in the *Devotions* he preached on the literal text of his own making. The distinctiveness of Donne's own Latin Scripture stands out boldly. Accustomed as he was in his sermons to cite a Latin passage before he gave an English version, Donne uses only two Latin words so in the body of the *Devotions*,[179] although his notes cite the Bible 342 times and his references to biblical passages exceed 500.[180]

In Expostulation 19, Donne describes both the simplicity and majesty of Scripture and provides the key to a right understanding of his procedure in "Stationes" and in the *Devotions*:

> My *God*, my *God*, Thou art a *direct God*, may I not say, a *literall God*, a *God* that wouldst bee understood *literally*, and according to the *plaine sense* of all that thou saiest? But thou art also (*Lord* I intend it to thy *glory*, and let no *prophane misinterpreter* abuse it to thy *diminution*) thou art a *figurative*, a *metaphoricall God* too: A *God* in whose words there is such a height of *figures*, such *voyages*, such *peregrinations* to fetch remote and precious *metaphors*, such *extentions*, such *spreadings*, such *Curtaines* of *Allegories*, such *third Heavens* of *Hyperboles*, so *harmonious eloquutions*, so *retired* and so *reserved expressions,* so *commanding perswasions*, so *perswading commandements*, such *sinewes* even in thy *milke*, and such *things* in thy *words*, as all *prophane Authors*, seeme of the seed of the *Serpent*, that *creepes*, thou art the *dove*, that flies.

[178]Ibid., pp. 151–52; see pp. 15–16 for date.

[179]"*Surgite Mortui, Rise yee* dead," at the end of Expostulation 2 (*Devotions upon Emergent Occasions* [London, 1624], p. 34).

Twice Donne reverses his usual procedure: "no *Proprietie*, no *Meum & Tuum*" in Meditation 11 (p. 257), and "a *propriety*, a *Meum & Tuum*" in Meditation 23 (p. 596).

[180]Elizabeth Savage, ed., *John Donne's Devotions upon Emergent Occasions*, Salzburg Studies in English Literature (Salzburg, 1975), I, xvii.

This hath occasioned thine ancient *servants*, whose delight it was to write after thy *Copie*, to proceede the same way in their *expositions* of the *Scriptures*, and in their composing both of *publike liturgies*, and of *private prayers* to thee, to make their accesses to thee in such a kind of *language*, as thou wast pleased to speake to them, in a *figurative*, in a *Metaphoricall language*.

In the "Stationes" Donne writes as "a *literall God*" who would be understood literally and according to the plain sense of what he says; in the *Devotions* he uses God's figurative style. Not only does he create his own text but he exploits generally the medieval method of exploring the fourfold meaning of biblical texts. The "Stationes" is Donne's plain sense, the spots or letters written by God and by himself, his literal scriptural text. Mere translation of the Latin text into English is insufficient. Donne must interpret it, and the Meditations are a first step. He says, in Expostulation 19, "Neither art thou thus a *figurative*, a *Metaphoricall God*, in thy *word* only, but in thy *workes* too," and in the Meditations he sees himself in station after station as part of the Book of Creatures which allegorically expresses but does not fully reveal God to man. In the Expostulations, Donne tries further to illuminate his text or station by taking into consideration the many biblical texts which are relevant to his station in an attempt to come to a rational understanding of his text, to see its moral significance. And, finally, in the Prayers, as a result of his concern for each spot, of his delineation of his natural condition and his attempt to view it rationally in the light of God's words, he can lay open the spiritual and mystical meaning of each station as he conforms his own will to God's and as he assumes the justness of each spot or station in God's providential scheme. The literal stations emblematize the stages of Donne's spiritual state, and he would show through his particular series of occasions the stages in his spiritual struggle and reconstitution by which his conscience is rectified.[181]

What, then, shall we make of Donne's strange use of verse in

[181]Here, and elsewhere in my discussion, I have profited from my notes and remembrance of a superb seminar paper written for me in 1958 by Forrest Read, who has, perversely, left in typescript what I urged him to publish.

the "Stationes"? On the one hand, it makes manifest the power and dignity he attributed to poetry. When he saw fit to create his own Scripture, he turned to verse; when he dared to re-create himself in words and through words, when he imitated his own Maker to create his own child, he wrote a poem. On the other hand, his use of the plainest of plain styles in the "Stationes" and of a figurative style in the *Devotions* which plunders all the resources of heart, mind, and language is a reversal of what we consider the customary attributes of poetry and prose. To be sure, not just the "Stationes" but all Donne's poems are marked by a tough spareness, by the use of ellipsis, by concision of expression, by precision and concretion of detail, and, over the centuries, many of his lines have been opened up by explicators and commentators. But it is the glory of most of the poems that each contains within itself topic, meditation, expostulation, and prayer. Each is not a starting place only, only a bare text; each has within it its share of murmurings, colloquies, exaltations; each contains in itself the various levels of meaning appropriate to it. The "Stationes" has that barrenness which Donne had once perversely and wittily called a blessing of nature and the glory of old age. Its ingenious sterility is of his own making, and, miraculously, the child which is the offspring of that sterility has inherited all the marvelous qualities which the aged father had passed on to the children of his youth. The "Stationes" is interesting in that it shows Donne willing in his old age to attempt a mode new to him, to fashion a bold conceit in the manner of God, stripped of correspondences; but the *Devotions* which follows it is even more interesting because it shows the extent to which prose had replaced poetry as the mode which expressed most completely the rich complexity of Donne's mind and the range and diversity of his feelings.

The Dating of "Hymne to God my God, in my sicknesse" and of "A Hymne to God the Father"

Donne continued to dazzle his contemporaries with the drama, emotionality, wit, and ingenuity of his prose for the rest of his days, right through *Deaths Duell*, the sermon he preached a month before he died. If the "Stationes" had been his last attempt in verse, we might well think, given its special characteristics and the eccentricity of its function as verse, that Donne had truly renounced poetry, or at least the kind of poetry that had given him the name of poet. But the same confinement that threw him back on his own resources and made him search himself and God, the same fevered excitement and heightened activity of mind that made him pour out the *Devotions* spilled over into one of his most extraordinary poems, "Hymne to God my God, in my sicknesse," and, it is usually thought, into the much admired "A Hymne to God the Father."

Walton has given us a good deal of misinformation about the two poems. He composed the last third of his original (1640) *Life of Donne* very artfully: it starts with the illness of Donne's which gave rise to the *Devotions* and leaps momentarily to his final illness before Walton, in a "digression" (as he calls it), recapitulates Donne's life by gradually building a picture of such piety that it can be exceeded only by the extreme holiness of his death. The digression begins with what Walton considers the most profane note in Donne's life, the marriage which was his "remarkable error," and moves next both to praise Donne's youthful poetry and to excuse it as having been written mainly "before the twentieth yeare of his age." Walton goes on to say that though Donne later regretted the pieces which he had loosely scattered in his youth, "he was not so falne out with heavenly Poetry, as to forsake it, no not in his declining age, witnessed then by many divine Sonnets, and other high, holy, and harmonious composures; yea even on his former sick bed, he wrote this heavenly Hymne, expressing the great joy he then had in the assurance of Gods mercy to him." He quotes in its entirety "A Hymne to God the Father," says that Donne "on this (which was his Death-bed) writ another Hymne which bears this Title, *A Hymne to God my God in my sicknesse*," and justifies Donne's writing "these high illuminations" by the examples of Prudentius, David, and Hezekiah.[182] There are several flaws

[182]*The Life and Death of Dr Donne*, sigs. B3^v–B4^r.

here. Throughout the *Life*, Walton's chronology is general and shaky, and it is fuzzy here, where he makes "A Hymne to God the Father" and the *Devotions* products of the same sickbed; when he introduces the story of the *Devotions* by saying of Donne that "in the fifty fourth yeare, a dangerous sicknesse seised him, which turned to a spotted Feaver, and ended in a Cough, that inclined him to a Consumption," he is probably conflating Donne's illness at the end of 1623 with another he had in 1625.[183] Again, Walton's incorrect attribution in this passage of Donne's Holy Sonnets to his declining age is mainly responsible for the post-dating of those poems by a decade or more, and the impression he creates that Donne wrote a good deal of religious verse to the day he died has led to a mistaken view of his poetic career which persisted for some three hundred years.

When Walton revised the *Life* for the edition of 1658, he added, after "A Hymne to God the Father," two moving paragraphs in which his purpose is clearly to object to the suppression of Church music during the Commonwealth.[184] He begins by saying, "I have the rather mentioned this *Hymne*, for that he caus'd it to be set to a most grave and solemn tune, and to be often sung to the *Organ* by the *Choristers* of that *Church* ['St *Pauls Church*,' 1670 ed.], in his own hearing," and he quotes, in a small feigned oration, Donne's words on the power of Church music.[185] At this point in the revision, he adds, too, a long passage about George Herbert and his poetry to show that there was a "Sympathy of inclinations" between Donne and Herbert (p. 82), and he quotes at some length from the poems they exchanged. Just before his original statement that Donne wrote "Hymne to God my God, in my sicknesse" on his deathbed, he adds, "that besides these verses to his dear Mr. *Herbert*, and that *Hymne* that I mentioned to be sung in the *Quire* of S.

---

[183]I. A. Shapiro, "Walton and the Occasion of Donne's *Devotions*," pp. 21-22.

[184]See *The Making of Walton's* Lives, pp. 94-95.

[185]Izaak Walton, *The Life of John Donne . . . The second impression* (London, 1658), pp. 77-79.

Pauls Church; he did also shorten and beguile many sad hours by composing other sacred Ditties," and he appends to the title of the deathbed poem the date "March 23. 1630 [31]" (p. 85). The additions add to the original misinformation. His dating "Hymne to God my God, in my sicknesse" eight days before Donne's death is factitious; it is one of a number of dates which Walton invented or tampered with to provide evidence for a point of view he would enhance.[186] His phrase "other sacred Ditties" reinforces the impression that Donne continued to write much religious poetry to the very end.[187] In 1640, he had been content to say that Donne had written hymns; his story in 1658 that Donne had "A Hymne to God the Father" set to music and that it was often sung to the organ by the choristers of St. Paul's may be true, but it probably exaggerates the degree of Donne's interest in and general concern for music.[188]

---

[186]See my discussion in *The Making of Walton's* Lives, pp. 99-102; see, too, pp. 29-30, 43-47, 56.

[187]Walton may have been misled by more than an easy and natural assumption that Donne must have written the Holy Sonnets after he took orders. We do not know when he got possession of the poems and correspondence which he printed as part of and as an appendix to the *Life of Herbert* in 1670. He prints in the *Life of Herbert* (*Lives*, 1670, pp. 17-18) a letter of Donne's to Magdalen Herbert, dated "Micham, July 11. 1607," in which Donne writes that he encloses "Holy Hymns *and* Sonnets"; prints, too, Donne's sonnet, here entitled "To the Lady *Magdalen Herbert*, of St. *Mary Magdalen*," in which Donne asks Mrs. Herbert to "*Harbour these* Hymns, *to his* [Christ's] dear name addrest"; and then he says, "These *Hymns* are now lost to us; but, doubtless they were such, as they two now sing in *Heaven*." (The date of the letter is wrong; see Chapter 4.) Donne's sonnet to Mrs. Herbert has survived only because Walton printed it; no manuscript version exists. Because Walton had a poem of Donne's which was otherwise "lost" and because he did not identify the hymns it refers to with *La Corona*, as modern editors have, he had some reason—if he had certain manuscripts of Donne's and Herbert's in his hands as early as 1640—to think that Donne had written more divine poetry than was known and that some of it had disappeared.

[188]Brian Morris thinks, rightly, that John Hilton Jr.'s setting of "A Hymne to God the Father" in Egerton MS. 2013 (British Library) is probably not the one to which Walton refers ("Not, Siren-like, to tempt: Donne and the Composers" in *John Donne: Essays in Celebration*, ed. A. J. Smith [London, 1972], p. 238). Hilton, who was born about 1599, took the degree of Mus. B. at Cambridge in 1626; he called his first book, *Ayres, or Fa La's for Three Voyces*, published in 1627, "these unripe First-fruits of my Labours"; in 1628,

"A Hymne to God the Father" was first printed with Donne's *Poems* of 1633, as the last poem in the collection. "Hymne to God my God, in my sicknesse" was first printed in the second edition (1635) of the *Poems*, and it was inserted just before "A Hymne to God the Father," which remains the last of the poems. I have shown elsewhere that Walton was largely responsible for the reordering of Donne's poems in 1635.[189] In 1635, then, when he was very much concerned to indicate a progression in Donne's verse from profane to sacred, when the details of Donne's deathbed would have been relatively fresh in his mind, his placement of the hymns seems to imply an order contrary to the one he announced so firmly in 1640. But, on the basis of external evidence, it is not possible to refute Walton's dating of "A Hymne to God the Father"; all editors follow him in attributing the poem to the time of Donne's *Devotions*. The evidence of the manuscripts merely reveals that the poem circulated widely.[190] There is, however, other extrinsic evidence for the dating of "Hymne to God my God, in my sicknesse," and that evidence contradicts Walton's deathbed date. The poem is

---

he was made parish clerk and organist at St. Margaret's, Westminster. Though he wrote some Church music, most of his music is secular (G. E. P. Arkwright, "Hilton, John [ii]," *Grove's Dictionary of Music and Musicians*, 5th ed. [1954]).

Morris's article (pp. 219–58) shows how little evidence points to Donne's interest in music. He finds surprisingly few references to music in the poems themselves (p. 221), and concludes that Donne "was not interested in music either as listener or as performer, that he thought of it (when he did) primarily in scientific, cosmological terms, and that it moved his imagination only in the most obvious ways" (p. 223). He shrewdly says, "It is a central quality of Donne's verse that it senses and exploits the unpredictability of human speech. Only with the advent of opera does it become possible for music to treat words rhetorically and freely, and this is what the *Songs and Sonnets* require. Rhythmically, Donne was half a century ahead of the musicians" (p. 236). Morris's suggestion that "Donne never conceived his poems in musical terms, and never delivered them as material for a marriage of the arts" needs, however, to be qualified by Donne's efforts in "A Hymne to Christ," "The Lamentations of Jeremy," and "A Hymne to God the Father."

[189]*The Making of Walton's* Lives, pp. 31–48, 101–2.

[190]Its absence in the Group I manuscripts is good presumptive evidence that it was written after Donne took orders. It is present in four manuscripts of Group II, in four of Group III, and in several miscellanies. Wherever in the manuscripts it has a title, the title indicates that the hymn is addressed to

present in Add. MS. 34324 (British Library), described by Gardner as "a collection of letters, minutes, and poems, collected and indexed" by Sir Julius Caesar, Master of the Rolls from 1614.[191] Caesar wrote on the back of the sheet which contains the hymn, "D. Dun Dene of Pauls / his verses in his greate / sicknes. / in Deceb. 1623." Gardner has shown, convincingly, that Caesar received the hymn in December 1623, that its title must derive from Donne's writing the occasion of the poem above it, and that Donne did not want it to circulate because he had written it in expectation of his death and his recovery had invalidated the occasion.[192] Her argument is persuasive even without evidence that Caesar and Donne were personally acquainted; it has been strengthened by R. C. Bald's finding that they were probably on friendly terms from at least 1621.[193] On the basis of external evidence, then, Walton's deathbed date for "Hymne to God my God, in my sicknesse" must give way to Caesar's date of December 1623, though there is nothing to contradict his dating "A Hymne to God the Father" at the time of the illness that gave rise to the *Devotions*. Internal evidence, I shall show, supports the case for dating "Hymne to God my God, in my sicknesse" in December 1623, and weakens the case for dating "A Hymne to God the Father" at about the same time.

"Hymne to God my God, in my sicknesse"

The "Hymne to God my God, in my sicknesse" is a remarkable poem, in which Donne reveals his idiosyncratic wit and

---

Christ. The printed title seems to have been chosen, wisely, by the editor of the 1633 edition. See *Divine Poems*, pp. 109-10.

[191]Ibid., p. 133. It appears in only one manuscript collection of Donne's poems, Stowe 961, which belongs to Group III. Gardner says, p. 107, "Spelling and punctuation do not suggest any direct contact between the two manuscript versions, or between either of them and *1635*"; the editor of *1635*, then, had access to still another manuscript. Shawcross says that the first stanza of the poem and the last two appear in Rawlinson Poet. MS. 142 (Bodleian) under the title "A Hyme in sicknes" (*Complete Poetry*, p. 491).

[192]*Divine Poems*, pp. 134-35.

[193]Bald, pp. 373, 454.

depth of passion even as he syncretizes hymn, sermon, and prayer. Louis Martz thinks that "the metaphysical style and the meditative method have here combined to assist Donne in the creation of one of his greatest poems." For him the poem clearly reveals in miniature all the essential components of a full religious meditation; he finds in it a formal preparation, the evocation in the imagination of a scene which provides a concrete setting for meditative activity, analytical reasoning, and a prayer in conversation with God. The whole becomes "a testimony of faith presented as a hymn of gratitude to the Creator."[194] Clay Hunt says that the poem is "by far Donne's most distinguished achievement in religious poetry."[195] He believes that Donne conceived it as a deathbed poem, that he seems to have laid aside the conscious self-dramatization of his other poems in order to write for himself. Donne, he says, cast "the poem in the form of a hortatory and analytical sermon addressed to his own soul": he "blocked it out as a step-by-step intellectual progression to a logical conclusion" to produce an argument which provides intellectual justification for his acceptance of the justness of God's ways (p. 97). Hunt's long essay analyzes Donne's structure and his ideas brilliantly as he makes clear Donne's wonderful exploitation of the theme that "death doth touch the Resurrection" in the extensive geographical conceit of stanzas 2-4 and in the scriptural analogies of the last two stanzas which provide theological justification for it. He says, in summary:

> This "Hymn" seems to me a magisterial performance, one of the few great religious poems in English. It is certainly Donne's richest and most finished work. And it has a quality which one rarely finds in Donne's verse: the quality of magniloquence, of that "impassioned majesty" which DeQuincey spoke of. DeQuincey found that effect throughout in Donne's work, but I think it is unusual in his poetry. The quality appears briefly in many pas-

[194]Louis Martz, "Donne: Hymne to God my God, in my sicknesse" in *Master Poems of the English Language*, ed. Oscar Williams (New York, 1966), pp. 137-40.

[195]Clay Hunt, *Donne's Poetry: Essays in Literary Analysis* (New Haven, 1954), p. 96. Chapter 4 considers the poem in great detail.

sages, but Donne does not often sustain the effect for long; something lively breaks in, and he shies off from the settled gravity which attends the Sublime. But as one follows the solemn procession of this poem, the sure and stately deployment of its firm patterns of thought and feeling behind its grave arabesques of wit, one meets a fullness of utterance and a sustained poise of mind which seldom appear in Donne's other verse. He touched on this effect in "A Hymn to God the Father," but for all its ritualistic dignity, that poem manifests little of the scope, the organizing power, and the richness which are the qualities of the imagination that is at work in this "Hymn." This poem seems to reflect a wholeness of mind and an entire commitment of the personality to poetic utterance which Donne had not attained before. [P. 115]

Hunt identifies what is extraordinary in this poem. His examination of a number of Donne's poems had shown that Donne customarily cast his materials into the intellectual structure of a debate or the actual dramatic situation of a debate. Here, he says, though the hymn has an inner argument which is essentially a debate between the worldly claims of his suffering body and the otherworldly appetites of his mind and soul, the debate has just about been won by the soul before the poem starts. What Hunt rightly emphasizes here, what he means by "wholeness of mind" and "entire commitment of the personality to poetic utterance" is that the hymn differs from the rest of Donne's poems (except for the *Second Anniversary*) in "the grave peace and quiet joy" which inform it, in the settled conviction of its point of view (p. 117). In this poem that "burden of consciousness" which Arnold Stein has called a hallmark of Donne's verse has been largely assimilated and transcended. The note of struggle, the pushes and pulls of mind that are characteristic even of the Holy Sonnets, have given way to an attitude which is more entirely unilateral. I suppose that is why we are disposed to think of the poem as mainly a hymn rather than as methodical meditation or sermon. Hunt suggests that the poem may reveal Donne's belief, in the circumstances of his illness, that "he will at last be quit of a World in which he had never felt fully at home," which he had renounced before and which, before, he had tried to persuade himself, unsuccessfully, was well lost (p. 117). Although he feels that the *Devotions*, written at the same time, "hardly show Donne with his face set boldly and calmly toward his West," he says that "the achievement of final fullness of voice in this deathbed poem can have come only from Donne's belief that he would soon find in death emotional completion by experiencing an ultimate release from all those inner and outer tensions which had beset his mind through life and had throttled the voice of his verse" (pp. 115-16). Hunt may be right; the hymn seems to reflect a particular time during Donne's illness when an uncommon singleness of attitude dominated his thought. But Donne more typically showed the wholeness of his mind by allowing us to see all the parts which made up the whole, and the inner and outer tensions of mind which he laid open in his verse did not throttle the voice of the verse; indeed, the shifts, alternatives, and disparities created the uniquely discordant harmony of his voice. In the past, too, he had made an entire commitment of his personality in all its complexity to poetic utterance; in the hymn, some parts of that personality are suppressed.

In the "Hymne to God my God, in my sicknesse" Donne seems supremely aware that he is making a special kind of divine verse. Its first stanza is linked in idea with the last lines of his poem, "Upon the translation of the Psalmes by Sir Philip Sydney, and the Countesse of Pembroke his Sister":

> And, till we come th'Extemporall song to sing,
> . . . may
> These their sweet learned labours, all the way
> Be as our tuning, that, when hence we part
> We may fall in with them, and sing our part.

Donne sees the Sidnean psalms as proper preparatives which attune man to God, which bring man on earth into harmony with God so that he can eventually take his part in the heavenly choir. So, too, at the beginning of the hymn, Donne envisions heaven as a place where, with God's "Quire of Saints," he will be made God's music for all eternity, and, in anticipation of being part of the music of heaven, he says, "As I come / I tune the Instrument here at the dore, / And what I must doe then, thinke now before." His main meaning is that he must tune his soul, get it into harmony with God, but, as Hunt says, the words refer, too, "to the writing of the poem itself, to Donne's act of composing his mind, here at the door of death, so that the instrument of his soul may resonate harmoniously with a hymn to God about his humble acceptance of death and his joyous hope of resurrection into eternal life" (p. 98). On this occasion, Donne does not see fit to attune his mind to God by rereading the Sidnean psalms, or by writing his own translation of the Psalms, but by writing a psalm of his own.

Donne ends his hymn with the lines:

> And as to others soules I preach'd thy word,
>> Be this my Text, my Sermon to mine owne,
>> Therfore that he may raise the Lord throws down.

Commentators on the lines have seen their general dependence on Paul's words in 1 Corinthians 9:27, "But I keep under my body, and bring it into subjection: lest that by any means, when I have preached to others, I myself should be a castaway," for Donne refers to this passage in Expostulation 3 of the *Devotions*: "But thine *Apostles* feare takes hold of mee, *that when I have preached to others, I my selfe should be a cast-[a]way*; and therefore am I *cast downe*, that I might not be *cast away*." Although Paul's words underlie the text on which Donne has preached in the poem, it is a strange procedure in a sermon to withhold the precise words of the text and, moreover, to withhold the text until the very end. If Paul's sentiment gives rise to the text of Donne's sermon, it is also, in its context in the poem, the evidence which validates the thrust of his thought. As Hunt says, "Donne caps the argument with a text from the Bible, which he quotes as a clincher in the final line of the poem" (p. 106). The last line summarizes, in a memorable paradox, the central idea of the poem: Donne, thrown down by illness, lying flat on his sickbed, says once again that "death doth touch the Resurrection," that God throws man down (makes him die) in order that He may raise him (so that He can grant man eternal life).

Although Hunt says that Donne cites "a biblical text" as "a final and unimpeachable argument-from-authority" for his conclusions, he is aware that Donne's last line, "Therfore that he may raise the Lord throws down" is not precisely biblical. Donne's text, he thinks, is based on Psalm 146:8 — "the Lord raiseth them that are bowed down" (AV).[196] He would account

---

[196]Gardner says (*Divine Poems*, p. 109), "The text of Donne's sermon to his own soul is not apparently Scriptural." She finds the "nearest" text to be the words of Eliphaz in Job 22:29: "When men are cast down, then thou shalt say, There is lifting up; and he shall save the humble person." A. B. Grosart says that Donne's text may be founded on Psalm 146:8, and on Psalm 145:14 — "The Lord upholdeth all that fall, and raiseth up all those that be bowed down" (*The Complete Poems of John Donne*, Fuller Worthies' Library [1873], II, 341). He thinks, however, that Donne's text is a reversal of Jonah 1:12: "Take me up, and cast me forth into the sea"; he cites line 22 of George Herbert's "The Crosse," "Taking me up to throw me down," and says that one can trace a reference to Jonah throughout Donne's stanzas.

Hunt's statement that Donne's line is "evidently based" on Psalm 146:8 probably comes close to Donne's source, but the other suggestions show that though Donne's sentiment is common enough, his way of expressing it is his own. Another passage similar to Donne's sentiment appears in Bosola's last words in *The Duchess of Malfi*, v.ii.348-49: "O Penitence, let me truly taste thy cup, / That throws men down, only to raise them up." Webster's borrowings from Donne's *Ignatius his Conclave* (1611) and from the *Anniversaries* (1611 and 1612) have been adduced as part of the evidence that he wrote his play in 1613. But when *The Duchess of Malfi* was first printed in 1623, its title page read that "diverse things" were printed "that the length of the Play would not beare in the Presentment," and it is not impossible that Donne read the play after it was printed, though he was not allowed to read after the onset of his sickness. The play was printed by Nicholas Okes, who had been the printer of the English translation of *Ignatius his Conclave* in 1611; it was printed for John Waterson, whose shop was in the churchyard of St. Paul's. It is possible that it was printed after Donne wrote "Hymne to God my God, in my sicknesse," but it is unlikely that Webster had access to a manuscript. Although John Russell Brown thinks that Webster oversaw some of the printing of the play (*The Duchess of Malfi*, The Revels Plays [Cambridge, Mass., 1964], pp. lxiv-v), he says there is no proof that he added to his text of 1613 (p. xxvii). He suggests, moreover, that Bosola's lines were possibly influenced by Sir William Alexander's *Croesus* (1604), v.i.2774-76: "Though I have tasted of afflictions cup, / Yet it may be, the gods for a good cause / Have

for Donne's modification of the structure of the line by stating that he wished "to make it more nearly parallel with the central argument of the poem and to give his final line the punch effect of paradox" (p. 111), and he would account for the discrepancy between the wording of the text in the poem and in the Authorized Version ("throws down" instead of "bowed down") by stating that Donne habitually translates from the Vulgate, which here reads, "Dominus erigit elisos"—the Lord raises those who have been struck down (p. 247). But this minimizes the radical differences between the biblical sentence and Donne's. Verse 8 of Psalm 146, like the verses before and after it, emphasizes God's aid and comfort to those in adversity. The use of the passive in the *elisos* of the Vulgate, of the near-reflexive "bowed down" in the Authorized Version, of the adjectival "croked" of the Geneva Bible make diffuse and almost put out of mind God's active role in the creation of adversity. The Geneva translation recognizes God's infliction of adversity, but relegates that to the marginal note in which it offers an explanation of it: "Thogh he visit them by affliction, hungre, imprisonment and suche like, yet his Fatherlie love and pitie never faileth them, yea, rather to his these are signes of his love." Donne's "the Lord throws down" bluntly vivifies the nature of God's activity implied in the "visit" of Geneva. Donne's line differs from the Bible, too, in that the "bowed down" of the Bible refers to the oppressed, the hungry, the imprisoned, the blind, to their affliction, not to their death, and the Bible's "raiseth them" has to do with the ameliorization of adversity, not with resurrection. Perhaps Donne had Psalm 146:8 in the back of his mind, but the changes he has wrought on it are so peculiarly his own that his text is more invention than quotation or interpretation. Nor is the text one which appears only in this hymn. He had used a variation of it long before in the Holy Sonnet "Batter my heart": "That I may rise, and stand, o'erthrow mee,'and

cast me downe to raise a thousand up" (p. 158). Webster seems to have used other passages from this play and from others of Alexander's tragedies (see p. 214).

bend / Your force, to breake, blowe, burn and make me new."
He used it again in a sermon on Acts 9:4 ("And he fell to
earth"), preached on January 30, 1625, little more than a year
after he wrote the hymn. Paul's falling to earth, he says, "is not
a figurative falling, not into a decay of estate, nor decay of
health, nor a spirituall falling into sin, a decay of grace; but it is
a medicinall falling, a falling under Gods hand, but such a falling under his hand, as that he takes not off his hand from him
that is falne, but throwes him downe therefore that he may
raise him." He says shortly after this that "onely the Lord
knowes how to wound us, out of love; more then all that, to
wound us into love," and in imagery reminiscent of that of the
hymn, he continues, "Therefore he brings us to death, that by
that gate he might lead us into life everlasting; And he hath not
discovered, but made that Northern passage, to passe by the
frozen Sea of calamity, and tribulation, to Paradise, to the
heavenly Jerusalem."[197]

The text of Donne's sermon to his own soul, "Therfore that
he may raise the Lord throws down," differs, then, from Psalm
146:8 in its emphasis on God's active part in throwing man
down and in his broadening its meaning from adversity and
comfort to death and resurrection. It differs also in its form; it
is not a simple declaration but it stresses purposiveness and cau-
sality. "My Text," Donne says; "my Sermon to mine owne" — his
text is essentially as much of his own making as are the texts he
created in "Stationes." Just before his announcement of his
text, Donne refers to Christ's passion, and his identification of
his own situation in the hymn with that of Jesus reminds us of
his use of the Stations of the Cross as the pattern on which he
had based the "Stationes." In both the "Stationes" and the
hymn Donne speaks, of course, of his fever and of his physicians, but there is a still closer link between the two. The hymn
contains at line 10 the Latin phrase, "*Per fretum febris*"; it is, I
think, the only Latin phrase of his own which Donne introduced into an English poem. Hunt says, shrewdly, that it is

[197]*Sermons*, VI, 212. Hunt cites the first of these passages, p. 247.

"probably the germ from which he developed the complex geo-graphical conceit" in stanzas 2-4 (p. 101). It is more than the germ of the conceit; it is the emblematic text, the equivalent of the Vulgate, on which Donne preaches in the poem. It is, in-deed, the text which is interpreted one way by his physicians and another by him: the physicians take it to mean that he will die of the raging heat of his fever, that the fever is the path to death; for Donne himself, death is the narrows to be traversed in order to reach resurrection. The Latin phrase of his own in-vention serves as his scriptural text even as the like phrases of "Stationes" had served the same function for the *Devotions*. It is first expounded, in stanzas 2-4, in the geographical terms of the Book of Creatures, the technique Donne used in the Medi-tations; then, in stanzas 5-6, where Donne compares his condi-tion with that of the first and last Adam, it is opened up by an examination of Scripture, in the way Donne proceeded in the Expostulations; and the last lines of the hymn are, like the third section of each of the *Devotions*, a prayer which announces the justness of God's ways. These several resemblances in method increase the likelihood that Donne wrote the hymn at the time he wrote "Stationes" and the *Devotions*. The hymn's fusion of disparate approaches and multivalent levels into a concise, complexly unified whole shows that Donne was still entirely ca-pable of achieving in verse what he did in the prose of the *Devo-tions*. If anything, the hymn is the greater achievement. It is the best evidence that, as late as the end of 1623, Donne's poetic powers had suffered no diminution.

In discussing the "Hymne to God my God, in my sicknesse," I have, for the sake of convenience, called it a hymn. It is a hymn, however, only in the sense that it is a divine poem in praise of God. It is a hymn in the sense that Donne seems to have called the sonnets of *La Corona* hymns, in the sense that we might call "Goodfriday, 1613. Riding Westward" a hymn.[198]

[198]The mark of a good hymn is that it renders praise memorably and freshly. Still, a hymn is a public poem, and its sentiments and expression may not be eccentric or idiosyncratic; its "I" must be applicable to the many "I's" who sing or chant it. It is precisely those individualistic qualities of Donne

Hunt has written admirably about the "music" of the poem (pp. 112–15). Although he is inclined to find fault with the musical quality of Donne's poetry, to think that he is far more interested in aspects of poetry other than sound, he is appreciative of Donne's performance here. For all his use of the terminology of music, Hunt does not consider the poem as a script for music; rightly, he listens, as readers of poetry usually do, to the sound and rhythm of words, phrases, and periods as a means of ordering and communicating meaning and feeling. Almost certainly, Donne did not intend the poem to be sung or to be adapted to song. He cast it, to be sure, into five-line pentameter stanzas, rhyming *ababb*, but a composer would have problems with the music from the very first line, with its three consecutive short syllables, and with the adjustment of his rendition of that line to the first lines of the following stanzas. And what would he have done with such metrically radical lines as the fourth, eighth, and eighteenth? Line 18 is full of bewitching *verbal* music, but Donne uses less consonance, assonance, and verbal repetition in this poem than in the other hymns and in "The Lamentations." Moreover, the long periods with which this poem begins contrast strikingly with the short periods (frequently limited to two lines) which Donne uses when he anticipates the possibility that a poem may be sung.

"A Hymne to God the Father"

"A Hymne to God the Father" is the most conventionally hymnlike of the three hymns. Except for the singularity of Donne's stance, it is as simple and regular a poem as Donne

---

which make "Hymne to God my God, in my sicknesse" a fine poem, one which is unmistakably Donne's, that undermine its ability to function as a conventional hymn. When Walton quoted only the first seven and a half and the last five lines of the poem, he was guided, I suppose, both by his desire to use the poem as efficient evidence of Donne's devoutness and by his dislike for conceited verse. But when the copyist of Rawlinson Poet. MS. 142 omitted stanzas 2–4, he probably thought to make a "better" hymn of the poem, and that may have been Emerson's purpose, too, in omitting the stanzas (though he printed all of "The Exstasie") when he printed the poem in an anthology of his favorite verse, *Parnassus* (Boston, 1874), p. 186.

ever wrote. In only a few other poems does he adjust the pattern of his first stanza so neatly to those that follow. The firmness of his rhyme is reinforced by the repetition of the *a* and *b* rhymes of the first stanza in the others. The last two lines of the first stanza are repeated in the second and modified in the third. The regular, thudding rhythm is only made more weighty by the numerous spondees, and even the effects of the odd placement of a caesura in the second line of stanza 3 and two of them in line 5 of that stanza are absorbed in the spondees which surround them. Only twice in the poem does Donne substitute a beginning trochee for the regular iamb. Donne not only repeats his rhymes from stanza to stanza, but he uses his *a* rhyme internally in the repetition of "done" in the fifth line of each stanza, and the last lines of his first two stanzas begin and end with his *b* rhyme. Even as the word "love" had resounded through all of "A Hymne to Christ," so, here, the word "sinne" appears seven times. Though it disappears after the first line of the last stanza, it is echoed and intensified, both in sound and in concept, by the "Sunne" which takes its place, and the *s*'s which sing through the first two stanzas are sounded once again in the last stanza and supported and enriched by several *sh* sounds. Four of the lines start with the words "Wilt thou forgive," serving both to simplify the structure of the thought of the poem and to emphasize its almost ritualistic music. The subtle modulations of pace and sound that characterize Donne's more complex poems are gone entirely; here, even so consciously consonantal a line as "And doe them still: though still I doe deplore" can be exceeded by the next: "When thou hast done, thou hast not done." Donne's music is loud and broad and simple, and so is his diction. Of the 144 words in the hymn, only 12 are not monosyllabic; of these 11 have two syllables ("forgive" is used four times), and even the only trisyllabic word, "heretofore," is merely a joining of three common monosyllabic words. Donne's metaphoric language is so scant and conventional that we are hardly aware of it. Gone, too, is the stupefying complexity of some of his typically long rhetorical periods; here, his units of meaning are regularly contained in two lines.

The concepts are put simply and memorably. The poem gets

its structure from an enumeration of generalized sins. In the first stanza, Donne mentions his participation in original sin and his constant repetition of sins which he constantly deplores, and the poem gets its onward progress from his announcement that he has more. The second stanza differs from the first only in the sins which it enumerates: the sin by which he has won others to sin and that which he shunned for a year or two but indulged in for twenty. The enumeration has taken place in the context of a colloquy with God; the third stanza continues the enumeration by its admission of a fifth sin — Donne confesses to the sin of fear, fear that when he dies, God will forsake him. As in a methodical meditation, though this poem is void of meditative elements except for the implication that the last sin stems from the others, the colloquy with God turns into a prayer. The poem gets its power from the desperation and extremity of Donne's demand; so intensely does he feel his sinfulness that he invokes God's promise of mercy by demanding that he swear it by the greatest of all oaths, by Himself. It gets its power, too, from the change in attitude in the last stanza. To this point, Donne's attitude is a cavalier one; to this point, he has been playing a kind of game with God. There has been an element of teasing, of taunting, in his stance: he has, as it were, been challenging God to forgive his sins; there is something almost irreverent in his throwing down the dare to God, something irreverent, too, in his smart dismissal of God's prowess in forgiveness with the casual, throwaway punning of "When thou hast done, thou hast not done." Donne's leading God on, testing him, step by step, move after move, only to shake off as insufficient what God has promised, only to belittle it with a bit of wit, contrasts remarkably with the end of the poem. The content of the poem, with its focus on the magnitude of Donne's sinfulness and, correlatively, on the extraordinary exertion God must make to purge him, is not unlike that of many of the Holy Sonnets. But the hymn lacks the passionate urgency of feeling and the intricate dialectic of many of the other penitential poems. The demands of the hymn as a vehicle for public expression, the premium it placed on commonality of idea and regularity and simplicity of articulation, made Donne prune the fancy of his ideas and control the range of his technique. But he wrote a hymn which is still recognizable as a spectacular performance by a particular man. Donne might, in a hymn, hold back some of the marks which set him apart from other men and other poets, but he could put his signature even here. This hymn, whatever else it says, still says "Thou hast Donne."

"A Hymne to God the Father" differs so radically from "Hymne to God my God, in my sicknesse" in technique and idea that it is hard to believe that they may have been written at about the same time. The links in technique between the "Hymne to God my God, in my sicknesse" and the "Stationes" and *Devotions* are many, and the doctrines about sickness, death, and resurrection are harmonious. "A Hymne to God the Father" is preoccupied with sin, even as the *Devotions* is, but there is a vast distance between the almost boastful catalog of sins which Donne ticks off in the hymn, intended to tax God's patience and test his capacity for forgiveness, and Donne's immersion in sin in the *Devotions*, the specificity there of his account of his sinning, the subtlety of his exploration of the multifarious aspects of sin.

Donne implies as early as Expostulation 1 that "the fever of lust, of envy, of ambition" is in him, and he specifies these sins again in Expostulation 11, after he has added (in Expostulation 9) "the *spirit of error*" and "*the spirit of giddines*" to "*the spirit of lust*." But the particularity of his account goes far beyond this, to include even, as he addresses God in Prayer 15, his sins as priest:

> I have sinned *behind thy backe* (if that can be done) by wilfull absteining from thy *Congregations*, and omitting thy *service*, and I have sinned *before thy face*, in my *hypocrisies* in Prayer, in my *ostentation*, and the mingling a respect of *my selfe* in preaching thy Word; I have sinned in my *fasting* by repining, when a penurious fortune hath kept mee low; And I have sinned even in that fulnesse, when I have been at thy table, by a negligent examination, by a wilfull prevarication, in receiving that heavenly *food* and *Physicke*.

The sins of his youth, he says in Prayer 10, were so many that he may not live hours enough to name them all, for he did them then faster than he can name them to God now. He does proceed to the naming "of Sinnes, of *Thought, Word,* and *Deed*, of sinns of *Omission*, and of *Action*, of sins against thee, against my *neighbour*, and against *my self*, of sinns *unrepented*, and sinnes *relapsed* into after *Repentance*, of sinnes of *Ignorance*, and sinnes against the testimonie of my *Conscience*, of sinnes against thy *Commaundements*, sinnes against thy *Sonnes Prayer*, and sinns against our owne *Creed*, of sins against the laws of that *Church*, & sinnes against the lawes of that *State*, in which thou hast given mee my station," only to say that his list is not complete. Not only is he aware that "our *fathers* have imprinted the *seed*, infused a *spring* of *sinne* in us" (Expostulation 22), but he recognizes that man has made sin immortal; it must, then, have a soul, and that soul is subject to transmigration: "when one *sinne* hath beene *dead* in mee, that *soule* hath passed into another *sinne*" (Expostulation 23). Sin, he says, "is the *root*, and the *fuell* of all *sicknesse* (Expostulation 22), and, over and over again he says, "I have sinned and sinned, and multiplied *sinne* to *sinne*, after all these thy assistances against *sinne*" (Prayer 20). But man is not content that he is powerful enough and cunning enough to demolish and undermine himself: "when wee our selves have no pleasure in the *sinne*, we *sinne* for others sakes," as Adam for Eve's sake, Solomon to gratify his wives, the Judges for Jezabel, Joab to obey David, and Pilate and Herod to humor the populace (Expostulation 22). So perverse is man that when his body is unable to sin, "his *sinfull memory* sinnes over his old sinnes againe," and what God would have him remember for compunction, he remembers with delight (Expostulation 21). Like the serpent and because of the serpent, he sins in secret so that others may not see him; but Satan's masterpiece is "to make us sin in secret so, as that we may not see our selvs sin" (Expostulation 10). Donne's net is fine enough to catch the ubiquity of sin, the slipperiness of sin, the sin which he can't recognize as sin; still, God's mercy is answerable to sin in all its forms. But God pardons no sin so immutably that a sinner can sin no more. He offers a reprieve, a *"present mercie,"* but it is not "an *antidote* against all *poisons"* (Prayer 22). Donne views with special horror the pardoned sinner who relapses: "My returning to any sinne, if I should returne to the abilitie of sinning over all my sins againe," he says in Prayer 4, "thou wouldest not pardon." A relapse is odious to God "because hee that hath *sinned,* and then *repented,* hath *weighed God* and the *Devill* in a *ballance;* he hath *heard God* and the *Devill plead;* and after *hearing,* given *Judgement* on that *side,* to which he *adheres,* by his *subsequent practice;* if he returne to his *sinne,* hee *decrees* for *Satan;* he prefers *sinne* before *grace,* and *Satan* before *God;* and in *contempt* of *God,* declares the *precedency* for his *adversary:* And a contempt wounds deeper than an injury; a *relapse* deeper, than a *blasphemy"* (Expostulation 23). Donne's anatomy of sin, his probings into the body and soul of sin, support his declaration to God, "Thou, O Lord, hast given mee *Wormewood,* and I have had some diffidence upon that," but, he continues, "thou hast cleared a *Morning* to mee againe, and my heart is alive" (Expostulation 11). He admits, "My heart hath strucke mee, when I come to number my sinnes," but if his heart is not single and docile, not perfect and clean, not a joyful heart, it is at least a *"melting"* heart, broken and contrite, not a faint one, and, hard as he is struck when he considers the number of his sins, he yet declares his trust in God: "that blowe is not to death, because those sinnes are not to death, but my heart lives in thee." Obviously, the design of the *Devotions,* their repetitive form and their number, gave Donne room to expatiate on sin, but his treatment of sin in "A Hymne to God the Father" is so radically simplistic that it is difficult to conceive that such differences in approach might arise from the same circumstances, regardless of the opportunities and demands made by genres so different.

In "A Hymne to God the Father" the last sin which Donne mentions is the "sinne of feare," and he limits himself to one aspect of it, his fear that when he dies a great darkness will fall upon him, that God will not be infinitely merciful and shed eternal light on him. Here Donne particularizes the sin of fear into the sin of despair, of lack of faith. In Prayer 14 of the *Devotions*, he comes close to admitting his vulnerability to this sin, but he does so in a concessive clause addressed to God — "though thou have suffered some *dimnesse*, some clouds of *sadnesse* & disconsolateness to shed themselves upon my *soule*" — and, he then declares, "I humbly blesse and thankfully glorifie thy holy name, that thou hast afforded mee the *light* of thy *spirit*, against which the *prince of darkenesse* cannot prevaile, nor hinder his illumination of our darkest nights, of our saddest thoughts." He prays that he may never fall into utter darkness, and, if he should, that God will disperse it. In the *Devotions*, Donne does not hide his fear that his sinfulness and unworthiness are such that he feels the inroads of despair, "accesses of *desperation*," but even in the last Expostulation, which centers entirely on his fear of relapsing into sin, he holds that God's mercy, like His majesty, is infinite, and he says, "thou who hast commanded me *to pardon my brother seventy seven times*, hast limited thy selfe to no *Number*."

In the *Devotions*, moreover, Donne spends the whole of the Sixth in an examination of his fear. He fears the increase of his disease, and his fear reflects, he thinks, his natural weakness as man. He does not fear death, for he gets his strength from God. His fear does not prevent him from receiving from God, from men, from himself "*spirituall*, and *civill*, and *morall* assistances, and consolations," nor is there any indication that he considers fear itself a sin. He admits that he fears God; his position here is the one he takes in the Holy Sonnet, "Oh, to vex me": he quakes "with true feare of his rod," and he feels "Those are my best dayes, when I shake with fear," for fear of God and love of God are inseparable and they are commingled in the wise man. Fear of the Lord is a benefit, and man is to be directed, not dejected, by it. Donne asks that he may not be ashamed of his fears, for Christ himself showed fear in leaving this life, and he asks to feel them in order to put an end to them as Christ did — by submitting all to God's will. In the *Devotions*, then, Donne expresses his fears, his fear of sickness, his fear of God, but he does not consider his fear a sin. We may catch "accesses of *desperation*" beneath the surface of the *Devotions*, but Donne enunciates his faith confidently and expresses strongly his belief in God's infinite mercy.

Even as Donne's consideration of sin and his attitude toward it differ greatly in "A Hymne to God the Father" and in the *Devotions*, so the hymn's "I have a sinne of feare, that when I'have spunne / My last thred, I shall perish on the shore" is much closer to the lines of the first Holy Sonnet, "Oh I shall soone despaire, when I doe see / That thou lov'st mankind well, yet wilt not chuse me," than to the sentiments of the *Devotions*. These differences, and the differences in kind between "A Hymne to God the Father" and "Hymne to God my God, in my sicknesse," do not, of course, constitute proof, perhaps ought not even be considered evidence, that "A Hymne to God the Father" was not written during Donne's illness or convalescence in late 1623 or early 1624. For one thing, we do not expect consistency of mood, uniformity of attitude, immutability of ideas in a lyric poet or in occasional poetry, particularly in a poet of Donne's volatile temperament, with his delight in ingenuity of argument and his mastery of dialectic and paradox. For another, even as we point to that similarity of concern, attitude, and technique which gives the impression of a coherent heightening by one shadow to both "Hymne to God my God, in my sicknesse" and the *Devotions*, we are aware that in the *Devotions* itself, each section moves from the expression of misery to questioning and murmuring and then to supplication and surrender. There is no reason that at a time when Donne's mind was moving hyperactively, though he was confined to one room and was deprived for the most part of the stimulus of books and of people, he could not for a few hours have felt and expressed the feelings and ideas which are in "A Hymne to God the Father." But when we consider that the only reason for the customary dating of the poem is that Walton associated its composition with the composition of the *Devotions*, and when we consider, too, the vagueness of Walton's chronology in the *Life of Donne*, his penchant for manipulating dates for their dramatic effectiveness, his invention of a speech for Donne so that he can use Donne's words as evidence for his own opinion of the high place of Church music, we may assume that Walton's date may not be precisely right even if he did not err so greatly here as in his date for "Hymne to God my God, in my sicknesse." I do not think it impossible that Donne could have written two hymns so very different in conception and technique at about the same time. I think it likelier that he wrote "A Hymne to God the Father" three or four years before he wrote "Hymne to God my God, in my sicknesse," for there seems to have been a time, just before and perhaps just after his trip to Germany in 1619, when he was interested in writing verse to be used as part of a Church service. The "Hymne to God my God, in my sicknesse" is not that kind of public poem; "A Hymne to God the Father" is. Since the Bridgewater manuscript, which aimed to be a complete collection of Donne's poems at the time it was compiled, contains "A Hymne to Christ" and "The Lamentations of Jeremy" but does not contain "A Hymne to God the Father" (or the Hamilton elegy of 1625, which also circulated widely), it is possible that this hymn was written at about the same time that Donne composed two poems with an eye toward Church performance and an ear attuned to Church music, but shortly after them, shortly after the last poems entered the Bridgewater collection.

"An hymne to the Saints, and to Marquesse Hamylton"

Donne wrote his last poem, "An hymne to the Saints, and to Marquesse Hamylton," reluctantly, and only because he could not refuse the request of his special friend, Sir Robert Ker. For many years, Ker and his fellow Scotsman, James, Lord Hay, had been Donne's chief advocates at Court, his access to royal favor. Early in James's reign, Sir Francis Bacon had introduced him to Hay, and it was Hay's services he called on in 1613 to bring himself to the attention of James's current favorite, another Sir Robert Ker, a second cousin of Donne's friend of the same name, who became Viscount Rochester in 1611 and was to become Earl of Somerset late in 1613.[199] In March 1614, it was Ker whom he asked to support his bid to Somerset for the ambassadorship at Venice, and just four days after he was ordained, he turned to Ker when he wanted to get Somerset's ear, and the King's, in order to forward his career in the Church.[200] Ker's influence in the Court dates from the beginning of James's reign, when he was made Groom of the Bedchamber in the household of Prince Henry; after Henry's death, he was made Gentleman of the Bedchamber to Prince Charles, and he also served in that capacity when Charles became king.[201] Donne knew him intimately enough in 1615 to ask him to be godfather to his daughter Margaret.[202] Before Donne left for Germany in 1619, he sent Ker copies of poems he had promised him and sent him, too, a manuscript of *Biathanatos* for safekeeping.[203] In January 1624, he turned to Ker when he wanted Prince Charles's permission to dedicate the *Devotions* to him.[204] Very shortly after he wrote his poem about Hamilton, he turned once more to Ker, for the Lord Chamberlain had asked him to preach the first sermon to the new king, a week after the death of King James, at Charles's residence, St. James's Palace, and he needed a place to collect himself before he gave his sermon. He wrote Ker, "I have no other way there, but you," and Ker offered not only his chamber, but dinner.[205] The friendship continued through all of Donne's life, and its warmth is indicated in Donne's many letters to Ker and in Ker's sole surviving letter to Donne.[206] It is indicated, too, in the bequest Donne made to Ker in his will: he left Lord Hay (by then the Earl of Carlisle) a

---

[199]Bald, pp. 100, 272-73 (and n. 1).

[200]Ibid., pp. 290 (and n. 2), 306-7; *Letters*, pp. 288-89.

[201] David Laing, ed., *Correspondence of Sir Robert Kerr, First Earl of Ancram* (Edinburgh, 1875), pp. viii, xi, hereafter cited as *Correspondence*; "Ancram" in *Complete Peerage*.

[202]Bald, pp. 315-16.

[203]*Letters*, pp. 21-22.

[204]Ibid., pp. 249-50.

[205]Bald, pp. 467-68; *Letters*, pp. 313-14, 311.

[206]About a fifth of the *Letters to Severall Persons of Honour* (1651) are addressed to Ker. Their presence in the volume shows that John Donne, Jr., who

Virgin Mary, Christ, and St. John painted by Titian, but he bequeathed to Ker a much more personal gift, a portrait of himself "made very many yeares before I was of this profession."[207] The Lothian portrait shows Donne as young romantic poet, and Donne knew that Ker appreciated his literary abilities. Ker belittled his own few attempts in verse,[208] but William Drummond of Hawthornden called him "the Muses sanctuarye" in one letter, and showed that he did not use the term idly in another: "Though I have no sute at Court to trouble you with, yet so long as Daniell lastes (who, dying as I heare, bequeathed to you his scrolls) or Done, who in his travells lefte you his, I will ever find a way of trafficking with yow by letters."[209] Ker had probably admired Donne's verse long before he was himself enshrined in Donne's eclogue-epithalamion for Somerset early in 1614. When Ker's friend, the distinguished Scottish courtier, the Marquis Hamilton died on March 2, 1625, he wanted a proper memorial in verse and he asked Donne to write it.

Donne did so promptly,[210] though the letter he sent Ker with the poem, printed with it in 1633 and in later editions, shows that he was less than enthusiastic with Ker's request:

---

edited it, was aware of his father's familiarity with Ker and was himself on good enough terms with Ker to ask for and receive the letters.

Ker's letter of October 7, 1628, to Donne is in *Correspondence*, I, 46–47.

[207]Bald, pp. 563, 567; see W. Milgate, "Dr. Donne's Art Gallery," *N&Q*, 194 (1949), 318.

[208]*Correspondence*, II, 521–22. Ker's main effort in verse was, he says, for "myne owne recreation." He was impressed when he attended Reformed services abroad to hear "in the Low Countryes the Dutch men and French sing in their severall languages to one tune," and he wished he might join in. In the early 1620s, he tried his hand at English metrical translation of the Psalms, fitted to continental tunes. Ten of his translations have survived. Ibid., pp. 488–506.

[209]Ibid., p. 519, and I, 24.

[210]Chamberlain sent a copy of the poem to Carleton on April 23, 1625 (*Letters of John Chamberlain*, II, 613). Almost certainly, Donne wrote it before James's death on March 27. I doubt that he would have written a poem honoring Hamilton in the weeks after James's death, or that he would have written one which omitted reference to the King's death. Moreover, he had important sermons to preach on April 3, 17, and 26 (*Sermons*, VI, Nos. 12–14).

SIR,

I Presume you rather trie what you can doe in me, then what I can doe in verse; you know my uttermost when it was best, and even then I did best when I had least truth for my subjects. In this present case there is so much truth as it defeats all Poetry. Call therefore this paper by what name you will, and, if it be not worthy of him, nor of you, nor of mee, smother it, and bee that the sacrifice. If you had commanded me to have waited on his body to Scotland and preached there, I would have embraced the obligation with more alacritie; But, I thank you that you would cõmand me that which I was loath to doe, for, even that hath given a tincture of merit to the obedience of

Your poore friend and
servant in Christ Jesus
I. D.[211]

Donne makes it clear that he acceded to Ker's request because it gave him the opportunity to demonstrate his regard for Ker: loath as he was to write a poem, he felt that friendship demanded compliance with the request, however uncongenial he might find it. Donne would have Ker understand that he no longer considered himself a poet, that his best days as poet — when he was given to feigning — were in the past, and that as priest and as regarder of truth he was estranged from the Muse.

The letter implies more than its apologies for the diminution of poetic capacity. Without much question, Donne would have preferred to honor Ker and Hamilton by preaching. He had never really cared to write memorial verse. His epicedes and obsequies are few in number, and all of them were written because they were expected of him by patrons or because he used them as occasions to ingratiate himself with patrons. His statement that he did best when he had least truth for his subject is probably a reference to the *Anniversaries*; he wrote a Latin epitaph, but no funeral elegy, on the death of Sir Robert Drury.

---

[211]Text reprinted (without italics) from *Poems, By J. D.* (1635), p. 349; this is somewhat better than the 1633 text (p. 148). In 1635, the letter precedes the poem, and it is headed "*To Sir* Robert Carr"; in 1633, the letter follows the poem and has no addressee.

He wrote no elegies for the children he lost; none for Spenser or Shakespeare; none for Queen Elizabeth or Queen Anne; none for his old acquaintance, Richard Martin, though he was urged to do so and apologized profusely;[212] none for Egerton, Bacon, Goodere, or the Countess of Bedford. He wrote no funeral elegy for King James, who died three and a half weeks after Hamilton; he paid his tribute at the end of a sermon, preached at Denmark House a month after the King's death. He memorialized Lady Danvers in a sermon of commemoration, not in an elegy. Nor did he write an elegy or an epicede or an obsequy for the Marquis Hamilton. The title of Donne's poem, "An hymne to the Saints, and to Marquesse Hamylton," accurately reflects its content, and Donne probably selected it with care. Both his lifelong disinclination to write memorial verse and his feeling of what the Dean of St. Paul's might write with propriety to accede to Ker's request made him write a "hymn." A hymn was, for Donne, a sacred poem, regardless of its form; he had used the term in "The Canonization" to refer to the sonnets he would build to memorialize his love, in "To Mrs. Magdalen Herbert: of St. Mary Magdalen" to refer to the *La Corona* sonnets, and in "Of the Progress of the Soule" to refer to the two poems he had written and to the anniversaries he still expected to write. The early editors of Donne's *Poems* recognized his intent, and "An hymne to the Saints, and to Marquesse Hamylton" was placed among the divine poems, not with the epicedes and obsequies.[213]

In 1625, Donne was reluctant to write poetry of any kind, regardless of its subject. His letter to Ker shows his disaffection for verse, not for the Marquis Hamilton. He does not seem to have known Hamilton more than casually. Donne may have been present when Hamilton participated in an entertainment pro-

[212]His response to Goodere's "commandment" is in *Letters*, p. 175.
[213]Noticed by Grierson, *The Poems of John Donne*, I, 288, and II, 216. In *Poems*, 1635, the poems were rearranged and the generic groups were emphasized by running heads. "An hymne to the Saints, and to Marquesse Hamylton" is among the "Divine Poëms," which are printed at the end of the volume (pp. 327–88), not with the "Funerall Elegies," which are on pp. 211–74.

vided for an honorable company by Lord Hay, Viscount Doncaster, on January 8, 1620, a week after he had returned from Germany.[214] On July 3, 1622, Donne and Hamilton were among the seven men chosen to be honorary members of the Council of the Virginia Company, but there is no record of familiarity between them.[215] Donne would have approved of Hamilton's interceding with the King on the occasion of Sir Robert Ker's killing a man in a duel in 1620,[216] and he would have welcomed his efforts to procure leniency for Bacon in 1621.[217] In 1617, Chamberlain wrote of him, "I have not heard of a man generally better spoken of then that marques even by all the English insomuch that he is every way held the gallantest gentleman of both the nations."[218] To students of Renaissance literature, knowledge of Hamilton's gallantry is largely limited to his participation in a number of masques and entertainments. He is remembered for his last-minute arrival at Windsor in September 1621, in time to have his fortune told in *The Gypsies Metamorphosed* as a man who would have laid by his scepter to have leapt a doxy who summoned him, but he had just returned from service as Lord High Commissioner to the Scottish Parliament[219] and Jonson says of him,

> Here is Man both for earnest, and sport.
> You were latelie imployed,
> And yo͏ʳ Master is joyed
> To have such in his traine
> So well can sustaine
> His Person abroad,
> And not shrincke for the loade.

Born in 1589, he had succeeded to his title in 1604; in 1608, the King confirmed to him the lands of the dissolved Abbey of

[214]Bald, p. 365.
[215]Ibid., p. 436.
[216]*Letters of John Chamberlain*, II, 288.
[217]"Hamilton, James, second Marquis," *DNB*.
[218]*Letters of John Chamberlain*, II, 98.
[219]*DNB*.

Aberbrothwick, in county Forfar, erecting them into a tempo-
ral lordship in his favor, with the title of a Lord of Parliament.
He was appointed a Privy Councillor of Scotland in 1613, and
of England in 1617; made Gentleman of the Bedchamber in
1621 and Lord Steward of the Household in 1624; created an
English peer as Earl of Cambridge in 1619, and installed as a
Knight of the Garter in 1623. With Buckingham, he had been
involved in the plans for the Spanish marriage, but in the year
following he actively opposed Buckingham's foreign policy. He
died on March 2, 1625, aged thirty-five, leaving to mourn him
not only many admirers but his wife of twenty-two years and
five children.[220] Chamberlain's letter to Carleton of March 12
recounts both the manner of his death and his general esteem:

> The Marquis Hamilton died on Ashwensday morning of a pesti-
> lient feaver as is supposed, though some suspect poison, because
> he swelled unmeasurablie after he was dead in his body but spe-
> cially his head. Upon the opening of both the phisicians saw no
> signes of any such suspicion, but ascribe the swelling to some ma-
> ligne or venomous humor of the small pocks or such like that
> might lie hid. . . . He is much lamented as a very noble gentle-
> man and the flowre of that nation.[221]

About a quarter of the forty-two lines of Donne's "An hymne
to the Saints, and to Marquesse Hamylton" lament Hamilton as
a very noble gentleman, but even so much is surprising in the
light of Donne's title. The title is somewhat misleading, for
Donne does not sing the praises of the saints; only in the first ten
lines is he concerned with them, and only because he addresses
them to pose the question of whether the new soul entered into
heaven takes its place in a rank already established there or is of
a new order. The saints then vanish from the poem, though its
conclusion is addressed to Hamilton as saint. Despite Donne's
use of "hymne" and "Saints" in his title to direct attention to the

---

[220]"Hamilton" in *Complete Peerage, DNB,* and *Burke's Peerage,* 105th ed.
(1970).
[221]*Letters of John Chamberlain,* II. 604–5.

poem as a divine one, he was aware that he must also write an epicede. Like his other epicedes, this poem is cast into pentameter couplets, it makes no demonstration of personal grief, and it spins a speculative thread of considerable ingenuity. The question Donne asks of the saints and the compliment to Hamilton it implies are preliminary to the idea that if one of the heavenly orders is increased, "by his losse grow all our *orders* lesse":

> The name of *Father, Master, Friend,* the name
> Of *Subject* and of *Prince,* in one are lame;
> Faire mirth is dampt, and conversation black,
> The *household* widdow'd, and the *garter* slack;
> The *Chappell* wants an eare, *Councell* a tongue;
> *Story,* a theame; and *Musicke* lacks a song;
> Blest *order* that hath him, the losse of him
> Gangreend all *Orders* here; all lost a limbe.
> Never made body such hast to confesse
> What a soule was; All former comelinesse
> Fled, in a minute, when the soule was gone,
> And, having lost that beauty, would have none;
> So fell our *Monasteries,* in an instant growne
> Not to lesse houses, but, to heapes of stone.

In his next lines, Donne deals inventively with body and soul; he suggests that the body immediately sent "that faire forme it wore," its ideal form, to the celestial "spheare of formes" to anticipate a resurrection, even before the soul, which was responsible for the fame of Hamilton's qualities and achievements as a man, has been enshrined in an earthly monument. Having predicated an ideal body as well as an earthly soul, Donne then addresses not the earthly soul but the ideal or "faire" soul, stationed, he implies, with the Penitents; he asks that the saintly Hamilton may wish that all his sinning and repentant friends join him in heaven, cleansed of sin.

If the "hymne" is not up to Donne's uttermost, it is still a poem recognizedly stamped with his mark. He wrote a divine poem about body and soul, sin and repentance, which was yet sufficiently particularized to serve as a tribute to Hamilton. He recalls Hamilton's distinction as Privy Councillor, as Gentleman of the Bedchamber and Steward of the Household, as Knight of the Garter; he probably suggests, in the bereavement of story and music, Hamilton's participation in courtly entertainments. His two-line simile about the fall of monasteries, highly effective as an analogy for the body's sudden loss of beauty, was probably not a reminiscence of the lands of the dissolved abbey granted to Hamilton; there is nothing to indicate that Donne had even vaguely in mind the idea that Marvell was to develop in *Upon Appleton House*. However, the lines "Never made body such hast to confesse / What a soule was; All former comelinesse / Fled, in a minute" do seem to point to what Chamberlain found remarkable in Hamilton's death, the great change in his body. But Donne saw that not as a morbid detail which perhaps had political origins; he saw it in the context which preoccupied his mind during the time he wrote the poem. He was writing in Lent, when, it is likely, he was thinking about the sermon he was to preach at St. Paul's on the evening of Easter day. He was concerned not only with the spiritual resurrection of the soul from sin, which must be accomplished every day by the ordinary means of preaching and sacraments, but with the resurrection of the body, "the last thing, that shall be done in Heaven."[222] He was concerned with "that Resurrection to life, which he hath promised to all them that do good, and will extend to all them, who having done evill, do yet truly repent the evill they have done." It was for him a matter of wonder "That God would have such a care to dignifie, and to crown, and to associate to his own everlasting presence, the body of man." The dignifying of the body of man had proceeded so far, he says, "as that amongst the ancient Fathers, very many of them, are very various, and irresolved, which way to pronounce, and very many of them cleare in the negative, in

[222]*Sermons,* VI (No. 13), p. 264. The quotations which follow are on pp. 279, 265, 266, 272.

that point, That the soule of man comes not to the presence of God, but remains in some out-places till the Resurrection of the body." Donne thinks that "consideration of the love of God, to the body of man" drew these Fathers into error, but he holds, too, that at a man's death we may properly say, "*Nunc est*, Now is the Resurrection come to him, . . . because after the death of the Body, there is no more to be done with the Body, till the Resurrection; for as we say of an Arrow, that it is over shot, it is gone, it is beyond the mark, though it be not come to the mark yet, because there is no more to be done to it till it be; so we may say, that he that is come to death, is come to his Resurrection, because he hath not another step to make, another foot to goe, another minute to count, till he be at the Resurrection." Donne's coming to terms with the sudden dispersion of the beauty of Hamilton's body was not, then, a momentary, idle, and ingenious speculation. His invention of a "faire forme" for the body and his reminder that the soul must be ministered to on earth since it governs the quality of a man's earthly attainments even as it is itself purified on earth are offshoots of the ideas that preempted his greatest attention at the time he was writing the poem.

The poem and the letter to Ker indicate a change in Donne's attitude toward poetry and a diminution in the quality of his verse when he was not fully involved in the occasion of a poem. Eleven years earlier, just a year before he took orders, he had been involved with Ker in the making of a poem, and his attitude and achievement then provide us with the means to measure the road he traveled. In 1613, Donne had managed to procure the Viscount Rochester's attention and aid, and he was intent to make sure that Rochester would continue to advance his career after the controversial decree of nullity of the marriage of the Earl of Essex and Lady Frances Howard (on September 27, 1613) made possible Rochester's marriage to the lady on December 26. It is clear that as late as January 19, 1614, Donne was not certain what he might do to rekindle the interest of Rochester (now Earl of Somerset) in him. He wrote his friend Goodere on that date that he had heard about a treatise concerning the nullity, said to originate in Geneva though its instigators were at Court, and, he said,

> My poor study having lyen that way, it may prove possible, that my weak assistance may be of use in this matter, in a more serious fashion, then an Epithalamion. This made me therefore abstinent in that kinde; yet by my troth, I think I shall not scape. I deprehend in my self more then an alacrity, a vehemency to do service to that company; and so, I may finde reason to make rime. If it be done, I see not how I can admit that circuit of sending them to you, to be sent hither; that seems a kinde of praying to Saints, to whom God must tell first, that such a man prays to them to pray to him. So that I shall lose the honour of that conveyance; but, for recompense, you shall scape the danger of approving it.[223]

Goodere had apparently written Donne that he thought it would be appropriate for Donne to write an epithalamion and had offered to act as intermediary in presenting it to Somerset, but Donne thought he might better advance his suit in a more sober fashion, by demonstrating his abilities in the law. On this occasion, and about the same time, Sir Robert Ker had also made suggestions to Donne, perhaps at his bidding, and he, too, thought an epithalamion would be fitting. Donne answered, "If my Muse were onely out of fashion, and but wounded and maimed like Free-will in the *Roman Church*, I should adventure to put her to an Epithalamion. But since she is dead, like Free-will in our Church, I have not so much Muse left as to lament her losse." He thought his gesture ought to be something more weighty: "Perchance this businesse may produce occasions, wherein I may express my opinion of it, in a more serious manner. Which I speake neither upon any apparent conjecture, nor upon any overvaluing of my abilities, but out of a generall readinesse and alacrity to be serviceable and grate-

---

[223]*Letters*, pp. 179–81; for addressee, see I. A. Shapiro, "The Text of Donne's *Letters to Severall Persons*," *RES*, 7 (1931), 296–97.

full in any kinde."[224] The Muse Donne called dead had in the last year produced two of his most memorable poems, the Valentine epithalamion for the Princess Elizabeth and "Goodfriday, 1613. Riding Westward." Clearly, however, in early 1614, Donne looked upon poetry as something of a toy, something fundamentally unserious, not the dignified sort of achievement which might lead to advancement in State or Church. But in 1614, if no more serious way of proving his merit turned up, he was ready, full of alacrity and vehemency, to do service by way of rhyme. Even as late as 1621, he was fired with the same alacrity when he wrote "Upon the translation of the Psalmes" for the Earl of Pembroke. In 1625, the Dean of St. Paul's and the Vicar of St. Dunstan's no longer needed to write poetry for self-advancement. He felt, even as he had felt eleven years before, that a public poem was not a sufficiently serious way of representing himself to the world; he was in no position to refuse Ker's request that he honor Hamilton by a poem, but he made it obvious that he would have embraced a more serious obligation with more alacrity.

When, in 1614, Donne finally found reason to make rhyme, his vehemency to do service was ardent enough to sustain 235 superb lines. If he would not "admit that circuit of sending them" to Goodere for him to pass on to Somerset, Goodere's suggestion that he act as presenter probably gave him the idea for the extraordinary eclogue which frames the epithalamion. The Allophanes whom he engages in dialogue is, without much question, Sir Robert Ker,[225] and Ker was to act as his intercessor with Somerset. The eclogue, nearly as long as the epithalamion itself, is Donne's ingenious way of explaining away the lateness of his offering and of showing his appreciation of the Court and its ubiquitous influence at the same time that he points to himself as out of Court. Although he insists that his nuptial song was not made "Either the Court or mens hearts to invade," that

---

[224]*Letters*, p. 270.

[225]Grierson writes, " 'Allophanes' is one who seems like another, who bears the same name as another, i.e. the bridegroom" (*The Poems of John Donne*, II, 94).

is precisely his purpose as he calls Somerset's attention to the fact that he is "dead, and buried." His offer to burn his poem as a perfect sacrifice must, of course, be rejected by Allophanes, who tells Idios that he will return to Court and lay the poem upon "Such Altars, as prize your devotion." The epithalamion itself is only slightly below Donne's blazing performance in the Valentine epithalamion; from the opening stanza, in which the inflaming eyes of the bride and the loving heart of the groom provide the heat and light to reprieve the old year, otherwise scheduled to die in five days, it is full of celebratory touches which freshen the commonplaces of the genre. Donne's wit matches his daring when he glances at the decree of nullity and comments on it: "Though it be some divorce to thinke of you / Singly, so much one are you two"; he revivifies old and favorite notions of his—the danger of looking directly on the face of God, and the difference between a Platonic Idea and its phenomenal manifestation—to describe the bride and her apparel; he hits just the right note of joyful naughtiness when he tells the wedded couple that "new great heights to trie, / It must serve your ambition, to die" and advises them to "Raise heires." For all Donne's desire to demonstrate his talents to Somerset in a serious manner, once he saw that he must adventure to put his Muse to an epithalamion, the Muse he considered more than "wounded and maimed" was, suddenly, "in nothing lame." All his chips were riding on the poem and he groomed its every detail.

Donne did not push himself so hard in the Hamilton poem. One senses that he is exercising his Muse, putting her through the paces. The poem is a good one, an adequate one, one that shows some of the marks of the poet, but it is a tired poem, self-protective, not aggressive. Donne's excuses that he could no longer measure up to his uttermost when it was best and that he did best when he had least truth for his subject are belied by the "Hymne to God my God, in my sicknesse," written not long before and written on the subject which was, above all others, full of truth for him. When, after his ordination, an occasion mattered to Donne, he could rise to the occasion in verse. When he was stirred, he would make his own occasion for verse. He was merely taking advantage of a critical stereotype when he equated his finest efforts with his greatest falsehoods. He could, to be sure, lie with the best of poets in a poem like "The Anagram," but he feigned best, most imaginatively and most inventively, when his subject was most important and urgent to him. That the most impressive feigning in the Hamilton poem seems to have arisen more from his preoccupation with the Easter season than from his concern to memorialize Hamilton or to turn the occasion of Hamilton's death into an opportunity for a truly memorable statement indicates, as tellingly as does his letter to Ker, that his commitment to the poem was only marginal and dutiful.

When Chamberlain sent Carleton a copy of "certain verses of our Deane of Paules upon the death of the Marquis Hamilton," he wrote, "though they be reasonable wittie and well don yet I could wish a man of his yeares and place to geve over versifieng."[226] His verdict on the poem hits the mark precisely. It was probably the mark Donne aimed at, and, had he heard Chamberlain's wish, he would have said "Amen." The verses about Hamilton are his last, save one. Many years before, Donne had written an "Epitaph on Himselfe" as a verse epistle to the Countess of Bedford, complimentary, witty, full of unexceptional holy doctrine, paradoxical down to its last ingenious couplet: "And thinke me well compos'd, that I could now / A last-sicke houre to syllables allow." Sometime before he died Donne did allow a last-sick hour to syllables, very different syllables from those of the "Epitaph." He wrote an epigraph to be placed beneath the picture of himself in his shroud. It is a single Latin hexameter, perfect for the occasion, stamped with his idiosyncratic marks, cryptic, conceited, conclusive: "Corporis haec Animae sit Syndon, Syndon Jesu."[227]

---

[226]*Letters of John Chamberlain*, II, 613.

[227]See Gardner's discussion in *Divine Poems*, pp. 112–13. She provides a literal translation, "May this shroud of the body be (i.e. typify) the shroud of the soul: the shroud of Jesus," and a paraphrase, "As the body is shrouded in white linen, may the soul be shrouded in a white garment also, which is not its own but is the white garment of Jesus."

Appendix: The Bridgewater Manuscript of Donne's Poems

B (Huntington Library EL 6893) is written on paper water-marked with a fleur-de-lis and the letters "W R." The mark is closest, I think, to that of Heawood 1721a, which Heawood identifies as Schieland, 1614, but it closely resembles, too, Heawood 1724 (Amsterdam, 1617).[1]

The arrangement of *B* seems to indicate that the main copyist had a text of "The Lamentations" in hand when he began his transcription. Although he placed "The Crosse" (here called "On the Cross") at the beginning of the volume, he then transcribed the secular poems available to him, left blank ff. 83-84, 105b (except for four lines), and 106a-115b, and started to copy the divine poems he had at f. 116a."The Lamentations" is the first of these (ff. 116a-125b), and "At his going wth my lo: / of Doncaster. 1619." is the last (ff. 140a-b). Ff. 141-61 are blank, and the "Problemes" start at f. 162a.

The compiler of *B* had access to more than one source, and he made an attempt to fill gaps he was aware of before the main copyist made his transcription. He wrote on the first leaf, now covered by the Bridgewater bookplate, "**When I died last year and dear I dye / all wanting 3 staues"; since all lines of "The Legacie" are present on f. 58b, he managed to secure a

---

[1]Edward Heawood, *Watermarks, Mainly of the 17th and 18th Centuries* (Hilversum, 1950).

complete text.[2] A second copyist added the following poems on ff. 105b–115a: "The Triple Foole" (untitled); "Going to Bed"; nine epigrams; "Epithalamion on a Citizen" (Lincoln's Inn); "Obsequies to the Lord Harrington," with the prefatory letter to the Countess of Bedford; "10th Epigram"; "Cruell, since thou doest not feare the curse," with the heading "This hath relation to ⌞ when by thy Scorne O Murdresse &c" (Donne's "The Apparition," then, led to the inclusion of the uncanonical poem). This copyist seems not to have been merely a professional scribe; no professional scribe would have taken the liberty to write in the margin of f. 106b, which contained the last part of "Going to Bed," "*why may not a man write his owne Epithalamion if he can doe it so modestly [?]"

B was probably compiled for John Egerton, 1st Earl of Bridgewater (created May 27, 1617) or for his wife, Frances, daughter of Ferdinando Stanley, 5th Earl of Derby. The manuscript has the Earl's signature, "J. Bridgewater" on the verso of its second leaf; its covers are stamped in gold with his wife's initials, "F B," separated by a center decoration.

Donne had probably made the acquaintance of John Egerton and his older brother, Thomas, when he was a student at Lincoln's Inn, and they must have paved the way for his appointment late in 1597 or in 1598 as a secretary to their father, the Lord Keeper.[3] He knew John Egerton's wife even prior to her marriage; her mother, the Countess Dowager of Derby, had married the Lord Keeper in October 1600.[4] Donne's relation with the Egerton family surely suffered after the marriage to Ann More which led to his dismissal, but his old employer lived to demonstrate the warmth of his feeling for him. When, in August 1614, Donne made a final attempt to secure some kind of state grant or office, he looked to Lord Ellesmere for support, and he wrote of his "so good contentment in the fashion" which

---

[2]He then drew a line through the words of his notation.
[3]Bald, pp. 53, 93, 537.
[4]Ibid., p. 110.
[5]Ibid., pp. 291–93; *Letters*, p. 173.

the Lord Chancellor used him.[5] In July 1616, the Lord Chancellor bestowed on Donne, without any prodding, a pretty sinecure, the benefice of Sevenoaks in Kent.[6] In June 1618, Donne gave evidence in favor of the Earl of Bridgewater in a suit in Chancery, and, R. C. Bald says, "this case renewed associations between Donne and the family of his old master, cementing a connection which remained constant for the rest of Donne's life."[7] On at least two occasions important to the family, Donne was asked to preach: he provided a sermon "at the Churching of the Countesse of Bridgewater," which Evelyn Simpson dates in 1621 or 1623,[8] and another, on November 19, 1627, at the marriage of the Earl's daughter Mary to the eldest son of Lord Herbert of Cherbury.[9]

The interest of the Earl or of the Countess or of both of them in Donne's work is clear in the presence of eight of his sermons, preached between December 1617 and April 1622, in the Ellesmere manuscript.[10] Donne seems to have sent them a copy of each of his printed sermons; of the six printed in his lifetime, copies of five presented to the Earl or the Countess have survived:

1. Sermon on Judges 20:15 (properly 5:20), "Preached at the Crosse the 15th. of September. 1622." Published in 1622. Huntington Library 59074 has the initials "FB FB," in ink, on the flyleaf and on the title page. (Keynes, no. 12)

2. Sermon on Acts 1:8, preached to "the Honourable Company of the Virginian Plantation" on November 13, 1622. Published in 1622. Simpson says that a copy in the Princeton University Library has the name "F. Bridgewater" on the flyleaf.[11] (Keynes, no. 15)

3. *Encaenia. The Feast of Dedication. Celebrated At Lincolnes Inne*, in a *Sermon there upon* Ascension day, 1623. Pub-

[6]Bald, pp. 317–18.
[7]Ibid., p. 337.
[8]*Sermons*, V, 14–15; Nos. 9, 10.
[9]Ibid., VIII, No. 3.
[10]See ibid., II, 365–71, and V, 18.
[11]Ibid., II, 466.

lished in 1623. The title page of Huntington Library 59075 is inscribed "J Bridgewater ex dono Authoris. 20. Junij 1623." (Keynes, no. 16)

4. *The First Sermon Preached to King Charles, At Saint James: 3°. April. 1625.* Published in 1625. The title page of Huntington Library 59076 is inscribed "J Bridgewater ex dono Authoris." (Keynes, no. 19) This sermon and the others described above which are at the Huntington Library are bound with the first issue of *Deaths Duell.*[12]

5. *A Sermon, Preached to the Kings M^{tie.} at Whitehall, 24. Febr. 1625* [26]. Published in 1626. Across the top of the title page of Huntington Library 60137 is the inscription "J Bridgewater ex dono Authoris 12° Martii 1625." (Keynes, no. 21)

The Bridgewater copy of *Devotions Upon Emergent Occasions*, 1624 (Keynes, no. 34) seems to have belonged to the Countess. Huntington Library 53917 has the initials "FB" stamped on the front and back covers, as they are on the Bridgewater manuscript of the poems, except that they are not gilt.

[12]See ibid., I, 13.

Index of Donne's Works

In general, poems are listed under categories familiar to readers of the volumes edited by Gardner and Milgate.

Index

General Index

Abbot, George, 156
Andrews, Dr. Francis, 85
Andrews, Dr. Richard, 106, 161
Aquinas, St. Thomas, 25, 27
Aristotle, 25-27, 49
Augustine, St., 27, 102

Bacon, Sir Francis, 156, 192, 197
Baker, Sir Richard, 84n
Bald, R. C., 71-72, 84, 95, 97n,
    98n, 108-9, 134, 140n, 145n,
    154n, 162n, 157, 175, 209
Bedford, Countess of (Lucy Har-
    rington), 95, 100, 102, 132,
    155-56, 205
Bennett, R. E., 91, 96n
Browne, William, 73
Buckingham, Duke of (George Vil-
    liers), 155-56, 158, 198
Bulstrode, Cecilia, 118
Burns, Robert, 59

Caesar, Sir Julius, 156, 175
Carre, Thomas, 160
Cary, Valentine, 156
Castiglione, Baldesar, 29-30
Chamberlain, John, 158, 194n,
    197-98, 200, 205
Chapman, George, 59, 60n, 73
Charles, Amy M., 112, 113n
Charles I, King, 138, 163, 193
Cirillo, A. R., 19

Cosin, John, 160
Crane, R. S., 18
Cruttwell, Patrick, 42
Cunnar, Eugene, 44n

Danby, Thomas, 72
Dante, 44, 50
Danvers, Sir John, 105n, 114, 160
Doncaster, Viscount, see Hay,
    James
Donne, Ann, 43, 97-98, 116, 118,
    123, 126, 145, 208
Donne, Francis, 97-98
Donne, John
    amount of poetry, 94, 173
    argument, use of, 22-24, 33, 38,
      54, 56-61, 176, 179-80
    attitudes toward poetry, 73, 94,
      99-103, 107, 170-71, 201-5
    audience, awareness of, 26, 31-
      33, 35n, 37, 38n, 77-78, 81,
      100, 103
    Bible, use of, 142, 168; Books:
      Epistles, 101-2, 179; Exodus,
      35; Lamentations, 119, 145,
      147-48; Psalms, 101-2, 142,
      180-82; Versions: Authorized,
      146, 180-81; Geneva, 146, 181;
      Tremellius, 144, 146-47, 149-
      50n; Vulgate, 168, 181, 183
    biblical interpretation, concept
      of, 168-69

The Disinterred Muse

Designed by Richard E. Rosenbaum.
Composed by Metricomp
in 11 point Baskerville, 2 points leaded,
with display lines in Baskerville.
Printed offset by Thomson/Shore, Inc. on
Warren's Number 66 Antique Offset, 50 pound basis.
Bound by John H. Dekker & Sons, Inc.
in Holliston book cloth
and stamped in Kurz-Hastings foils.

Library of Congress Cataloging in Publication Data

Novarr, David.
   The disinterred muse.

   Includes bibliographical references and index.
   1. Donne, John, 1572-1631 — Criticism and interpretation.
I. Title.
PR2248.N6   821'.3   80-66967
ISBN 0-8014-1309-5